Light C

Gambling—Gamesters—Wagers—The Turf

Ralph Nevill

Alpha Editions

This edition published in 2022

ISBN : 9789356892361

Design and Setting By
Alpha Editions
www.alphaedis.com
Email - info@alphaedis.com

I

The gambling spirit inborn in mankind—Its various forms in reality identical—Resemblance of gamblers to the alchemists of old—Capriciousness of fortune—Importance of small advantages at play—An extraordinary run at hazard—Napoleon and Wellington little addicted to cards—Blücher's love of gaming—He wins his son's money—Avaricious gamesters—Anecdotes of the miser Elwes—Long sittings at the card-table—Modern instance in London—Two nights and a day at whist at the Roxburgh Club—Casanova's forty-two hour duel at piquet—Anecdotes of Fox, the Duke of Devonshire, Sir John Lade, Beau Nash, and others—Country houses lost at play—"Up now deuce and then a trey"—The Canterbury barber.

The passion for speculation which, throughout all ages, has captivated the great bulk of humanity, would seem to be an innate characteristic of mankind. It assumes various forms and guises which often deceive those over whom it exercises its sway, and becomes in numberless cases a veritable obsession, causing its victims to devote the whole of their time, thoughts, and money—sometimes even their lives—to its service. Devotees of the simpler forms of gambling, such as are to be procured at the card-table and on the race-course, are often looked down upon by people who are themselves under the sway of other insidious, if more reputable, modes of tempting fortune. For all speculation, whether it be in pigs or wheat, stocks and shares, race-horses or cards, is in essence the same—its main feature being merely the desire to obtain "something for nothing," or in other words to acquire wealth without work. Gambling, of no matter what kind, is thus a conscious and deliberate departure from the general aim of civilised society, which is to obtain proper value for its money. The gambler, on the other hand, receives either a great deal more than he gives or nothing at all.

All conditions of life being more or less disquieted either with the cares of gaining or of keeping money, it is but natural that mankind should be allured by the idea of discovering and utilising an easy and quick road to riches. Alas, the prospect of speedy wealth, which exercises such an irresistible fascination over certain natures, is in the vast majority of cases nothing but a delusive mirage, as tempting to covetous folly as the "philosopher's stone." Indeed, the votaries of chance in a great measure resemble the alchemists of old, who were ever seeking, but never found, a method of producing untold gold.

So convinced were these searchers of the possibility of eventually discovering the secret of manufacturing riches, that they laughed even at successful gamblers, deeming them to be mere drudges and sluggards on the golden road. There was a time, indeed, when students of what Gibbon termed "the vain science of alchemy," were actually called "multipliers," and their unbounded confidence naturally made a deep impression upon the credulous ignorance of their age. So much so that our Henry IV. appears to have become seriously alarmed at the prospect of the country being flooded with precious metals manufactured by the "multipliers," for a statute passed during his reign decrees that "none from henceforth shall use to multiply gold or silver or use the craft of multiplication, and if any the same do he shall incur the pain of felony." His Majesty might just as well have issued an edict against gamblers making use of a sure method of winning!

One of the most remarkable things about gambling is that no one ever seems to win—certainly the vast majority of those addicted to play, even the most lucky, generally declare that on the whole they have lost. A number of these, however, probably leave out of their calculations the large amounts which they have spent whilst fortune was in a generous mood; for gamblers when in luck are apt to fling their money about very freely, and even when they are losing they do not as a rule practise a rigid economy. This is not the case, of course, with followers of methods and systems who take their gambling seriously; these are often frugal men who, though quite callous about losing large sums in the pursuit of their hobby, regard money spent on enjoyment or luxuries as wasted. This is the type of gambler who racks his brains with calculations, and takes immense trouble to obtain really sound information about the chances of some race-horse, or of the rise or fall of some stock.

But even to such sober gamblers the result is usually disappointing. All methods, systems, and combinations do little to assist gamblers to win—the most they can effect is to put a limitation on their losses; and as regards special information, those who are addicted to racing know only too well how expensive it is to be acquainted with any one in a position to give really good "tips." More than that, information which emanates from owners, trainers, and jockeys would soon break the Bank of England were that institution to decide to risk its capital on such advice. Not that in many cases these men are not really anxious to give their friends winners; but somehow or other the good thing hardly ever comes off. It is indeed not at all unlikely that the race-goer who knows no one connected with the Turf has a distinct advantage; for when regular racing men possess reliable information as to a horse which has been reserved for some coup, they are obviously not at liberty to divulge its name, and consequently the "tips" they give are little more than hints of vague possibilities.

Although as a matter of fact the goddess of chance—not erroneously called "fickle"!—is in the long run pitilessly severe upon her votaries, one and all, there are times and occasions on which she seems not indisposed to smile. To propitiate her is, therefore, the first ambition of all gamblers, and in their efforts to attain this end many of them exhibit an almost childish superstition. Yet we must remember that the wisest of the Roman emperors kept a golden image of Fortune in their private apartments, or carried it about them. They never sent it to their successor till they were near expiring; and then it was accompanied with this declaration—that in the whole course of their achievements, they were more indebted to fortune than to any skill or dexterity of their own.

Always feminine, Fortune is to all appearances essentially wayward and capricious. She requires to be constantly tended, silently expected, and approached with due caution and prudence. Rough and refractory behaviour scares her away; irritation at her eccentricities banishes her altogether; whilst levity and ingratitude, when she is in a beneficent mood, soon causes her to escape. Moderation is the only chance of securing her constant presence. In short, fortune, or luck, is a phenomenon, the ground and essence whereof is to a great degree inexplicable. For the most part we know it only from its effects, and can give no certain account either of its nature or of its mode of action, and of the always increasing or diminishing greatness of it. To the gambler fortune appears to be an occult power, the aid of which is not infrequently invoked by means of various fanciful fetishes, which for the moment acquire a real virtue, as being likely to propitiate the invisible influence which presides over speculation.

The movements of fortune have been well compared to those of the sea, which for the most part seems to affect a serene and smiling aspect, broken only by tranquil ripples. From time to time, however, furious tempests and storms disturb its surface, calm being often re-established as quickly and suddenly as it was originally broken. Like the sea, Fortune would at heart appear to be inclined towards tranquillity, though her fury, when roused, is inclined to conceal this tendency.

Whilst Fortune generally seems to distribute her favours in a somewhat haphazard way, there is no doubt that those who study the so-called laws of chance are the most likely to receive them. For although chance is generally considered to be effect without design, this is not strictly true. Throughout the universe of nature, indeed, all events appear in the end to be governed by immutable laws which have existed from the beginning of time, no matter what partial irregularities may arise at certain periods.

In any game, for instance, equality in play is likely to restore the players in a series of events to the same state in which they began; while inequality, however small, has a contrary effect, and the longer the game be continued, the greater is likely to be the loss of the one player and the gain of the other. As has been very soundly said, this "more or less," in play, runs through all the ratios between equality and infinite difference, or from an infinitely little difference till it comes to an infinitely great one. The slightest of advantages, whether arising from skill or chance, will as surely "materialise" in the course of play as does the carefully calculated profit of a commercial expert.

An event either will happen or will not happen; this constitutes a certainty. Some events are dependent, others independent. The difference is very important. Independent events have no connection, their happenings neither forwarding nor obstructing one another. Choosing a card from each of two distinct packs includes two independent events; for the taking of a card from the first pack does not in any way affect the taking of a card from the second—the chances of drawing, or of not drawing, any particular card from the second pack being neither lessened nor increased. On the other hand, the taking of a second card from a pack from which one has already been drawn is a dependent event, as the composition of the pack has been altered by the abstraction of one particular card.

The surprising way in which an apparently small advantage operates may be judged from the following example:—A and B agree to play for one guinea a game until one hundred guineas are lost or won. A possesses an advantage on each game amounting to 11 chances to 10 in his favour. Mathematical analysis of this advantage proves that B would do well to give A upwards of ninety-nine guineas to cancel the agreement.

Further, many speculative events, which at first sight seem to be advantageous to one side, are demonstrated by mathematical investigation to be of an exactly contrary nature. A bets B thirty-two guineas to one that an event does not happen, and also bets B thirty guineas even that it does happen in twenty-nine trials. Besides this A gives B one thousand guineas to play in this manner six hours a day for a month. Here B would appear to have some advantage. Mathematical investigation, however, proves that in reality the advantage of A is so great that B ought not only to return the thousand guineas to A, but give him, in addition, another ten thousand guineas to cancel the agreement.

Every game of chance presents two kinds of chances which are very distinct—namely, those relating to the person interested (the player) and those inherent in the combinations of the game. That is to say, there is either "good luck" or "bad luck," which at different times gives the player a "run" of good or bad fortune. But besides this, there is the chance of the combinations of the game, which are independent of the player and which are governed by the laws of probability. Theoretically, chance is able to bring into any given game all the possible combinations; but it is a curious fact that there are, nevertheless, certain limits at which it seems to stop. A proof of this is that a particular number at roulette does not turn up ten or a dozen times in succession. In reality there would be nothing astounding about such a run, but it is supposed never to have happened. On the other hand, the numbers in one column at roulette have been known not to turn up during seventeen successive coups.

All the same, extraordinary runs do occur at all games. In 1813, a well-known betting man of the name of Ogden laid one thousand guineas to one guinea, that calling seven as the main, a player would not throw that number ten times successively from the dice-box. Seven was thrown nine times in direct sequence! Mr. Ogden then offered four hundred and seventy guineas to be let off the bet, but the thrower refused. He took the box again but threw only twice more—nine—so that Mr. Ogden just saved his thousand guineas.

In a game of chance, the oftener the same combination has occurred in succession the nearer we are to the certainty that it will not recur at the next coup. It would almost appear, in fact, as if there existed an instant, prescribed by some unknown law, at which the chances become mature, and after which they begin to tend again towards equalisation. This is the secret of the pass and the counter-pass, and also of the strange persistence which certain numbers at roulette sometimes show in recurring—they are merely making up for lost time. At the end of a year all the numbers on a roulette board would be found to have come up about the same number of times—provided, of course, that the wheel is kept in proper working order, a state of affairs which is assured at Monaco by scrupulous daily inspection.

The considerations set forth above apply more especially to games like roulette and trente-et-quarante played at public tables, where all players have an equal chance against the bank, and where the personal element, which is so important in private play, is to a large extent eliminated. It is at public tables that the real gambler finds his best chance. There, whilst having a fair field and no favour, he may, if lucky, win very large sums with the certainty of being immediately paid; and he is not exposed to various unfavourable influences, which tell against men of his disposition when gambling amongst acquaintances and even friends. Wherever a number of careless, inattentive people possessed of money chance to be assembled, a few wary, cool, and shrewd men will be found, who know how to conceal real caution and design under apparent inattention and gaiety of manner; who push their luck when fortune smiles and refrain when she changes her disposition; and who have calculated the chances and are thoroughly master of every game where judgment is required.

Occasionally men of this stamp have been known to have accumulated a fortune, more often a respectable competency, at play. If they had been interrogated as to the exact means by which they had made their success, they would, had they been desirous of speaking the truth, have replied in the words of the wife of the Maréchal d'Ancre, who, when she was asked what charm she had made use of to fascinate the mind of the queen, "The charm," she replied, "which superior abilities always exercise over weaker minds."

The minor forms of gambling, which serve to gratify the speculative instincts of ordinary mortals, have generally possessed little attraction for great men, whose minds would seem to have been occupied by more ambitious, though perhaps in essence not less speculative, designs. Napoleon, for example, was a very poor card-player, and from all accounts never indulged in any serious gambling. The great Duke of Wellington, though he was once accused of being much addicted to playing hazard, would also seem to have entertained no particular fondness for play. In the course of a letter which he wrote in 1823 to a Mr. Adolphus, who had publicly referred to his supposed love of play, the great Captain wrote "that never in the whole course of his life had he ever won or lost £20 at any game, and that he had never played at hazard or any game of chance in any public place or club, nor been for some years at all at any such place." Nevertheless, the Duke became an original member of Crockford's in 1827, though there is no record of his ever having played there.

Another great soldier, on the other hand, repeatedly lost large sums at play. This was Blücher, who was inordinately fond of gambling. Much to his disgust this passion was inherited by his son, who had often to be rebuked by his father for his visits to the gaming-table, and was given many a wholesome lecture upon his youth and inexperience, and the consequent certainty of loss by coming in contact with older and more practised gamblers. One morning, however, young Blücher presented himself before his father, and exclaimed with an air of joy, "Sir, you said I knew nothing about play, but here is proof that you have undervalued my talents," pulling out at the same time a bag of roubles which he had won the preceding night. "And I said the truth," was the reply; "sit down there, and I'll convince you." The dice were called for, and in a few minutes old Blücher won all his son's money; whereupon, after pocketing the cash, he rose from the table observing, "Now you see that I was right when I told you that you would never win."

If, however, it would seem to be the case that few, if any, of the world's very greatest minds have been addicted to gambling, it is no less true that outside this select band all classes have been, and are, equally subject to the passion. Nothing, indeed, is more extraordinary than the fact that it has been observed to exercise the same fascination on men of the most diverse characters and dispositions—on rich and poor, educated and uneducated, young and old, learned and ignorant.

Moreover, unlike other passions, the love of gambling generally remains unimpaired by age, and instances of people of advanced years expending their few remaining energies at the card-table are not rare. There is the story of the venerable old north-country lady whom a visitor found looking very red-eyed and weary. "I fear you are suffering from a bad cold?" he inquired, solicitously. "Eh, I'se gat na cauld," was the reply; "some friends kem from Kendal on Tuesday that love a game a whist dearly, and I'se bin carding the morn and e'en, the e'en an' the morn, twa days." "Indeed, and what might you have won?" "Eh," she replied, with considerable satisfaction, "it mun be a shilling."

At first sight, also, one would think that avarice and passion for play were absolutely incompatible; yet there are not a few striking instances of the two vices being combined—by men to whom the spending of a few shillings was agony, but who would risk thousands at cards with comparative equanimity. Such an one was the celebrated Mr. Elwes, who combined a passion for gambling with habits of the greatest penury. He was originally a Mr. Meggot, the name of Elwes being assumed under the terms of the will of his uncle. Sir Harvey Elwes.

Sir Harvey was himself the perfect type of a miser. Timid, shy, and diffident in the extreme, he kept his household, which consisted of one man and two maid-servants, chiefly upon game from his own land and fish from his own ponds; the cows which grazed before his door furnished milk, cheese, and butter for the establishment; and what fuel he burned his own woods supplied. As he had no acquaintances and no books, the hoarding-up and the counting of his money was his greatest delight. Next to that came partridge catching—or setting, as it was then called—at which he was so great an adept that he was known to take five hundred brace of birds in one season. What partridges were not consumed by his household he turned out again, as he never gave anything away. At all times he wore a black velvet cap much over his face, a worn-out, full-dress suit of clothes, and an old great-coat, with worsted stockings drawn up over his knees. He rode a thin thoroughbred horse, and the horse and his rider looked as if a gust of wind would have blown them away together.

At the time Mr. Meggot succeeded to the name and fortune of his uncle he was over forty, having for about fifteen years previously been well-known in the most fashionable circles of the West End. He was a gambler at heart, and only late in life did he succeed in obtaining any mastery over his passion for play. His losses were great, but this was mainly because while he himself always paid when he lost, his opponents were not always so scrupulous, and it was notorious that the sums owed to him in this way were very considerable. But he professed the quixotic theory that "it was impossible to ask a gentleman for money"; and to his honour, but financial disadvantage, he adhered strictly to this rule throughout his life.

The acquaintances which he had formed at Westminster School and at Geneva, together with his own large fortune, all conspired to introduce Mr. Elwes (then Mr. Meggot) into whatever society he best liked. He was at once admitted a member of the club at Arthur's, and of various other similar institutions; and as a proof of his notoriety as a gambler, it may be mentioned that he, Lord Robert Bertie, and some others, are noticed in a scene in *The Adventures of a Guinea* for the frequency of their midnight orgies. Few men, even on his own acknowledgment, had played deeper than himself, or with such varying success. He once played two days and a night without intermission; and the room being a small one, the company were nearly up to their knees in cards. He lost some thousands at that sitting. The Duke of Northumberland was of the party—another man who never would quit the gaming-table while any hope of winning remained.

Even at this period, Mr. Elwes' passion for gaming was equalled by his avarice, and in a curious manner he contrived to mingle small attempts at saving with pursuits of the most unbounded dissipation. After sitting up a whole night playing for thousands with the most fashionable and profligate men of the time—in ornate and brilliantly-lighted salons, with obsequious waiters attendant upon his call—he would walk out about four in the morning, not towards his home, but into Smithfield, to meet his own cattle, which were coming up to market from Thaydon Hall, a farm of his in Essex. There would this same man, forgetful of the scenes he had just left, stand in the cold or rain, haggling with a carcass butcher for a shilling. Sometimes when the cattle did not arrive at the hour he expected, he would walk on in the mire to meet them; and more than once he actually trudged the whole way to his farm, seventeen miles from London—a tedious walk after sitting up the whole of the night at play!

Though he never engaged personally upon the Turf, Mr. Elwes was in the habit of making frequent excursions to Newmarket, and a kindness which he once performed there is worthy of recollection. Lord Abingdon, who was slightly known to Mr. Elwes, had made a match for £7000 which it was supposed he would be obliged to forfeit from an inability to produce the sum—though the odds were greatly in his favour. Unsolicited, Mr. Elwes made him an offer of the money; he accepted it, and won the engagement.

On the day this match was to be run a clerical neighbour had agreed to accompany Mr. Elwes to Newmarket. As was the latter's custom they set out on their journey at seven in the morning, and, with the hope of a substantial breakfast at Newmarket, the clergyman took no refreshment before starting. They reached Newmarket about eleven, and Mr. Elwes busied himself in inquiries and conversation till twelve, when the match was decided in favour of Lord Abingdon. The divine then fully expected that they should move off to the town for breakfast; but Elwes still continued riding about on one business or another. Eventually four o'clock arrived; and by this time his reverence had become so impatient that he murmured something about the "keen air of Newmarket heath" and the comforts of a good dinner. "Very true," replied Elwes, "have some of this," offering him at the same time a piece of old, crushed pancake from his great-coat pocket. He added that he had brought it from his house at Marcham two months before, but "that it was as good as new." The sequel of the story was that they did not reach home till nine in the evening, when the clergyman was so tired that he gave up all other refreshment for rest. On the other hand, Elwes, who had hazarded seven thousand pounds in the morning, retired happily to bed with the pleasing recollection of having saved three shillings.

In later life Mr. Elwes was elected to Parliament, where he proved himself an independent country member and exhibited great conscientiousness. During this time he had the greatest admiration for Mr. Pitt, and was wont to declare that in all the statesman's words there were "pounds, shillings, and pence." When he quitted Parliament, he was, in the common phrase, "a fish out of water." He had for some years been a member of a card-club, at the Mount Coffee-House, and it was there that he consoled himself for the loss of his seat. The play was moderate, and he enjoyed the fire and candles which were provided at the expense of the Club; but fortune seemed resolved to force from him that money which no power could persuade him to bestow. He still retained his fondness for play, and imagined that he had no small skill at piquet. It was his ill-luck on one occasion to meet a gentleman who had the same idea of his own powers in this direction, and on much better grounds; for after a contest of two days and a night, in which Elwes continued with the perseverance which avarice will sometimes inspire, he rose the loser of no less than three thousand pounds. The debt was paid by a draft on Messrs. Hoare, which was duly honoured the next morning.

This is said to have been the last bout of gaming indulged in by Mr. Elwes, and not long afterwards he retired to his country seat at Stoke, remarking that "he had lost a great deal of money very foolishly, but that a man grew wiser by time." After this no gleam of pleasure or amusement broke through the gloom of a penurious life, and his insatiable desire of saving became uniform and systematic. He still rode about the country on an old brood mare (which was all he had left); but then he rode her very economically, on the soft turf adjoining the road, so as to avoid the cost of shoes. His household expenses were reduced to a minimum, his few wants being attended to by a man who became almost as celebrated as his master. This extraordinary servant acted as butler, coachman, gardener, huntsman, groom, and valet; and was, according to Mr. Elwes, "a d——d idle rascal" into the bargain.

Mr. Elwes died in 1789 and left an enormous fortune for that day, about five hundred thousand pounds being divided between his two natural sons.

Mr. Elwes' record of having played piquet for two days and a night (thirty-six successive hours) was a remarkable one, for the physical strain involved by playing for such a long period is very considerable. Yet the fascination of remaining at the gaming-table for a long stretch of time frequently takes possession of those addicted to play. As a rule it is not by any means caused solely by the consideration of the stakes played for; it would rather seem that the players become mere automatic gaming machines, the mechanism of which runs steadily on. Several years ago a noticeable instance of this occurred in a London Club, where, on a certain evening, a small party had been playing écarté for fairly moderate stakes. The game began about eleven o'clock; some three or four hours later only two players remained. As the time went on, fine after fine was incurred by this couple, but still they continued playing—until they passed the hour when expulsion was the penalty exacted from any member still remaining in the Club-house. They were still playing when morning broke, and though horrified and sleepy-eyed waiters informed them that they could no longer continue, their only answer was to stop the clock, an irritating reminder of the fleeting hours. In this fashion they continued till one o'clock the next afternoon, when, having realised that their escapade was a serious one, they strolled through a crowd of outraged members into the brilliant sunlight which, as if in irony, chanced that morning to be flooding the street. It should be added that before leaving the Club-house—for ever, as it turned out—the two culprits prudently wrote out their resignations. The curious thing was that the stakes during this sitting were by no means high, and the sums which changed hands were consequently comparatively small.

Rowlandson, the artist, who was a well-known figure at most of the fashionable gaming-houses of his time, frequently played through a night and the next day. On one occasion he remained at the hazard table for thirty-six hours without a break, the only refreshment which he took being brought to him in the gambling-room. Rowlandson, who was a most honourable man, was generally unlucky, and lost several legacies at play. His imperturbability was remarkable, and he never exhibited the slightest emotion whether he won or lost.

At the Roxburgh Club in St. James's Square—at the time when it was kept by Raggett, the well-known proprietor of White's—Hervey Combe, Tippoo Smith, Mr. Ward (a member of Parliament), and the distinguished Indian General, Sir John Malcolm, once sat from Monday evening till Wednesday morning at eleven o'clock, playing whist. Even then, they would very likely have continued playing, had not Hervey Combe been obliged to attend the funeral of one of his partners. Combe, who had won thirty thousand pounds from Sir John Malcolm, jocularly told him that he could have his revenge whenever he liked. "Thank you," replied Sir John, "another sitting like this would oblige me to return to India again!"

In all probability, however, the longest duel at cards which ever took place occurred in the eighteenth century at Sulzbach, where the famous adventurer, Casanova, made the acquaintance of an officer, d'Entragues by name, who was very fond of piquet. For four or five days in succession the Venetian and this officer played after dinner. At the end of that time, however, Casanova declined to play any more, having come to the conclusion that his opponent made a regular practice of rising from the table directly he had won ten or twelve louis. He adhered to this resolution for a day or two, but d'Entragues became quite importunate in offers to give him his revenge.

"I do not care to play," was the reply of Casanova, given with some effrontery. "We are not the same kind of gamblers. I play only for my pleasure and because the game amuses me, whilst you play merely to win."

"If I understand you rightly," was the retort, "this is deliberate rudeness!"

"I did not mean to be rude; but every time we have played you have left me in the lurch at the end of an hour."

"A proof of my solicitude for your pocket, for as you are a worse player than I, you would have lost a great deal had we continued."

"Possibly, but I don't believe it."

Eventually it was agreed that they should resume their contest, but that the player who was the first to rise from the piquet-table should forfeit fifty louis to his opponent. The stakes were five louis a hundred points, ready money only to be played for.

The game began at three in the afternoon; at nine d'Entragues proposed supper. Casanova said he was not hungry; whereupon his opponent laughed, and the game was continued. The onlookers, who were fairly numerous, went to supper, afterwards returning to remain till midnight, when the players were left alone with a croupier who attended to the accounts, the only utterances heard being those connected with the game.

From six in the morning, when the visitors who were taking the Sulzbach waters began to be about, the contest excited the greatest public interest. Casanova was now losing a hundred louis, though his luck had not been very bad.

At nine o'clock a lady, Madame Saxe by name, to whom d'Entragues was very devoted, arrived upon the scene and persuaded each of the combatants to partake of a cup of chocolate. D'Entragues was the first to consent to this; he believed that his opponent was near to giving in.

"Let us agree," he proposed, "that whoever asks for food, leaves the room for more than a quarter of an hour, or goes to sleep in his chair, shall be deemed the loser."

"I take you at your word," was Casanova's reply; "and shall be ready to hold to any other irritating conditions you may suggest."

The game proceeded. At twelve o'clock another meal was announced, but both players still declared that they were not hungry; at four, however, they took some soup. Towards supper-time the onlookers began to think that matters were going too far. Madame Saxe then made a suggestion that the stakes should be divided, but to this proposal Casanova firmly declined to consent. At this moment d'Entragues might have risen from the table a winner even after having paid the forfeit, for besides being the better player luck had favoured him. Nevertheless, his pride prevented him from abandoning what had degenerated into a mere contest of endurance. His appearance had become that of a corpse which had been disinterred, in striking contrast to the still normal looks of Casanova, who, to the remonstrances of Madame Saxe, replied that he would only give up the struggle by falling down dead.

The night wore on, and once more the players were left alone. By this time d'Entragues was showing evident signs of complete exhaustion, which was increased by an altercation about some trifling point raised by Casanova with the express purpose of further weakening his opponent's resistance.

At nine o'clock next morning Madame Saxe arrived to find her lover losing, and so dazed that he could hardly shuffle the cards, count, or properly discard. Once more she appealed to Casanova, pointing out to him that he could now rise a winner. In a tone of great gallantry the latter replied that he would agree to abandon the struggle if the forfeit were declared void, a condition to which d'Entragues declined to assent. The latter, though very weak, showed considerable annoyance at the manner in which Casanova had spoken to Madame Saxe, and declared that for his part he should not leave the table till either he or his opponent lay dead upon the floor.

In due course of time soup was again brought to the players, but d'Entragues, who was now in the last stage of weakness, fell down in a dead faint almost immediately after the cup had been raised to his lips, and in this condition he was carried away to bed. On the other hand, Casanova, after having given half a dozen louis to the croupier (who had been awake for forty-two consecutive hours), leisurely put the gold he had won in his pockets, and strolled out to a chemist's where he purchased a mild emetic. He then went to bed and slept lightly for a few hours, getting up about three o'clock in the afternoon with an excellent appetite. His opponent did not appear till the next day, when, much to his credit, he told Casanova that he bore him no ill-will, and was on the contrary grateful to him for a lesson which he should remember all the days of his life.

Casanova was not always as successful as this in his gambling enterprises, which indeed occasionally involved him in unpleasant situations; but like most adventurers of his type and age he was seldom depressed by losses. He would appear to have generally dominated other gamesters whom he met—a state of affairs which was probably not unconnected with the Venetian's well-known truculence. Besides, he was, as a rule, not over-burdened with money, a circumstance which perhaps made him the more ready to engage in a contest. People who are over-prosperous are not given to exhibiting any particular spirit in such affairs. A gentleman, who had been fortunate at cards, was asked to be a second in a duel, at a period when the seconds engaged as heartily as the principals. "I am not," replied he, "the man for your purpose at this time; but go and apply to a friend of mine from whom I won a thousand guineas last night, and I warrant you he will fight like any devil!"

Though ready to resent any slight, and tenacious of keeping up a reputation for being "cock of the walk" in the circles in which he moved, Casanova was possessed of great self-control, and always made a point of being urbane, even whilst sustaining a severe reverse—a pleasing characteristic which, he declared, obtained him access to much pleasant society. It was his constant practice to hold a bank at the various resorts of the pleasure-loving world which he visited during his adventurous career. At Aix in

Savoy (which is still a place in high favour with the votaries of chance owing to its two Casinos), Casanova was once particularly successful. He himself, with all a gambler's superstition, attributed his good fortune on this occasion to the appearance of three Englishmen—one of them Fox (then on the threshold of his career), who borrowed fifty louis of the great adventurer, whom he had previously met at Geneva.

From his earliest years Charles James Fox had been accustomed to gambling, having been elected a member of Brooks's when but sixteen years old. At that time the Club in question, now so decorous and staid, was the head-quarters of the fashionable London gamester, and the high-spirited youth fully availed himself of the excellent opportunities for dissipating a fortune which were here at easy command. On one occasion Fox sat playing at hazard for twenty-two consecutive hours, with the result that he rose the loser of eleven thousand pounds. At twenty-five he was a ruined man, his father having paid for him one hundred and forty thousand pounds out of his own property.

The SPENDTHRIFT

Deaf to his aged Sire's advice,
And biggotted to Cards and Dice;
With many a horrid Oath and Curse,
He loudly wails his empty Purse.

From an Eighteenth-Century Print.

Though a most unsuccessful gambler. Fox played whist and piquet exceedingly well, it being generally agreed at Brooks's that he might have made about four thousand a year at these games had he but confined himself to them. His misfortunes arose from playing at games of chance, particularly at faro, of which he was very fond. As a rule after eating and drinking plentifully, he would repair to the faro table, almost invariably rising a loser. Once indeed, and only once, he won about eight thousand pounds in the course of a single evening; part of this money he paid away to his creditors, and the remainder he lost again almost immediately in the same manner. Mr. Boothby, also an irreclaimable gamester and an intimate friend of Fox, speaking of the latter said, "He was unquestionably a man of first-rate talents, but so deficient in judgment as never to have succeeded in any object during his whole life. He loved only three things: women, play, and politics. Yet at no period did he ever form a creditable connection with a woman; he lost his whole fortune at the gaming-table; and with the exception of about eleven months he remained always in opposition."

Before he attained his thirtieth year, Fox had completely dissipated every shilling that he could either command or procure by the most ruinous expedients. During his career he experienced, at times, many of the severest privations attached to the vicissitudes which mark a gamester's progress, and frequently lacked money to defray common expenses of the most pressing nature. Topham Beauclerk—himself a man of pleasure and of letters—who lived much in Fox's society at that period of his life, used to say that no man could form an idea of the extremities to which his friend had been driven in order to raise money, after losing his last guinea at the faro table. For days in succession he was reduced to such distress as to be under the necessity of having recourse to the waiters of Brooks's Club to lend him assistance—even sedan-chairmen, whom he was unable to pay, used to clamour at his door.

Notwithstanding the numerous petty claims which at times made Fox's life unbearable, he could never resist high play, which seems to have completely destroyed his judgment as to the value of money, and prided himself upon the largeness of his stakes. The Duke of Devonshire, who, much to his honour, made a point of never touching a card, went one day out of curiosity to the Thatched House Club to see the gambling. After some time, finding himself awkward at being the only person in the rooms who was not participating in the play, he proposed a bet of fifty pounds on the odd trick to Charles Fox. "You'll excuse me, my Lord Duke," replied Charles, "I never play for pence." "I assure you, sir," answered his Grace, "you do, as often as I play for fifty pounds."

Fox, whilst a gambler of the most hopeless description, and extravagant almost beyond words, had, as is well known, many good points. Amongst them was hatred of meanness, which was an abomination of the worst sort in his eyes.

Finding himself on one occasion in considerable funds owing to a run of luck at faro, he remembered an old gambling debt due to Sir John Lade, familiarly known at that time as Sir John Jehu, and accordingly wrote, desiring an appointment so that he might pay what he owed. When they met, Charles produced the money, which Sir John no sooner saw, than calling for a pen and ink, he very deliberately began to reckon up the interest.

"What are you doing now?" cried Charles.

"Only calculating what the interest amounts to," replied the other.

"Oh, indeed!" returned Fox with great coolness, at the same time pocketing the cash, which he had already thrown upon the table. "Why, I thought, Sir John, that my debt to you was a debt of honour; but as you seem to view it in another light, and seriously mean to make a trading debt of it, I must inform you that I make it an invariable rule to pay my Jew creditors last. You must therefore wait a little longer for your money, sir; and when I meet my money-lending Israelites for the payment of principal and interest, I shall certainly think of Sir John Jehu, and expect to have the honour of seeing him in the company of my worthy friends from Duke's Place"—a locality which at that time swarmed with usurers.

Though Fox rather excelled at card games of skill, horse-racing was his darling amusement, until, from prudential motives, he quitted the Turf and all other forms of speculation. He played at games of chance with indifference, and would throw for a thousand guineas with as much sang-froid as he would twirl a teetotum for a shilling. But when his horse ran he was all eagerness and anxiety, always placing himself where the animal was to make its effort, or where the race was likely to be most strongly contested. From this spot he would watch the early part of the race with an immovable look, merely breathing quicker as they accelerated their pace. But when the horses came opposite to him, he rode in with them at full speed, whipping, spurring, and blowing, as if he would have infused his whole soul into the courage, speed, and perseverance of his favourite racer. The race being over, the fact that he had won or lost seemed to be a matter of perfect indifference to him, for he immediately began to discuss the next event, whether he had a horse entered for it or not.

The fact that Fox was often in the most dire financial straits through his reckless gambling does not seem to have excited any extraordinary astonishment amongst his contemporaries. The men of the eighteenth century were quite accustomed to the vicissitudes connected with gaming, which seems to have been viewed with the greatest leniency in every way.

The celebrated Beau Nash was sometimes in sore straits owing to a run of ill luck at play, and on one occasion, at York, he lost all the money he possessed. In these circumstances some of his companions agreed to equip him with fifty guineas, upon condition that he should stand at the great door of the Minster in a blanket as the people were coming out of church; and to this proposal he readily agreed. The Dean passing by unfortunately knew him. "What," cried the divine, "Mr. Nash in masquerade?" "Only a Yorkshire penance, Mr. Dean, for keeping bad company," said Nash, pointing to his companions. Some time after this the Beau won a wager of still greater consequence by riding naked through a village upon a cow, an escapade which was considered as a harmless and natural frolic.

In the year 1725, a giddy youth who had just resigned his fellowship at Oxford, brought his whole fortune to Bath; and without the smallest degree of skill in play, won a sufficient sum to make any ordinary man happy. His desire of gain, however, being increased by his good fortune, he plunged more deeply in the following October, and added four thousand pounds to his former capital. Hearing of this, Beau Nash, who was a good-natured man, one night invited him to supper, and told him there would come a time when he would repent having left the calm of a college life for the turbulent profession of a gamester. "You are a stranger to me," said he, "but to convince you of the part I take in your welfare, I'll give you fifty guineas to forfeit twenty every time you lose two hundred at one sitting." The young gentleman refused this offer, and was eventually ruined.

This system of tying up was very usual. The Duke of Bedford, being chagrined at losing a considerable sum, pressed Mr. Nash to tie him up for the future from playing deep. With this view the Beau gave his Grace one hundred guineas to forfeit ten thousand whenever he lost a sum to the same amount at one sitting. The Duke, however, loved play to distraction, and within a short time again lost eight thousand guineas at hazard. As he was on the point of throwing for three thousand more, Nash caught hold of the dice-box and entreated him to reflect on the penalty he would incur should he loose. For that time the Duke desisted, but so possessed was he by the love of play, that shortly afterwards, having lost a considerable sum at Newmarket, he was contented to pay the penalty.

On another occasion Nash undertook to cure a young peer of the gambling fever. Conscious of his own superior skill he determined to engage the Earl in single play for a very considerable sum. His Lordship lost his estate, and the title-deeds were put into the winner's possession; finally his very equipage was deposited as the last stake, and he lost that also. Nash, however, who showed himself to be the most generous of gamesters, returned all, only stipulating that he should be paid five thousand pounds whenever he should think proper to make the demand. He never did anything of the kind during the nobleman's life; but some time after his decease, Mr. Nash's affairs being on the wane, he demanded the money of his Lordship's heirs, who honourably paid it without hesitation.

At the present day gambling is more or less confined to large towns, but a different state of affairs prevailed in the eighteenth century, when whole properties frequently changed hands at the card-table. The owner of Warthall Hall, for instance, having lost all his money, in a frenzy of excitement finally risked the whole of his estate upon a low cut of the cards. He cut the deuce of diamonds, and in remembrance of his good luck fixed a representation of the lucky card upon the front of his house with the following inscription:—

Up now deuce and then a trey,[1]
Or Warthall's gone for ever and aye.

Shelley Hall in Suffolk, the remains of which still exist, was lost at play by Thomas Kerridge, the last squire, who died in 1743. According to tradition, he gambled away the house room by room; and when all the contents were gone and the house gutted, he pulled down certain portions and gambled away the bricks. Blo' Norton Hall, Norfolk, is also said to have been lost at play by its owner, Gawdy Brampton, who, when he was finally ruined, committed suicide in an attic, from which his ghost is still said to emerge and haunt an adjoining staircase—perhaps because his widow married the man who had won his money and the old Hall.

Many of the small tradesmen in the country towns were eager devotees of chance, and sharpers frequently reaped a rich harvest in provincial centres. Indeed, the happy-go-lucky spirit of the eighteenth century was very favourable to such gentry, who pillaged all ranks without distinction.

About 1780 there resided at Canterbury a barber who was famous for the way in which he made natty one-curled hunting wigs, but who was also much given to making bets and to boasting of his discernment and judgment. Two blacklegs, coming to Canterbury for the races, heard of this barber and immediately formed a plan to shave him in his own way. To accomplish the business, they went to one of the principal inns, where, ordering a capital supper, they sent for the perruquier to bespeak wigs for themselves and their servants. The knight of the strop readily and cheerfully attended; and, having taken the external dimensions of the gentlemen's heads, whilst totally ignorant of the schemes which lay within them, was about to depart, but was prevented by a pressing invitation from his new customers to take supper with them. He was of a convivial turn and fond of company, which in his own opinion afforded opportunities of displaying his great sagacity in the mysteries of betting; and for this reason he politely accepted the invitation.

After supper, a game of whist was suggested, but as the barber did not feel himself so great an adept at this as at his favourite game of "done and done," the proposal fell to the ground. As the guest of the evening was a great politician, and his companions were well informed of his manners and character, the conversation turned upon politics, from that unaccountably veering round till wagers became the general topic. Highly delighted at the introduction of a subject of which he deemed himself a perfect master, the barber listened with the greatest attention to the conversation, and eagerly offered several bets himself. As his two companions appeared rather shy, and hinted that it would not be safe to bet with a man who calculated matters so shrewdly as generally to win, he became very anxious to get the better of men whom he considered as "pigeons"—though, unluckily for him, they turned out to be "rooks."

After many propositions, they offered to bet him ten guineas that he would not repeat one sentence, and that only, during the space of ten minutes. Cunningly thinking that he had his men, the barber started up and swore he could repeat any sentence for an hour. After having blithely stepped home for a supply of cash, he returned, and a bet of fifty guineas having been made, both stakes were deposited under a hat on the table, the conditions being that the barber should without intermission repeat the words "*There he goes*," for half an hour's continuance. He accordingly took his station at the table, and, with a watch before him to note the time, began his recital of *There he goes*, *There he goes*, *There he goes*.

When he had kept on in a steady and unalterable tone for a quarter of an hour, one of the gentlemen, with a view to lead the barber from his stated subject, lifted up the hat, counted out half the money, and saying "D—n me if I don't go," put the cash in his pocket and walked off. This circumstance, however, had no effect upon the barber. A few minutes later the man who remained coolly pocketed the residue of the money, and added, as the barber repeated the words *There he goes*, "And d—n me if I don't follow him." The barber was now left alone with his eyes riveted on the watch, anxious for the expiration of the short time which still remained to elapse before his bet was won, but more confident than ever.

In the meantime, the departure of the two strangers without settling the bill excited the notice of the landlord; he went into the room, and the barber, looking him in the face, kept repeating *There he goes*, "Yes, sir, I know it; they have both been gone some time; pray are you to pay the bill?" No answer being given but *There he goes*, the host immediately ran for the barber's wife and a doctor, supposing him in a state of hopeless delirium. They arrived; his wife, taking him round the neck, in vain endeavoured to make him deviate from his purpose; the doctor, after feeling his pulse, pronounced him in a high fever, and was getting ready his apparatus for opening a vein, when the time expired, and the barber in a frenzy of excitement, jumped upon the table and exclaimed, "Bravo, I have won fifty guineas of the two gentlemen who are gone out!" The persons present now concluded, beyond a doubt, that he had lost his senses; his wife screamed, and the landlord called for assistance to have him secured.

When matters were explained, however, the landlord had a horse saddled, and rode in pursuit of the gentlemen, to remind them of their forgetfulness. After riding about ten miles, he overtook them in a lonely part of the road. Here he reminded them that they had not paid their bill, upon which they presented pistols to his head, robbed him of between twenty and thirty guineas, and advised him not to travel again upon such a foolish errand, but to look better after his inn, and tell the barber to be careful how he made his bets in future.

FOOTNOTES:

[1] A three.

II

The spirit of play in the eighteenth century—The Duke of Buckingham's toast—Subscription-Houses, Slaughter-Houses, and Hells—The staff of a gaming-house—Joseph Atkinson and Bellasis—Raids on King's Place and Grafton Mews—Methods employed by Bow Street officers—Speculative insurance—Increase of gaming in London owing to arrival of *émigrés*—Gambling amongst the prisoners of war—The Duc de Nivernois and the clergyman—Faro and E.O.—Crusade against West-End gamblers—The Duchess of Devonshire and "Old Nick"—Mr. Lookup—Tiger Roche—Dick England—Sad death of Mr. Damer—Plucking a pigeon.

During the last ten years of the reign of George II., "that destructive fury, the spirit of play" wrought great havoc in London. Gaming was declared to have become the business rather than the amusement of persons of quality, who were accused (probably with considerable truth) of being more concerned with speculation than with the proceedings of Parliament. Estates were almost as frequently made over by whist and hazard as by deeds and settlements, whilst the chariots of the nobility might be said to roll upon four aces. As a means of settling disputes, the wager was stated to have supplanted the sword, all differences of opinion being adjusted by betting.

In fashionable circles and at Court, gambling was especially prevalent. In January 1753 it was recorded that "His Majesty played at St. James's Palace on Twelfth Night for the benefit of the Groom-Porter." All the members of the Royal Family present on this occasion appear to have been winners, the Duke of Cumberland getting £3000. Amongst the losers were the Duke of Grafton and the Lords Huntingdon, Holdernesse, Ashburnham, and Hertford. The exact amount of benefit which accrued to the Groom-Porter from the evening's play does not transpire.

Henry Bennet, Earl of Arlington, had a house near the site of the present Buckingham Palace, which went by his name. It was afterwards purchased by John Sheffield, Duke of Buckingham, who, after obtaining an additional grant of land from the Crown, rebuilt it in a magnificent manner in 1703. During his residence here, the Duke was a constant visitor at the then noted gaming-house in Marylebone, the place of assemblage of all the infamous sharpers of the time. His Grace always gave them a dinner at the conclusion of the season, and his parting toast was, "May as many of us as remain unhanged next spring meet here again." Quin related this story at Bath, within the hearing of Lord Chesterfield, when his Lordship was surrounded by a crowd of worthies of the same stamp. Lady Mary Wortley alludes to the amusement in this line:—

Some Dukes at Marybone bowl time away.

As the century waned, play became more and more popular in London. So great indeed was the toleration accorded to gaming in the West End of the town that what were virtually public tables may be said to have existed. These were well-known under the names of Subscription-Houses, Slaughter-Houses, and Hells, and were frequented by less aristocratic gamesters than the Clubs, where whist, piquet, and other games were played for large sums. At the houses not inaptly called Hells, hazard was played every night, and faro on certain nights in each and every week, nearly all the year round. These Hells were the resort of gentlemen, merchants, tradesmen, clerks, and sharpers of all degrees and conditions, very expensive dinners being given twice or thrice a week to draw together a large company, who, if they meant to play, were abundantly supplied with wines and liquors gratis.

The advantage to the faro bank varied at different stages of the game: the least advantage to the proprietor of the bank, and against the punter, was about three and a half per cent and the greatest twenty-six per cent. It is said that the annual expense of maintaining one of these Hells exceeded £8000, which of course came out of the pockets of its frequenters.

Quite a large army of retainers were attached to every well-regulated gaming-house. The first, and of the greatest importance, was the commissioner, always a proprietor, who looked in at night, the week's account being audited by him and two other proprietors. Then followed the director, who superintended the rooms; the operator, who dealt the cards at faro, or any other game; the croupier, who watched the cards and gathered the money for the bank; a puff, handsomely paid to decoy others to play; a clerk, who acted as a check upon the puff, to see that he embezzled none of the money given him to play with; a squib, who was a puff of meaner rank, and received but a low salary, whilst learning to deal; a flasher, to swear how often the bank had been stripped; a dunner, who went about to recover money lost at play; a waiter, to fill out wine, snuff candles, and attend the gaming-room; an attorney, the sharper the better; a captain, ready to fight any gentleman who might be peevish at losing his money; an usher, to light gentlemen up and downstairs, and give the porter the word; a porter, who was generally a foot soldier; an orderly man, whose duty consisted in walking up and down on the outside of the door to give notice to the porter, and alarm the house at the approach of the constables; a runner, employed to obtain intelligence of the justices' meeting. Beside these, there were link-boys, coachmen, chairmen, drawers, and others, who might bring information of danger, at half a guinea each for every true alarm. Finally, there was a sort of affiliated irregular force, the members of which—affidavitmen, ruffians, and bravoes—were capable of becoming assassins upon occasion.

A celebrated sporting resort at the end of the eighteenth century was Mundy's Coffee-House, in Round Court, opposite York Buildings, in the Strand, then kept by Sporting Medley (the owner of Bacchus and some other horses of eminence upon the Turf). Here thousands were nightly transferred over the hazard and card tables by O'Kelly, Stroud, Tetherington, and a long list of adventurous followers.

Another famous gaming-house was kept by a certain Joseph Atkinson and his wife at No. 15 under the Piazza, in Covent Garden. Here they daily gave elaborate dinners, cards of invitation being sent to the clerks of merchants, bankers, and brokers in the city. Atkinson used to say that he liked citizens—whom he called "flats"—better than any one else, for when they had dined they played freely, and after they had lost all their money they had credit to borrow more. It was his custom to send any pigeons who had been completely plucked to some of their solvent friends, who could generally be induced to arrange matters in a satisfactory way. The game generally played here was E.O.,[2] a sort of roulette.

Keepers of gaming-houses in London were very liable to be black-mailed by men whose principal means of livelihood was obtaining "hush money." A certain class of individuals existed who for a specific amount undertook to defend keepers of Hells against prosecutions. One of the most notorious of these was Theophilus Bellasis, sometimes clerk and sometimes client to a Bow Street attorney—John Shepherd by name—who would, when it was likely to be profitable, act as prosecutor of persons keeping gaming-houses. The magistrates at last realised the collusion which existed between Bellasis and Shepherd, and refused to move in cases where the two rogues were concerned.

The houses, called by sharpers Slaughter-Houses, were those where persons were employed by the proprietors to pretend to be playing at hazard for large sums of money, with a view to inducing some unthinking individual to join in the play. When the scheme succeeded, the pigeon, by means of loaded dice and other fraudulent methods, was eventually dispossessed of all his cash, and perhaps plunged into debt, for which a bond was given, the embarrassments of which he felt for some years after. If, however, he returned to play again with the hope of regaining what in such company was past redemption, his ruin was quickly and completely sealed.

At one time, the parish officers of St. Ann's, Soho, set up a number of lanterns and boards with the words "*Beware of bad houses*" painted upon them, for the purpose of ridding the neighbourhood of dissolute and abandoned women. In consequence of this having had the desired effect, it was proposed to put up similarly-worded notices near the Hells and Slaughter-Houses of St. James's, but the idea was never carried into effect.

Places where faro was played abounded about Pall Mall and St. James's Street, and from time to time exciting scenes were witnessed when the authorities decided upon making a raid.

In 1799 considerable uproar was caused in Pall Mall by a raid upon Nos. 1 and 3 King's Place, which were attacked by what were facetiously termed the "Bow Street troops" acting under a search warrant. These in a very short time carried the place by storm, and took ten prisoners, together with a great quantity of baggage, stores, which consisted mainly of tables for rouge-et-noir and hazard; cards, dice, counters, strong doors, bars and bolts. The attack began by a stratagem put into execution by "General Rivett," who was in supreme command of the attacking force. He sought to gain an entrance at the street door of No. 1; but this having failed, and all attempts to force it having proved ineffectual, one of the light troops mounted the counterscarp of the area, and descended into the kitchen, while another scaled a ladder affixed to a first floor of No. 3; and having each made good their footing, opposition being then abandoned by the besieged who had betaken themselves to flight, the attacking force without molestation opened the gates and let in the main body, after which a general search and pursuit ensued. Several gamblers retreated to the top of the houses adjoining, whither they were followed and taken prisoners; one poor devil, the supposed proprietor of No. 3, was smoked in a chimney, from whence he was dragged down—a black example to all gamesters! Three French *émigrés* were among the captured, one of whom had his retreat cut off just as he was issuing from a house in Pall Mall, through which he had descended unobserved, and by which way some others escaped. Mother Windsor and her nymphs, who were well-known residents in the locality, were much alarmed by the operations; and the old lady, who declared that the presence of gaming in the vicinity had long been a scandal, vociferously applauded to the skies the vigilance of the police in putting down such pests of society.

A RAID ON A LONDON GAMING-HOUSE.
From a Print in the possession of Messrs. Robson & Co., 23 Coventry Street, W.

About the same time No. 13 Grafton Mews, Fitzroy Square, obtained an unenviable reputation as being a veritable Temple of Fraud, an illegal lottery insurance business being carried on there, which impoverished the poorer class of people residing in the neighbourhood. The house in question, which it was said had been specially built, was to all appearance a square brick tower about fifty feet high—on three sides it presented not the slightest sign of habitation; towards Grafton Mews, however, it bore the usual semblance of a stable.

To this place flocked grooms, valets, and all the silly fry of the district, carrying with them as much money as they could scrape together. Business was generally over by the afternoon, when the proprietors, who never made their exit by the door, climbed up to the top of the tower, and got through a hole in the roof—from which, by a ladder, they descended to a slated roof of a back place about twenty feet lower; they then crawled along about twenty feet of wall, and by an aperture in another, like a gun-port, descended into a back yard, and completed their cat-like line of march through a house in Hertford Street. This, to the astonishment of the neighbours, was done regularly every morning.

The place having become a public scandal, Townshend, with several Bow Street runners and four carpenters, went to Warren Street one morning, three hackney coaches being posted at some distance from the scene of action.

On the arrival of the peace officers, the four proprietors of No. 13 came out through the roof, and planted their ladder; but it gave way, and they were obliged to jump upon the slated roof twenty feet below them. By some marvellous chance, however, they escaped uninjured, the slates only being broken. They then jumped upon an adjacent wall, and flung their books into the garden of a gentleman's house. No. 17 Warren Street, and followed themselves; their idea was to escape through his back door, but the owner was fortunately at home, and resisted this design. They then leaped the wall of the next house, Drover's, the hairdresser, with their books, and in this house they were secured. One of them fired a pistol at the officers, which fortunately did no harm. The runners had cutlasses and axes, with which they made their way into the house.

The inhabitants of the district, it may be added, did not exhibit any enthusiasm for the officers of the law—on the contrary, they showed considerable displeasure against those who had come there to preserve most of them from misery and ruin. The informer, never a popular character, was a lean, cadaverous old woman. She accompanied the swindlers in the first coach, with the hootings of the rabble in her ears, and the whole cavalcade moved off the ground, escorted by a very hostile crowd which accompanied it to Bow Street. Here the four men, who had been arrested with so much difficulty, were sentenced to six months' imprisonment each in the house of correction in Coldbath Fields.

It would appear that previous to 1778 gaming was never conducted upon the methodical system of partnership concerns, wherein considerable capital was embarked. After that period, the vast licence allowed to keepers of fraudulent E.O. tables, and the great length of time which elapsed before they met with any check from the police, afforded a number of dissolute and abandoned characters many excellent opportunities of acquiring property, which was afterwards increased in the low gaming-houses, by nefarious methods at Newmarket and other fashionable places of resort, and in the lottery. At length, though these individuals had started without any property, or any visible means of lawful support, a sum of money, little short of one million sterling, was said to have been acquired by a class originally (with some few exceptions) of the lowest and most depraved description. This enormous mass of wealth was employed as a great and an efficient capital for carrying on various illegal establishments, particularly gaming-houses, and houses for fraudulent insurances in the lottery.

Part of this capital was even said to be utilised in subsidising various faro banks kept by ladies of fashion, whilst a certain proportion was also devoted to fraudulent insurance in the lotteries, where the chances were calculated to yield about thirty per cent to the gambling syndicate, most of the members of which maintained a number of clerks, employed during the drawing of the lotteries, who conducted the business, without risk, in counting-houses where no insurances were taken, but to which books were carried, not only from the different offices in every part of the town, but also from the "Morocco-men," who went from door to door taking insurances, and enticing the poor and the middle ranks to become adventurers.

In calculating the chances upon the whole numbers in the wheels, and the premiums which were paid, there was generally about £33:1:3 per cent in favour of the lottery insurers: but when it is considered that the people generally, from not being able to understand or recollect high numbers, always fixed on low ones, the chance in favour of the insurer was greatly increased, and the deluded poor plundered.

In the early part of the eighteenth century, speculative insurance, which could be effected upon anything, including lives, was a favourite form of gambling in England. Any one's life could be insured, including that of the King, and, to such an extent was this carried, that daily quotations of the rates on the lives of eminent public personages were issued by members of Garraway's and Lloyd's. The highest premium ever paid is supposed to have been twenty-five per cent on the life of George II., when he fought at Dettingen. On the fall of the leaders of the Rebellion of 1745 very large sums changed hands; whilst a number of insurance brokers were absolutely ruined owing to the escape of Lord Nithsdale from the Tower—an exploit which this nobleman accomplished by the aid of his devoted wife. As time went on these speculative insurances became a public scandal, and they were finally made illegal by the Gambling Act of 1774.

At the time of the French Revolution hordes of *émigrés* of all classes took up their temporary or permanent residence in London, with the result that over thirty gaming-places were, more or less, publicly established in the Metropolis. Here, besides faro and hazard, the foreign games of roulette and rouge-et-noir flourished, a regular gradation of houses existing, suited to all ranks, from the man of fashion to the pickpocket.

The mania for gaming amongst the exiles was confined to no particular class—high and low alike being affected by it. Nothing, for instance, could exceed the rage for gambling which possessed the prisoners of war at Dartmoor. About two hundred of them, including a number of Italians, having lost all their clothes by gaming, were sent to the prison ships in the Hamoaze, to be clothed anew, many more being left in rags. These unfortunate men played even for their rations, living three or four days on offal, cabbage-stalks, or, indeed, anything which chance might throw in their way. They staked the clothes on their backs, and even their bedding. It was the custom at Dartmoor for those who had sported away the latter article to huddle very close together at night, in order to keep each other warm. One out of the number was elected boatswain for the time being, and at twelve o'clock at night would pipe all hands to turn, an operation which, from their proximity to each other, had to be simultaneous. At four o'clock in the morning the pipe was heard again, and the reverse turn taken.

Such of the *émigrés* belonging to the upper classes as possessed funds could easily indulge their passion for play in the fashionable circles where many of them had made themselves popular during previous and more pleasant visits to England. Many, like the Duc de Nivernois, had intimate friends in high places. Before the Revolution he had been Ambassador in England. This nobleman was well known for his love of chess, which on one occasion led to a very pleasant incident. Staying with Lord Townshend, the Duc, when out for a ride was obliged by a heavy shower to seek shelter at a wayside house occupied by a clergyman, who to a poor curacy added the care of a few scholars in the neighbourhood. In all this might make his living about eighty pounds a year, on which he had to maintain a wife and six children. When the Duc rode up, the clergyman, not knowing his rank, begged him to come in and dry himself, which he was glad to do, borrowing a pair of old worsted stockings and slippers and warming himself by a good fire. After some conversation the Duc observed an old chess-board hanging up, and asked the clergyman whether he could play. The latter told him that he could play pretty tolerably, but found it difficult in that part of the country to get an antagonist. "I am your man," said the Duc. "With all my heart," answered the clergyman, "and if you will stay and take pot-luck, I will try if I cannot beat you." The day continuing rainy the Duc accepted the proffered hospitality, and found his antagonist a much better player than himself. Indeed, the clergyman won every game. This, however, in no way annoyed the Duc, who was delighted to meet with a man who could give him so much entertainment at his favourite game. He accordingly inquired into the state of his host's family affairs, and making a memorandum of his address, he thanked him and rode away without revealing who he was.

Some months elapsed and the clergyman never thought of the matter, when one evening a footman rode up to the door and delivered the following note—"The Duc de Nivernois presents his compliments to the Rev. Mr. Bentinck, and as a remembrance of the good drubbing he received at chess, begs that he will accept the living of X——, worth £400 per annum, and that he will wait upon his Grace the Duke of Newcastle on Friday next, to thank him for the same." The good clergyman was some time before he could imagine this missive to be more than a jest, and hesitated to obey the mandate; but as his wife insisted on his taking the chance, he went up to town, where to his unspeakable satisfaction he found that his nomination to the living had actually taken place.

The habits of dissipation which had prevailed at Versailles in some measure affected the English upper classes, many of whom were thoroughly versed in the amusements so popular in France.

For a time a positive rage for gaming seized fashionable London, and a number of ladies kept what were practically public gaming-tables to which any one with money could obtain comparatively easy admission.

Faro is supposed to have been invented by a noble Venetian, who gave it the name of *bassetta*; and for the evils resulting from it he was banished his country. In 1674 Signor Justiniani, Ambassador from Venice, introduced the game into France, where it was called *bassette*. Some of the princes of the blood, many of the *noblesse*, and several persons of the greatest fortune having been ruined by it, a severe law was enacted by Louis XIV. against its play. To elude this edict, it was disguised under the name of *pour et contre*, "for and against"; and this occasioning new and severe prohibitions, it was again changed to the name of *le pharaon*, in order to evade the *arrêts* of Parliament. From France this game soon found its way to England, where it was first called basset, but in the fashionable circles, where at that time it enjoyed a great vogue, it was invariably known by the name of faro.

Faro, pharo, or pharaoh, which was Fox's favourite game, was supposed to be easy to learn, fair in its rules, and pleasant to play. Two packs of cards were used, and any number of people could play, one pack being for the players whilst the banker had another. Fifty-two cards were spread out, and the players staked upon one or more which they might fancy. The banker dealt out his pack to the right, which was for himself, and to the left (called the *carte anglaise*) for the players, who instead of their pack often used a "livret," specially adapted for staking. The "livret" consisted of thirteen cards, with four others called "figures." The "little figure" had a blue cross on each side, and represented ace, deuce, and three. The "yellow figure"—yellow on both sides—signified 4, 5, and 6. The "third figure" had a black lozenge in the centre, and stood for 7, 8, and 9. The "great figure" was a red card, and indicated knave, queen, and king. The banker won all the money staked on any card corresponding with a card dealt by him to the right, and had to pay double stakes on any card dealt to the left which players had selected in their own pack. If he dealt two equal cards (called a doublet) he won half of all the money staked upon the card of that value, and on the last card of his pack, did the players win, he only paid even money. In reality the chances were very favourable to the holder of the bank.

Complaints were very rife as to the way in which these faro parties were conducted. An especial grievance was "card money," a small sum paid by each visitor into a pool for every new pack of cards used. This money was supposed to be a perquisite of the servants, though malicious rumours declared that it never reached them. The advent of French *émigrés* after the French Revolution was also the cause of considerable irritation, it being declared that many of the exiled *noblesse* completely monopolised some of the tables, round which they formed a circle, and excluded English ladies and gentlemen from taking part in the game.

The losses of many of those who played at faro were so heavy and constant that the banks contracted many bad debts; and in addition the fashionable parties in time became full of little tricks and artifices which were to the detriment of those holding the bank. Some of the latter found it advisable to employ eight croupiers instead of the four usually attached to each faro table, for the pigeons were all flown and those who remained were little better than hawks.

Faro, in the female circles of fashion, had given way to a more specious and alluring game called lottery, which, instead of wheels, consisted of two bags, from which prizes and blanks were drawn. The holder of the bank derived an advantage of upwards of thirty per cent.

About 1794 some of the ladies who gave gambling parties in St. James's Square began to add roulette as an increased attraction to those fond of gaming. It was remarked at the time that this was merely the old game of E.O. under a different name. As a matter of fact the two are somewhat alike, though roulette is a far more complicated and amusing method of losing money.

An E.O. table was circular in form and as a rule four feet in diameter. The outside edge formed the counter on which the stakes were placed, the letters E.O. being marked all round it. In the centre was a stationary gallery in which the ball rolled, and an independent round table moving by means of handles on an axis. The ball was started in one direction and the table rotated in the other, there being forty compartments of equal size, twenty marked E and twenty marked O, the whole principle being that of roulette without a zero. This very necessary adjunct to a successful bank, was in time furnished by the adoption of "bar holes" into which two of the forty spaces were converted, the practice being that the banker won all the bets on the opposite letter whilst not paying over that into which the ball fell. With such a proportion of two in forty, or five per cent in its favour, the banks did very well.

Gaming raged throughout Society at this time, and it was even declared that young ladies were taught whist and casino at fashionable boarding-schools, where their "winning ways" were cultivated in this direction. One schoolmistress, it was averred, was in despair at the dullness of her pupils, who were quite unable to grasp the comparatively easy intricacies of faro. Gillray was quick to grasp the opportunity which such a state of affairs afforded to his powers of satire, and was pitiless in his caricatures of female gamblers. "Faro's Daughters, or the Kenyonian Blow-up to Gamblers," published in 1796, was one of the most striking of these. In this Lady Archer and Mrs. Concannon were shown in the pillory, upbraiding one another. Lord Kenyon had made some very scathing comments upon the vice of gaming during a recent trial to recover fifteen pounds won at play on a Sunday, and had declared that the highest society was setting the worst example to the lowest, being under the impression that it was too great for the law. He himself, he added, should the opportunity arise, would see that any gamblers brought before him, whatever their rank or station, should be severely dealt with if convicted, and though they might be the first ladies in the land they should certainly exhibit themselves in the pillory.

Gambling in the West End of London amongst ladies had indeed become a public scandal, and in due course the authorities found themselves bound to take action.

In 1797 a regular crusade was made against faro, and the Countess of Buckinghamshire, Lady Elizabeth Luttrell, Mrs. Mary Sturt, Mr. Concannon, and Mr. O'Burne, were charged at Marlborough Street with having "played at a certain fraudulent and unlawful game called faro, at the house of the Earl of Buckinghamshire, in St. James's Square."

With them was also charged Henry Martindale, who had financed the bank—the four or five people employed to run the table were each paid half a guinea a night by him, tenpence out of which was deducted for the use of the maids.

A witness, Joseph Evatt by name, deposed that he had seen Lady Buckinghamshire play every Monday and Friday, as regular as the days came. Her ladyship, said he, used to continue *punting* and betting, paying and receiving, from night till morning.

The lady's counsel, Mr. Onslow, endeavoured to invalidate this man's testimony by showing that he was a terrible democrat, and disaffected to His Majesty's person and government; and also by proving that he wanted to palm an old suit of livery on his master, and to persuade the tailor to charge for a new one, and give him part of the money. To prove the first charge Mr. Onslow examined the witness Evatt himself, and asked him if he had not declared that the Government was a bad one, and that he should like to cut the King's head off? The magistrate, Mr. Conant, would not suffer him to answer such a question. To prove the latter, the foreman of Mr. Blackmore, a tailor, said that Evatt having saved a suit of livery as good as new, wanted Mr. Blackmore to take it, allow him four guineas, and send it home as a new suit. The magistrate did not consider this such a notorious piece of fraud in a footman, as to prevent his being believed on his oath.

Joseph Burford swore to the fact of Lady Buckinghamshire playing repeatedly.

Mr. Onslow ended by saying that he trusted the magistrate would not, upon the evidence of such men as Evatt and Burford, convict Lady Buckinghamshire, and hold her up as an object for the finger of democratic scorn to point at.

Notwithstanding this defence, the lady was sentenced to pay a fine of fifty pounds, as were Lady Elizabeth Luttrell, Mrs. Mary Sturt, and Mr. O'Burne. The case against Mr. Concannon was quashed owing to his having been described as Lucas Concannon instead of Lucius.

Martindale was fined two hundred pounds, and in consequence of the scandal produced by the whole affair was eventually made a bankrupt, by which the ladies of the fashionable world were thrown into a state of considerable alarm. Martindale it was who supplied the beautiful Duchess of Devonshire, and many other dashing women of distinction, with sums to support their gambling propensities. His assignees were said to have claims on some of the first families of England to the amount of £180,000, and the curious disclosures which were made engrossed much attention in all the sporting circles.

Many of the great ladies of that day lived only for pleasure, spending enormous sums in dress, and also in carriages and horseflesh, it being a point of honour amongst them to possess a superb turn-out. One lady, well known for the splendour of her equipage at race meetings where she cut a distinguished figure, once apologised to a friend for appearing at Doncaster with a humble four-in-hand and four out-riders, saying that her coachman wished to come with six horses as usual, but she thought it right, in such hard times, to come "incog."

The gambling ladies of that day came into contact with all sorts of shady characters, many of whom were very unpolished diamonds. Such a one was the man known as "Old Nick," whose principal revenue was drawn from a hazard table where strangers were treated with a hospitality which they generally had good cause to remember.

Old Nick also had a considerable interest in a number of lottery insurance offices, lent money, and gambled himself when able to get in contact with any unplucked pigeon. Having once stripped a young man at cards of about £100, with which he had been entrusted for the purpose of paying a bill for the beautiful Duchess of Devonshire, her Grace applied in person to the winner to refund the whole, or, at least, a part of his booty. Old Nick's answer was: "Well, Madam, the best thing you can do is to sit down with me at cards, and play for all you have about you; after I win your smock, so far from refunding, I'll send you home *bare*—to your Duke, my dear."

One of his friends being under trial for a very serious charge and having no defence left but his character, produced Old Nick in order to vouch for his respectability. The latter's ready eloquence represented him as the most amiable and innocent of the creation. The counsel for the prosecution having smelt a rat, began to ply the witness with such questions as he positively refused to answer. Being asked the reason, he answered honestly for once in his life: "My business here was to give the man a good character, and you, you flat, imagine that I'm come to give him a bad one."

THE BEAUTIFUL DUCHESS THROWING A MAIN.
By Rowlandson.

In the early part of the year 1805 the West End was much excited by a statement in a morning paper referring to the supposed discovery by the Duke of Devonshire of immense losses at play, principally to gamesters of her own sex, incurred by his lovely Duchess. Her Grace's whole loss, chiefly at faro, was declared to amount to £176,000, of which a private gentlewoman and bosom friend, Mrs. —— was said to have won no less than £30,000. The discovery was made to the Duke one Sunday; the Duchess rushed into his library, and, in a flood of tears, told him she was ruined in fame and reputation, if these claims of honour were not instantly discharged. His Grace was thunderstruck when he learned the extent of her requisition, and the names of the friends who had contributed in so extraordinary a manner to such extreme embarrassments. Having soothed her in the best manner he was able, he sent for two confidential friends, imparted to them all the circumstances, and asked them how he should act. Their answer was promptly given—"Pay not one guinea of any such infamous demands!" and this advice, it was supposed, would be strictly adhered to by the Duke. Her Grace was said to have executed some bonds, to satisfy, for a moment, these gambling claimants; but, of course, they could be of no avail. Two gentlemen and five ladies formed the snug flock of rooks that had so unmercifully stripped this female pigeon of distinction.

A few days later, however, *The Morning Herald*, which was responsible for the startling news, declared that the fiction of the female gamblers of distinction in a house fitted up near St. James's Street for their ruinous orgies, began to die away; for it had been discovered that the supposed pigeoned Duchess, declared to have sacrificed half a million sterling of her lord's fortune, had never gambled at any game of chance, whilst her amiable companion, who was a pattern of domestic propriety, instead of having helped to pluck her Grace, had never played for a guinea in the course of her life. This denial was probably inspired from influential quarters.

The gambling ladies seem to have fallen into obscurity when the nineteenth century began; the "faro dames," as they were called, found their occupation gone. Their game, at which few of them had "cut with honours," was up, and their "odd tricks" were no longer of any avail in London. One of the most notorious, Mrs. Concannon, migrated to Paris, where her house continued for some time to be the meeting-place of those fond of deep play.

Whist now began to be a good deal played at fashionable parties, but in 1805 four-handed cribbage became the fashionable game in the West End, and whist, during a temporary eclipse, as it declined in the West, rose with increase of splendour in the East. At a city club the stakes played for were ten pounds a game, and guineas were betted on the odd trick. A select party of business men, well known on the city side of Temple Bar, once played at whist from one Wednesday afternoon till the next Friday night, and only left off then because two of the players were unfortunately Jews.

At another whist party, a lady who had not been accustomed to move in quite as good society as the other guests, won a rubber of twenty guineas. The gentleman who was her opponent pulled out his pocket-book and tendered £21 in bank-notes.[3] The fair gamester observed, with a disdainful toss of her head: "In the great houses which I frequent, sir, we always use gold." "That may be, madam," replied the gentleman, "but in the little houses which I frequent we always use paper!"

At this time adventurers abounded, many of whom profited by the speculative tendencies of the age. A character of the first magnitude in the annals of gaming, for instance, was a Mr. Lookup, who lived towards the close of the eighteenth century. A Scotchman by birth, a gamester by profession, he accumulated a considerable fortune by methods of none too reputable a kind.

Originally an apprentice to an apothecary in the north of England, he acted in that profession as journeyman in the city of Bath. Soon after the death of his master, he paid his addresses to his mistress, the widow; and, having none of that bashful modesty about him which is sometimes an obstacle to a man in such pursuits, and being a remarkably tall stout man, with a tolerably good figure, he prevailed on the Bath matron to favour him with her hand.

From his infancy Lookup manifested a strong propensity for play, and as he grew up became very expert at several games. Till his marriage, however, he was hampered by lack of funds, which prevented him from exercising his skill and judgment to much advantage. Finding himself master of five hundred pounds brought to him by his wife, he soon shut up shop, and turned his application from pharmacy to speculation. He became a first-rate piquet and whist player, and soon mastered various other games of chance and skill; in a short time, by incessant industry, greatly increasing his capital.

Lord Chesterfield and Mr. Lookup, for a long time, played constant matches at piquet together, the former being something of an adept at the game; but Mr. Lookup's superior skill at length prevailed, with the result that very considerable gains passed into his pocket.

Lord Chesterfield would also sometimes amuse himself at billiards with Mr. Lookup, and upon one of these occasions the peer had the laugh turned against him by the sharp tactics of his antagonist. Mr. Lookup had met with an accident by which he was deprived of the sight of one of his eyes, though to any cursory observer it appeared as perfect as the other. Having beaten the peer playing evens, Lookup asked how many his lordship would give him, if he put a patch upon one eye. Lord Chesterfield agreed to give him five, upon which Lookup beat him several times successively. At length his lordship, with some petulance, exclaimed, "Lookup, I think you play as well with one eye as two." "I don't wonder at it, my lord," replied Lookup, "for I have seen only out of one for these ten years." With the money he won of Lord Chesterfield he bought some houses at Bath, and jocularly named them Chesterfield Row.

After he had accumulated a considerable sum by play, Mr. Lookup went to London, and, having buried his wife, married another widow with a very large fortune. His plan of operations was now much enlarged; and, though he played occasionally for his own amusement, or when he met with what is termed a "good thing," he abandoned gaming as a regular profession. He now struck out several schemes, some visionary and others advantageous; among the former being a project for making saltpetre. A foreigner having drawn up a specious plan, presented it to Lookup, who, from his superficial knowledge of chemistry, thought the scheme practicable. A considerable range of buildings was erected for carrying on these works near Chelsea; salaries were appointed for the directors and supervisors, and large sums expended to bring this favourite scheme to perfection. So sanguine were Lookup's hopes of success, that he persuaded a particular friend of his (Captain Hamilton) to become a partner, with the result that the latter lost many thousands. At length, tired with the fruitless expense and repeated disappointments, he abandoned this project for others less delusive.

Mr. Lookup was concerned in many privateering ventures, several of which proved successful; at any rate he was thought to be a substantial gainer in these enterprises. At the close of the war he engaged in the African trade, and had considerable dealings in that commerce to the time of his decease.

As he grew old, however, his darling passion would at times predominate; and within a few weeks of his death he was known to sit up whole nights playing for very considerable sums. It was even averred that he died with a pack of cards in his hand, at his favourite game of humbug or two-handed whist; on which Sam Foote jocularly observed, "that Lookup was *humbugged* out of the world at last."

Some description of Mr. Lookup's favourite game, of which he is said to have been the inventor, may not be out of place. Though now obsolete, it was once very popular at the rooms in Bath, and in the West End of London.

Humbug may properly be called two-handed whist, as only two persons play. The cards are shuffled and cut; the lowest deals out all the cards, and turns up the last for the trump. Each player has now twenty-six cards in his hand, and the object is to make as many tricks as they can, all the laws of whist prevailing, the cards being of the same value as when four play. But the honours do not reckon any further than they prevail in making tricks by their superiority over inferior cards; the tricks reckon from one to as many as are gained; for instance, if one player has twenty tricks, and the other only six, the first wins fourteen, and if they play a guinea a trick of course wins fourteen guineas. The game finishes every deal, when the balance is settled, and they then commence another game. As each player knows, at first, all the cards his adversary has in his hand, it is common, in order to sort them, to lay them with their faces up; but after they have ranged them, and begun to play, they are as careful of concealing their cards as they are at the common game of whist, it then depending upon memory to know what cards have been played and what remain in hand. As it is allowed only to turn up the last trick to see what has been played, a revoke is punished with the same rigour at this game as at whist; and the forfeiting three tricks is often worth more at humbug than at the former game.

The London of the past swarmed with sharpers of every description on the look-out for rich young men. Billiard-rooms which are now quite decorous resorts were favourite haunts of these gentry.

The noted Captain Roche, known as Tiger Roche, was once at the Bedford billiard-table, when it was extremely crowded. As he was knocking the balls about with a cue. Major Williamson, who wanted to talk to him about some business, desired him to leave off, as he monopolised the table and hindered gentlemen from playing. "Gentlemen!" exclaimed Roche with a sneer. "Why, Major, except you and I, and two or three more, there is not a gentleman in the room: the rest are all low blacklegs." On leaving the place the Major expressed some astonishment at his companion's rudeness, and wondered that, out of so numerous a company, it was not resented. "Oh, d—n the scoundrels, sir," said Roche; "there was no fear of that, as there was not a thief in the room that did not suppose himself one of the two or three gentlemen I mentioned."

A particularly dangerous individual was the notorious Dick England, an Irishman of obscure origin, who rose to comparative prosperity through gaming and betting. A hard-headed man, England possessed great control over his temper, which, however, when given a free run, could be terrible. Having played at hazard one evening with a certain young tradesman of his acquaintance, England lost some three or four score pounds, for which he gave his draft upon Hankey, the banker. Having persuaded his antagonist to give him his revenge, the luck turned, and England not only won his money back, but as much more in addition. It then being late, he desired to retire, and requested his antagonist to pay in cash or to give a cheque upon his banker for the money which he had lost. The tradesman resolutely refused to do either, on the plea that he had been tricked, and that the money had not been fairly won. England once more demanded the money, and when it was again refused, he tripped up the young man's heels, rolled him up in the carpet, and snatching a case-knife from the sideboard, cut off his long hair close to the scalp. This violent action, coupled with the menacing attitude of England still flourishing the knife, and uttering the most deep-toned imprecations, had such an effect upon the young man in the stillness of past three o'clock in the morning, that he arose, and with the meekness of a lamb wrote a draft for the amount of his loss, took his leave very civilly, wishing the Captain a good morning, and never mentioned the circumstance again.

SHARPERS AND BUCKS IN A BILLIARD ROOM.

Dick England was a constant frequenter of all places likely to afford him pigeons worth plucking. At a tennis court he met the Honourable Mr. Damer, who was in the habit of playing tennis for amusement and exercise. One evil day, however, when no one was about, Mr. Damer played a game with England, who was profuse in his admiration for his opponent's skill. Though Mr. Damer knew England's reputation, and would not have been seen at Ranelagh with him, or had him at his table for a thousand pounds, he was not proof against the man's flattery, and England soon became his habitual opponent at tennis.

The latter, in league with other sharpers, soon sent to Paris for the best tennis player in the world, who on his arrival was instructed to lose unless given signals—the display of a certain coloured handkerchief, the raising of a bat, and similar signs—should be made.

England now proceeded to begin the stripping of his dupe by pretending to back him for fifty or a hundred guineas a set, complaining bitterly of his losses when unsuccessful. Mr. Damer meanwhile was losing three, four, and sometimes five thousand guineas in a day; and with such blind avidity did he pursue this destructive game, that he soon found himself a loser of near forty thousand guineas. At last, he found it prudent to resist the propensity to play with England and his band of sharpers, some of whom were constantly at his house in Tilney Street, requesting payment. Mr. Damer offered them post-obits, bonds, or in short the best security he could then offer, his father, Lord Milton, afterwards Lord Dorchester, being alive; no, they would have cash. Mr. Damer could not find it; but, to his high sense of honour be it told, he threw himself at his father's feet; the worthy parent weighed the matter well, and sent his steward from Milton Abbey with power to pay every shilling, though he knew his son had been cheated of every guinea. The steward, however, arrived only in time to learn that his young master, having sent for five girls and a blind fiddler, had blown out his brains after a roystering carouse at a tavern in Covent Garden. According to Horace Walpole it was Fox who, with infinite good nature, went to meet Mrs. Damer on her way to town and prepared her for the dismal news. "Can," says Walpole, "the walls of Almack's help moralizing when £5000 a year in present and £22,000 in reversion are not sufficient for happiness and cannot check a pistol!"

England was very fertile in expedients in plucking his pigeons. On one occasion, being with other blacklegs at Scarborough, and a rich dupe, from whom a good deal was expected, refusing to play after dinner, the party, having made the pigeon drunk and given the waiter five guineas to answer any awkward questions which might be asked in the morning, wrote out on slips of paper "D—— (the pigeon's name) owes me a hundred guineas." "D—— owes me eighty guineas," and so on. England, however, wrote "I owe D—— thirty guineas."

The next morning England, meeting the guest of the night before on the cliff, said to him: "Well, we were all very merry last night." "We were indeed," replied the pigeon, "and I only hope I did not offend any one, for I must confess that I drank a good deal more than usual."

"You were in good spirits, my dear fellow," said England, "that was all; and now, before I forget, let me pay you the thirty guineas I lost to you last night—I am not very lucky at cards."

D—— stared, and positively denied having played for a shilling; but England assured him upon his honour that he had. He added that he had paid hundreds to men who having drunk deep remembered nothing till he had shown them his account. Mr. D—— thus fell into the trap laid for him, and, being a novice, put the notes in his pocket, thinking England the most upright man he had ever met. Shortly after, Mr. England's friends presented their cards. Mr. D——, thunderstruck at their demands, swore that he had never played with them, and indeed that he did not know of his having played at all, until Captain England, very much to his credit, had paid him thirty guineas, though he himself did not remember any cards or dice having been in the room. The leader of the band replied with great warmth, "Sir, it is the first time my honour was ever doubted. Captain England, and the waiter, will tell you I won a hundred guineas of you, though I was a great loser by the night's play."

The victim of the plot, however, fortunately for himself, met some friends who were men of the world, and one of them having cross-examined the waiter, and promised him another five guineas if he spoke the truth, the latter at last admitted that England and his companions were notorious blacklegs, and that Mr. D—— did not play at all, or, if he did, it could not have been for five minutes, as the rest of the party were constantly ringing and making punch in their own way.

On the advice of this friend D—— ended the matter by sending England back his thirty guineas with five more to pay the cost of the supper; and the blacklegs, finding that the affair was likely to do them no good, left Scarborough the next morning.

A young Kingston brewer, Rolles by name, having publicly insulted England by calling him a blackleg at Ascot, the latter, who could snuff a candle with a pistol ball, called him out and shot him, after which he fled to the Continent, remarking: "Well, as I have shot a man I must be after making myself scarce." As an outlaw living in Paris, England continued to make money by play till the outbreak of the French Revolution, which for a time rather injured the avocation of sharpers in France.

It is said, however, that he furnished the heads of our army with some valuable intelligence in its celebrated campaign in Flanders; and that, as a reward, his return to this country was facilitated, and an annuity promised him.

On his arrival in London, he was tried and acquitted of the murder of Mr. Rolles. For the remainder of his life he appears to have completely abandoned gambling, and to have lived a very quiet existence near Leicester Square.

FOOTNOTES:

[2] Described at page 55.

[3] £1 notes existed at this time.

III

Former popularity of dice—The race game in Paris—Description of hazard—Jack Mytton's success at it—Anecdotes—French hazard—Major Baggs, a celebrated gamester of the past—Anecdotes of his career—London gaming-houses—Ways and methods of their proprietors—Ephraim Bond and his henchman Burge—"The Athenæum"—West-End Hells—Crockford's—Opinion of Mr. Crockford regarding play—The Act of 1845—Betting-houses—Nefarious tactics of their owners—Suppression in 1853.

The most popular gambling game of the eighteenth century, at which great sums were lost and won, was "hazard," which emptied the pockets of multitudes in the West End, and proved the ruin of many a country squire fresh to the allurements of town.

Before 1716 itinerant vendors usually carried dice with them, and customers, even children, were encouraged to throw for fruit, nuts, or sweets; and when the floors of the Middle Temple Hall were taken up nearly a hundred sets of dice which had fallen through the chinks in the flooring were found. Dice have been out of fashion for many years in the modern world, though quite recently they have begun to enjoy some slight popularity in France in connection with an elaborated form of the race game which at one time was a favourite amusement in English country houses. Two Clubs, the Racing Plomb Club and the Pur Plomb Club, now exist in Paris, the members of which declare that the movements of little leaden horses over a course, in accordance with the throw of the dice, are more amusing and exciting than roulette or baccarat. The little metal steeds used at this game are named after prominent race-horses on the French Turf. The races, called after events like the Grand Steeplechase and Grand Prix, are begun with three or four dice, continued with two, and end with one, the courses of Auteuil and Longchamps being realistically reproduced on the race-boards. A leaden horse which wins a certain number of races is accorded some advantage over the rest. For instance, a winner, say of stakes amounting to one hundred francs, advances seven points instead of six on the board when its owner throws a six, and so on in proportion, whilst if it has won sixteen hundred points a throw of six advances it eleven points. This racing game, which, however, is played rather for amusement than mere gambling, was revived by M. Fernand Vandéreux, who has brought it into popularity in Parisian literary and artistic circles.

Hazard, which is now practically obsolete, seems to have made an irresistible appeal to the gaming instincts of former generations, and the financial ravages for which it was responsible eventually provoked such scandals that the game was rendered illegal in 1845. It was a somewhat complicated form of gambling, and in these days, when so many easy forms of speculation exist, would in all probability have died a natural death even without the intervention of the law.

The following is an account of the game as played some fifty years ago, when it still enjoyed some popularity amongst racing men.

The players assembled round a circular table, a space being reserved for the "groom-porter" (the term applied to the croupier), who occupied a somewhat elevated position, and whose duty it was to call the odds and see that the game was played according to rule. Two dice were used and the player who took the box placed as much money as he wished to risk in the centre of the table, where it was covered with an equal amount, either by some individual speculator, or by the contributions of several. The player (technically called the "caster") then proceeded to call a "main," that is to say, any number from 5 to 9; of these he would mentally select the one which either chance or superstition might suggest, call it aloud, then shake the box, and deliver the dice. If he threw the exact number he called, he "nicked" it, as the term went, and won; if he threw any other number (with a few exceptions, which will be mentioned), he neither won nor lost. The number, however, which he threw became his "chance," and if he could succeed in repeating it before he threw what was his main, he won; if not, he lost. In other words, having completely failed to throw his main in the first instance, he should have lost, but did not in consequence of the equitable interference of his newly-made acquaintance, which constituted itself his chance. If a player threw two aces (commonly called "crabs") he lost his stake. For example, suppose the caster "set"—that is, placed on the table—a stake of £10, and it was covered by an equal amount, and he then called 7 in as his main and threw 5; the groom-porter would at once call out "5 to 7"—meaning that 5 was the number to win and 7 the number to lose. The player then continued throwing until the event was determined by the turning up of either the main or the chance. Meanwhile, however, a most important feature in the game came into operation—the laying and taking of the odds caused by the relative proportions of the main and the chance. These, as has been said, were calculated with mathematical nicety, never varied, and were proclaimed by the groom-porter. In the instance given, as the caster stood to win with 5 and to lose with 7, the odds were declared to be 3 to 2 against him, inasmuch as there are three ways of throwing 7, and only two of throwing 5. If a player should "throw out" once, the box passed on to the next person on his left, who at once took up the play. He could, however, "throw in" without interruption, and if he was able to do this half a dozen times and back his luck, his gains would amount to a large sum, sixty to one being the odds against it.

The choice of a main was quite optional: many preferred 7 in because they might make a coup at once by throwing that number, or by throwing 11, which is a "nick" to 7, but to 7 only. Many shrewd players, however, preferred some other main, with the view of having a more favourable chance to depend upon of winning both stake and odds. For example, let us reverse the case given above, and suppose the caster called 5 and threw 7; he would then have 7 as his chance to win odds of 3 to 2 in his favour.

Such was the game of English hazard, at which large fortunes were lost. Cheating could only be effected by the use of loaded dice, which were called "dispatches," or by high and low dice having only certain numbers. Sharpers often carried these and also "cramped" boxes to make the dice fall in a particular way. So popular were dice with the gamesters of old that one of them left an injunction in his will that his bones should be made into dice and his skin into coverings for dice-boxes.

The round table on which English hazard was played had a deeply bevelled edge, intended to prevent the dice from landing on the floor, which rendered a throw void. If either of the dice, after having left the box, should strike any object on the table, such as a man's elbow or stick, except money, it was also no throw. Every player had the right of "calling dice," even when the dice were being thrown. This, of course, nullified the throw, another set being handed to the caster by the groom-porter. Many a lucky coup was destroyed by some captious player having exercised this privilege—with most irritating effects to the disappointed caster on finding that he had "nicked" his main. When one of the dice remained in the box after the other had been landed, the caster might either throw it quickly, or gently coax it from the box. If one die landed on the top of another, it was removed by the groom-porter and declared a throw. Dice were known as the "ivories."

At a Westminster election, the keeper of a notorious gambling-house in St. Anne's parish, on being about to give his vote, was asked in the usual way what his trade was; when after a little hesitation, he replied, "I am an ivory turner."

Many curious incidents occurred at hazard. On one occasion when two gamesters had deposited a very large stake to be won by him who threw the lowest throw with the dice, one of them, who had thrown three aces, thought himself secure of success.

"Wait for my throw," cried his opponent.

He threw, and with such dexterity, that by lodging one of the dice on the other, he showed only one ace on the uppermost of them. He was allowed by the company to have won the stakes.

It used to be said that at hazard, men under the influence of wine were invariably more fortunate than those who played with cooler heads or more collected judgments. Of this, perhaps the most remarkable instance ever known was the notorious spendthrift and sportsman Jack Mytton, of whom the Hell-keepers used to say, "there was no use playing against the Squire when he was drunk."

Mytton was indeed rather a formidable figure at the hazard-table, where he was supposed to have won more than he lost. When heated with wine and full of courage he was the dread of the proprietors of the minor gambling-tables at country race meetings, whose banks he was given to breaking in more ways than one—it being his practice to demolish all their gambling apparatus if he observed the slightest suspicion of foul play. At Warwick races in 1824, for instance, Mytton and some friends not only smashed a rouge-et-noir table to atoms, but soundly thrashed the proprietor and his gang.

On another occasion he showed considerable presence of mind when surprised by the Mayor of Chester during a raid on a hazard Hell one Sunday. In the confusion which ensued the Squire of Halston, who was a winner, deftly put his gains in his hat, which he quite coolly placed upon his head, and walked out unnoticed. He was not so careful, however, on one occasion after a great run of luck in London when, having broken the banks of two well-known London Hells, he went off with the money—a large sum in notes—to Doncaster. On his return from the races in a post-chaise he set to work to count his winnings, the windows of the carriage being open. He soon fell asleep, and when he awoke, the night being far advanced, found that notes to the value of several thousand pounds had been blown out of the window. Truly a case of "light come, light go!"

LIGHT COME, LIGHT GO.

When quite a young man Mytton had been subjected to plucking by many a rook. As a subaltern of the 7th Hussars in the army of occupation at Calais he borrowed £3000 of a banker at St. Omer one day and lost half of it the next at a swindling E.O. table. However, he relieved his feelings by demolishing the whole concern. About the same time he lost no less than sixteen thousand napoleons to a certain Captain at billiards, but Lord Uxbridge, who was Colonel of his regiment, having reason to believe that the whole thing was a robbery, forbade him to pay.

There are now probably very few people in England who could conduct a game of hazard, the rules of which are practically forgotten. The last man who was thoroughly versed in the intricacies of the game is said to have been a certain well-known bookmaker, Atkins by name, who, as late as the 'seventies, used to keep a hazard-table going at Brighton during the race week, where considerable sums of money were lost and won. He also presided over a hazard-table at Bognor during the Goodwood meeting. An associate of his, who was known as "Chanticleer" owing to his vocal powers in calling the odds, afterwards proved very successful in another walk of life, where he accumulated a considerable fortune.

Some thirty-six years ago hazard used to be played at Doncaster during the race week, an excellent account of the scenes which used to take place there being given by Sir George Chetwynd in his *Recollections*.

French hazard was less rough-and-ready than the English game. Every stake that was "set" was covered by the bank, so that the player ran no risk of losing a large amount, though, if successful, he could win but a trifling one; on the other hand, the scale of odds was so altered as to operate most prejudicially against the player. An equal rate of odds between main and chance was never laid by the French "banker" as was insisted on by the

English groom-porter; while, again, "direct nicks" alone were recognised by the former. Most extraordinary runs of luck have occurred at hazard, a player having sometimes thrown five, seven, and even eleven mains in a single hand. In cases of runs like this the peculiar feature in the French game became valuable, the bank being prepared to pay all winnings, while, generally speaking, a hand of six or seven mains at English hazard would exhaust all the funds of the players, and leave the caster in the position of "setting the table" and finding the stakes totally unnoticed or only partially covered.

To show what sums changed hands at hazard in the eighteenth century, it may be mentioned that a celebrated gambler. Major Baggs by name, once won £17,000 at hazard, by throwing in, as it is called, fourteen successive mains. This Major Baggs was an extraordinary character who went to the East Indies in 1780 on a gaming speculation; but not finding it answer, he returned home overland, encountering many adventures. At Cairo he narrowly avoided death by escaping in a Turkish dress to Smyrna. A companion of his was seized, and sent prisoner to Constantinople, where he was at length released by the interference of Sir Robert Anstie, the English ambassador. Baggs once won £6000 of a young gentleman at Spa, and immediately came to England to get the money from the peer (Lord Onslow) who was the father of the young man. Terms of accommodation were proposed by his lordship in presence of a well-known banker whose respectability and consequence were well known. The peer offered him a thousand guineas and a note for the remainder at a distant period. Baggs, however, wanted the whole to be paid down, and some altercation ensued, in the course of which the banker observed that he thought his lordship had offered very handsome terms. "Sirrah," said Baggs in a passion, "hold your tongue; the laws of commerce you may be acquainted with, but the laws of honour you can know nothing about."

Major Baggs at one time in his life was worth more than £100,000. He had fought eleven duels, and was allowed to be very skilful with the sword. He was a man of a determined mind, great penetration, and considerable literary culture; and when play was out of the case, could be an agreeable, gentlemanlike, and instructive companion. He was very generous to people whom he liked; and a certain naval lord, highly respected, when in rather a distressed situation at Paris, found a never-failing resource in the purse of the Major, who was open-handed enough at times. For several years he lived at Paris in the greatest splendour, and during a stay at Avignon, frequently gave splendid suppers to the Duke and Duchess of Cumberland and their friends, whom he followed to Naples, getting introduced to the King's private parties, and winning £1500 of His Majesty.

Major Baggs eventually fell a victim to gaming, dying of a chill produced by a night passed in a round-house, having been locked up with other frequenters of a gaming-house which was raided by the police.

Numbers of such places existed in the London of that day, which were the constant resort of those who, like the Major, found access to Clubs somewhat difficult.

From about 1780 to 1845 the West End was full of gambling-hells, the most popular of which were generally in the parish of St. James's, and St. George's, Hanover Square. Others also existed in St. Martin's-in-the-Fields, Piccadilly, St James's Street, Pall Mall, St. James's Square, Jermyn Street, Bury Street, Charles Street, King Street, Duke Street, Bennett Street, and the neighbourhood of the Quadrant. The games principally played, besides English and French hazard, were rouge-et-noir, roulette, and une-deux-cinque. The principal proprietors of these houses were Bond, Oldfield, Goodwin, Bennet, Smith, Russell, Phillips, Rougeir, Burge, Carlos, Humphries, Fielden, Taylor, Bird, Morgan, Kerby, Aldridge, Barnet, and many others, amongst whom, of course, the celebrated Crockford stood forth in almost regal splendour.

Nevertheless there was a crusade against gambling and betting always carried on by the section of the population which were known as the "Methodists," some of whose preachers were very clever and apt.

"Ah, my brethren," once said one of these, addressing a congregation into which several sporting men had strolled, "why waste your lives thinking so much of what you call 'flimsies.' These, my friends," turning over the leaves of his Bible, "are God's bank-notes, and when you carry them to heaven, he will cash them at sight!"

Another preacher, whilst painting a vivid picture of the tortures which awaited gamesters in a future life, declared that the apartments of Satan were filled with cards and dice, and that Hoyle was the only book in his library. Nevertheless, the denunciations of the "godly" effected little, and though from time to time the authorities organised raids upon the more scandalous resorts, gaming continued to flourish.

As late as the early 'thirties of the last century, the West End of London was full of Hells, a number of them in the Quadrant. Hazard was the principal game played. The lowest gaming-houses were generally located in obscure courts or other places not much exposed to public observation. As a rule they were kept shut up as if unoccupied, or else some appearance of a trade was carried on to prevent suspicion. It used to be said that at one or two of these Hells individuals were kept on the premises whose sole duty lay in being able to swallow the dice in case of a raid by the authorities.

Whether this was the case or not, it is certain that there was usually some convenient receptacle contrived in the shutters or elsewhere into which the implements of gaming could be speedily thrown. A house containing a back room sufficiently large to contain forty or fifty people, was the ideal of the proprietors of such places. The man who acted as croupier was, as has been said, known as the "groom-porter," an appellation dating from the eighteenth century, when the Court was, on occasion, wont to gamble at the Groom-Porter's in the Palace of St. James.

The profits of the house were supposed to be derived from a tax levied on successful players, any one winning three times running being expected to pay a certain sum of money to the table or "cagnotte." A player doing this was called a "box hand," the amount of his contribution varying from a shilling to half a crown according to the rules and standing of the house.

A ROW IN A FASHIONABLE HELL.

The main profits of these Hells, however, were in the majority of instances derived from shady practices, many of the proprietors being in league with sharks of various kinds who preyed upon the more credulous or foolish players.

The least important gambling-houses were generally kept by retired prize-fighters and bullies, who hectored their weaker clients out of such sums as they might chance to win.

In the higher class of Hells, silver counters, representing certain fractions of a pound, were used; these were called pieces, and one of them was the amount of the tax levied on a "box hand."

When a gentleman first appeared at these Hells, the Hellites and the players were curious to learn who and what he was, especially the former, to calculate the rich or poor harvest to be reaped by him, and they regulated their conduct accordingly. Should he be introduced by a broken player, and lose a good sum, his introducer seized the opportunity to borrow a few pounds of the Hellites. But if the gentleman was successful, "a few pounds to give his kind friend a chance" was not refused. If the visitor proved unlucky the Hellites ventured, after he had lost hundreds, to lend him twenty or thirty pounds, for which his cheque was demanded and given. Generally they not only knew his name, but soon ascertained, by underhand inquiries at his bankers, the extent of his account, his connections and resources. Upon this knowledge, if his account was good, they would cash him cheques to within a hundred pounds of the balance. Instances have been known, after cheques have been cashed and paid in this way, to large amounts, and the balance drawing to a close, that when a cheque for a small amount has been wanted, cashed by the very same parties, it has been refused, the Hellite actually telling the party, within a few pounds, the amount he had left at his banker's. One gentleman was once told within five pounds of what he had there.

A number of Hells masqueraded as Clubs, and made some show of only admitting regular members to the delights of play.

The following prospectus, issued in the 'twenties of the last century, is a fair sample of those used by the proprietors of gaming-houses in London to attract clients. The house in question was under the superintendence of Weare, who was murdered by Thurtell.

> A party of gentlemen, having formed the design of instituting a Select Club, to be composed of those gentlemen only whose habits and circumstances entitle them to an uncontrolled but proper indulgence in the current amusements of the day, adopt this mode of submitting the project to consideration, and of inviting those who may approve of it, to an early concurrence and co-operation in the design. To attain this object the more speedily, and render it worthy the attention and support it lays claim to, it may be only necessary to mention that the plan is founded on the basis of liberality, security, and respectability, combining with the essential requisites of a select and respectable association, peculiar advantages to the members conceded by no similar institution in town. Further particulars may be learned on personal application between the hours of twelve and two at 55 Pall Mall.

In 1831 a gaming-house called the Athenæum was a public scandal. This gaming-hell was situated at the upper end of St. James's Street, on the same side as White's. It was owned by three brothers named Bond, one of whom only, Ephraim, was publicly recognised as the proprietor.

This man Bond had had many vicissitudes. Once, when quite at the end of his tether, a gentleman came into a house where he was looking on at the play, and having no confidence in his own judgment or good fortune, commissioned Bond to make his bets for him, and, being very successful, the gentleman, who was a member of the House of Commons, presented him with fifty pounds. This became the nucleus of his future fortune.

After working his fifty pounds for some time in various advantageous gaming speculations, he became a small partner in a Bury Street house and subsequently in gaming-houses in Bennett Street, Pall Mall, and Piccadilly, until, as before stated, he located all his machinery and performers in the Athenæum, in St. James's Street, near Nos. 50 and 51.

Burge, an individual closely connected with Bond, was another well-known figure in the gambling world of those days.

The "Subject," as this man was nicknamed, in consequence of his wretched and cadaverous appearance, was born at Glastonbury, in Somersetshire, where he was brought up a tailor. Shortly after the termination of his apprenticeship he married, but finding business not answer his expectations he removed to London, where he commenced business in a little way, but in about two years became a bankrupt. At this period of his life, when distressed in pocket and harassed in mind, he was introduced into a shilling table hazard-house kept at that time by the celebrated J.D. Kelly and George Smith in Lisle Street, Leicester Square.

From the very moment that the "Subject" first saw a hazard-table his nature changed, and wife, children, home, and business were totally obliterated from his mind. The few shillings which from time to time he could scrape together from the charity of his own or his wife's friends were all carried to the table, although at this time he was still a perfect novice in all concerning play. He generally lost his money soon after he entered a gaming-house, but even when penniless he always remained until the table was broken up, generally some time before midnight, when he would make his way to a miserable home, only to sleep till the hour for witnessing play again arrived. This state of restlessness and perturbation brought on a serious fit of illness, whilst his wife was compelled to take in washing for the support of the family, who lived amidst scenes of acute misery. Nothing, however, diverted the "Subject" from the gaming-table; no sooner did he recover and was able to crawl out than he was at hazard again, though many were his quarrels with the table-keepers, who resented his presence in their rooms, as he so rarely brought a shilling to play with. Nothing, however, could overcome his infatuation, and had he been turned out for good he would have lain down at the door, and listened to the sound of the dice-box until he died of exposure to the weather. At length Smith, a gaming-house proprietor who had removed to Oxendon Street, Coventry Street, finding Burge determined, by some means or other, to be present during play, installed him as a permanent official in his rooms, with regular duties, the chief of which were to trim the lamps hanging over the hazard-table and to hand a glass of gin to the man who threw in six mains in succession, when he was allowed to say, "Remember the waiter, your honour." Subsequently, the groom-porter being indisposed, the "Subject" mounted the stool and called the main, continuing afterwards sometimes to act alternately in each capacity until the proprietor took the house in 71 Jermyn Street, when he got a rise in the world and was made a regular groom-porter in a crown-house.

The history of the so-called "Athenæum" run by Bond was curious.

At the time when the real Athenæum in Pall Mall was being established there was a swindler upon the town named William Earl. Although the son of a respectable bookseller, who formerly resided in Albemarle Street, Piccadilly, he committed some very flagrant acts of imposition upon the public. Among many other schemes he conceived the plan of pretending that he was the person deputed and authorised by the gentlemen composing the members of the true Athenæum Club, to take and fit up a house for their accommodation. The house in St. James's Street being to let at the time, he (Earl) took it on the residue of a lease having between two and three years to run, and, forthwith, when in possession, got tradesmen to fit it up in the most superb manner possible, making it a great favour to recommend them to so good a job, the Athenæum management promising that all the money shares should be paid down the moment the house was ready for the reception of the members. The furniture, however, as fast as it was brought into the house, disappeared, being taken away by Earl to dispose of for cash to put into his own pocket, preparatory to a final retreat from the scene of action. This being discovered before larger debts were contracted, the creditors, who were already minus about £1400, convened a meeting, at which, under a threat of a criminal prosecution, they compelled Earl to assign the premises and everything else to three gentlemen, Messrs. Baines, Vincent, and Laing, in trust for the benefit of the creditors. These gentlemen, subsequently representing the case of the creditors to the Lord Chamberlain, obtained a licence for music, the premises being designated and inserted in the licence as known by the name of the Athenæum; but this and a juggling speculation failing, it was at length let to Ephraim Bond, Esq., at a rental of £50 per month. This was in the early part of the year 1830, during which Earl was committed to Newgate for swindling a jeweller in St. Paul's Churchyard out of a gold chain and other property, being subsequently transported for the term of seven years. The notoriety of these circumstances, and the length of time Earl's name had been before the public, as being somehow connected with the institution described as the Athenæum Club in St. James's Street, led a vast number of thoughtless young men to visit the house. Certain is it, that not a few joined the place under a full impression that they were actually admitted into the real Athenæum Club: and to this confusion of names did the new proprietor, in a very large measure, owe the extraordinary run of play he had at his tables. Among the persons who were employed at this house were Kelly, Peck, Hancock, Mayne, and Thompson: the two latter were retained by Bond as waiters, after having been placed in the house under the following circumstances. Earl, as the spurious Athenæum progressed, advertised for waiters; when these men applied, he represented in forcible language the responsible nature of their situations, and the great trust which would be reposed in them, informing one that all the linen and glass would be placed in his hands, and the other that he would have charge of plate to the value of some thousands. By these means he induced one to deposit £150 and the other £100 as security before they entered upon the service of the Club. Bond thought that the ill-usage of these men gave them some claim upon the premises, and, therefore, installed them into the office which they originally came to fill, that is, as waiters.

At many of the gambling-houses the waiters reaped a rich harvest by lending money. At Crockford's one of these servants once received £500, nominally as a Christmas-box, but really as a recognition of timely financial assistance rendered to frequenters of the hazard-table; £100 of this sum was given to him by a nobleman who had in one week won £80,000 on a moderate sum which had been borrowed from the waiter in question.

About 1838 gaming-houses were kept open all day, the dice were scarcely ever idle, day or night. All the week, all the year round, persons were to be found in these places, losing their money, and up to 1844 there were no less than twelve gaming-houses in St. James's and St. George's. Before that the play was higher, but not so general.

The increase of gambling-houses was said to be owing to the existence of Crockford's. Such was the opinion of the Honourable Frederick Byng, as given before the Committee of the House of Commons. He declared "that the facility to gamble at Crockford's led to the establishment of other gambling-houses fitted up in a superior style, and attractive to gentlemen who never would have thought of going into them formerly." He added that in his older days gambling was very high, but the amusement of a very few. Mr. Byng also said he "could have named all the gamblers in his early days at the clubs. No person coming into a room where hazard was carried on would have been permitted to play for a small sum, and therefore poor people left it alone."

The gambling which was carried on in the private rooms of the wine and oyster houses, about 1840, was of the same character as that which had at the same time flourished in the vicinity of St James's. For this reason the blackguards frequenting the former attained the most profound knowledge of the art of robbing at the West-End Hells. They visited the saloons every night, in order to pick up new acquaintances amongst inexperienced youth. Well-dressed and polite, they carefully scanned every visitor on the look-out for pigeons to pluck, and having found one went soon to work to establish an acquaintance. Cards being proposed, the leader of the band provided a room, play ensuing, accompanied by the certainty of loss to the unfortunate guest. If the invitation was rejected, the pigeon was attacked through a passion of a different kind. The word being given to one of their female friends, she threw herself in the quarry's way, and prevailed upon him to accompany her to her house. In the morning the "gentleman," who in vain had solicited him to play at the saloon the night before, would call—as if to pay "a friendly visit." Cards would be again proposed, the "lady" offering to be the partner of her friend in the game. Numbers of young men were plundered by such schemes of thousands of pounds; and a good deal of demoralisation prevailed amongst small tradesmen and gentlemen's servants, numbers of whom frequented the low gambling-houses. If one of these could scrape together two or three hundred pounds he was able, with the assistance of the keeper of the Hell, to lend it to needy losers at sixty per cent.

A careful inspection was made of the visitor's appearance by a gaming-house keeper's spies, his dress being strictly scrutinised. He was obliged, before entering the saloon, to deposit his great-coat and cane, or anything else which might facilitate the introduction of some weapon; the value or elegance of these did not save him from the humiliation of having it taken from him at the door. The assaults which were sometimes made on the bankers led to such precautions.

The blame for the great increase of gambling in the West End was mostly attributed to Crockford, who presided over the most palatial gaming-house ever run in England.

William Crockford was the son of a small fishmonger who lived next door to Temple Bar. After his father's death the young man soon abandoned fish-selling for more exciting pursuits. He became a frequenter of the sporting-houses then abundant in the neighbourhood of St. James's, went racing, and, after setting up a successful hazard bank in Wattier's old Club-house,[4] became connected with a gaming-house in King Street, which, though it frequently got him into trouble with the authorities, put a very large sum of money into his pocket. At King Street, Crockford, together with his partner Gye, is said to have once won the very large sum of £100,000 from five well-known men-about-town, amongst whom were Lords Thanet and Granville and Mr. Ball Hughes.

With the capital amassed in the manner described Crockford founded the celebrated institution in St. James's Street which was sometimes jokingly called "Fishmonger's Hall."

It was opened at the end of the year 1827. There were about 1200 members, exclusive of ambassadors and foreigners of distinction; the annual subscription was £25. The Club-house was luxurious beyond anything which had been known up to that time. The decorations alone, it is said, cost £94,000, and a salary of £1200 a year was paid by Crockford to his cook, M. Eustache Ude.

The Club-house, which still exists in an altered form as the Devonshire Club, was decorated and upholstered in the somewhat gaudy style popular during the reign of George IV., the apartment known as the State Drawing-room being particularly gorgeous and florid in its general effect.

The gaming-room was comparatively small. Here were card-tables at which whist was occasionally played, whilst in the centre stood the hazard-table, the real *raison d'être* of the whole establishment.

The expenses of running this gambling-club were large, the dice alone costing some two thousand a year! Three new pairs at about a guinea each pair were provided at the commencement of every evening's play, and very often as many more were called for either by players or by Crockford himself in order to change the luck.

By the terms of his agreement Crockford was bound to put £5000 into a bank every night whilst Parliament was sitting; as long as any of this capital remained he was not allowed to end the play until an hour previously appointed.

During his first two seasons Crockford is said to have made about £300,000; he may, indeed, be said to have extracted nearly all the ready money from the pockets of the men of fashion of the day. So much so was this the case, that when Crockford retired in 1840 it was said that he resembled an Indian chief who retires from a hunting country when there is not game enough left for his tribe.

Mr. Crockford's private views as to the likelihood of any player at hazard increasing his fortune were certainly interesting. Being one day asked by a young man of his acquaintance what was the best main to call at the game, he solemnly replied: "I'll tell you what it is, young man. You may call mains at hazard till your hair grows out of your hat and your toes grow out of your boots. My advice to you is not to call any mains at all."

COUNT D'ORSAY CALLING A MAIN AT CROCKFORD'S.

This, though undoubtedly sound, was a curious speech from a man who had laid the foundation of a large fortune at the gaming-table, and had himself successfully called all the mains under the sun.

Whilst many were ruined at Crockford's, nobody appears to have made much by the place except the proprietor, who, though latterly rather unsuccessful in speculation, died a very rich man at the age of sixty-nine in May 1844.

In 1844 a Select Committee on gaming took a great deal of evidence, Crockford himself being examined, though nothing was got out of him. The result of all this was that on the 8th of August 1845 was passed an Act to amend the law against games and wagers. The Act in question was particularly aimed against hazard, which had undoubtedly done a good deal of harm, lending itself as it did to much trickery and foul play. Gaming-houses were now rigorously repressed, but it was not long before gambling began to rage in another form, many betting-houses being started.

The first institution of this kind appears to have opened its doors in 1847, the proprietors being Messrs. Drummond and Greville. About 1850, about four hundred of these houses (the vast majority not very solvent), where regular lists of the prices were openly exhibited, flourished, and an epidemic of gambling was declared to have attacked even the poorest class, who were being offered facilities for risking their hard-earned sixpences and shillings. The rise and fall of the odds before any great race was eagerly watched by the keepers of the betting-houses, and scenes of wild excitement occasionally occurred. Many of the smaller betting-shops were simply traps for the unwary. The stock-in-trade needed was merely a few flyblown racing prints and some old ledgers. A room was soon hired, often in some derelict tobacconist's shop, and business then commenced. Most of these places existed in obscure and dirty thoroughfares; the neighbourhood of Drury Lane being especially affected by those indulging in this nefarious industry. Just before a big race meeting, such as the Derby or Ascot, numbers of these betting shops would burst into bloom for a short space of time. When the meetings ended, the crowd coming to get paid would find the proprietor gone and the place in charge of a boy, who, generally not at all disconcerted, would announce that his master had gone out on "'tickler bizness," and would not be back till late at night. His wife also had gone out of town for her health till the winter. "Will he be back to-morrow?" would cry the crowd. "No, he won't be here to-morrow 'cos it's Sunday, and he always goes to church on Sunday," a favourite reply which made even the losers laugh. "Will he be back on Monday, then?" "Monday," would say the boy, reflecting, "No, I don't think he'll be here on Monday—he's going to a sale on Monday." After further inquiries and replies of this sort the crowd would, for the time being, reluctantly disperse, murmuring something about a "sell" instead of a "sale," to return again time after time with the same ill-success, till eventually, realising that they had been duped, the bell-pull was torn out and the windows broken, the proprietor meanwhile doing a flourishing business in some other locality. Various subterfuges were employed by betting-shopkeepers to attract clients. One of these places grandiloquently styled itself "The Tradesmen's Moral Associative Betting Club." The circular issued by this beneficent organisation set forth that a number of persons in business, realising the robberies hourly inflicted upon the humbler portion of the sporting public by persons bankrupt alike in character and property, had banded themselves together to establish a club wherein their fellow tradesmen and the speculator of a few shillings might invest their money with the assured consciousness of meeting with fair and honourable treatment. In all probability the clients of the Moral Associative Club found that, like other institutions of the same sort, its idea was to receive the money of all and close its career by paying none.

A man named Dwyer, who kept a cigar shop and betting-house in St. Martin's Lane in 1851, was in the habit of laying a point or two more than the regular odds, and in consequence did the largest business of any list man in London. He was considered to be absolutely safe. It was his custom to pay the day following a big race, but when Miss Nancy won the Chester Cup, his doors were found to be closed; and the house being broken into by an enormous crowd of infuriated creditors, everything valuable was discovered to have been removed. Dwyer, as a matter of fact, had bolted with about £25,000 of the public's money. The occurrence of scandals such as this naturally caused a considerable outcry for the suppression of the betting-houses, which, it was declared, were demoralising the public, who, even when they were not swindled, were led into risking sums which they could not afford. A Bill for checking the evil was eventually drafted, and in July 1853 was passed an Act entitled "An Act for the Suppression of Betting-Houses," which inflicted on any one keeping or assisting to keep any house, office, room, or place for the purpose of betting, a penalty not exceeding one hundred pounds, or imprisonment with or without hard labour for any time not exceeding six calendar months.

FOOTNOTES:

[4] No. 81 Piccadilly.

IV

Craze for eccentric wagers at end of eighteenth century—Lord Cobham's insulting freak and its results—Betting and gaming at White's—The Arms of the Club—The old betting-book and its quaint wagers—Tragedies of play—White's to-day—£180,000 lost at hazard at the Cocoa Tree—Brummell as a gambler—Gaming at Brooks's—Anecdotes—General Scott—Whist—Mr. Pratt—Wattier's Club—Scandal at Graham's—Modern gambling clubs—The Park Club case in 1884—Dangers of private play.

Towards the end of the eighteenth century a curious mania for making eccentric wagers seized hold of the bucks of the day. Unlike many another craze this was not imported from France, but had its rise and progress entirely in England. During the last illness of Louis XIV., Lord Stair laid a wager on his death, which rather astonished the French, who did not approve of such a form of speculation. At a subsequent period bets about the most trivial incidents became quite common in the West End of London. Not infrequently some thoughtless wager would lead to considerable trouble.

Lord Cobham, for instance, once foolishly bet Mr. Nugent a guinea that he would spit in Lord Bristol's hat without the latter, who had a reputation for effeminacy, resenting it. The wager itself was singularly lacking in refinement, and the moment chosen for carrying it out was quite in keeping.

Lord Bristol being one day at Lady Cobham's talking to some ladies, he chanced to lean over a chair holding his hat behind him, into which Lord Cobham deliberately spat, at the same time asking Mr. Nugent, who was present, for his guinea; after which he began to make the most profuse apologies to the victim of the outrage, who, remaining apparently quite unmoved, merely asked if his host had any further use for his hat, and then resumed his conversation, and every one considered the incident at an end. Lord Bristol being to all outward appearance absolutely unruffled.

The next morning, however, both Lord Cobham and Mr. Nugent received messages demanding satisfaction, to which they returned the most humble answers. The incident, they declared, was all merely a foolish joke, and they were quite ready to make all sorts of submissive apologies.

Lord Bristol, however, would only assent to condone the insult if the aggressors were ready to make a public apology in the Club-room at White's, where he was prepared to receive it, and here, amidst a crowd of members, Lord Cobham and Mr. Nugent publicly expressed their regret.

As the eighteenth century waned. White's Club developed into a great gambling centre; its members indeed professed a universal scepticism and decided everything by a wager. There was nothing, however trivial or ridiculous, which was not capable of producing a bet. Many pounds were lost upon the colour of a coach-horse, the birth of a child, the breaking off of a marriage, and even a change in the weather.

A favourite mode of speculation was backing one man against another, that is, betting that he would live the longest. People of all classes were made the subjects of such bets. An actor was pitted against a duke, an alderman against a bishop, a pimp against some member of the privy council. Scarcely a remarkable person existed upon whose life many thousand pounds did not depend. The various changes in the health of any one who was the subject of heavy betting naturally gave rise to many serious reflections in the minds of the people who had wagered large sums on his life or death. Some would closely watch all the stages of a total stranger's illness, more impatient for his death than the undertaker who expected to have the care of his funeral; others would be very solicitous about his recovery, and send every hour to know how his health progressed, taking as great care of him as any clergyman's wife who has no other fortune than the living of her husband. Great consternation was caused by an unexpected demise. Considerable odds were laid upon a man with the constitution of a porter, who was pitted against an individual expected to die every week. The porter, however, unexpectedly shot himself through the head, and the knowing ones were taken in.

The main supporters of gaming at White's at this time were George Selwyn, Lord March, Fox, and Lord Carlisle.

The latter was of a rather more serious disposition than the others, and had a wife and children to whom he was devoted. Though at times a high gambler himself, he wrote several letters to Selwyn, warning him of the dangers of hazard.

On one occasion Lord Carlisle won £13,000 from a peer, which he never seems to have got, and again indulged in some disastrous play in 1776, after which he wrote to George Selwyn to say that he had never lost so much at five different sittings as on this occasion in one night. A note by Selwyn in the letter puts the sum at £10,000. In after-life Lord Carlisle entirely abandoned gaming, and settled down into an exemplary country gentleman.

Another constant player for high stakes at White's was Sir Everard Fawkener, the writer's great-grandfather, who held an important office in connection with the Post Office. He played cards very badly, and George Selwyn used to say that playing with him was as bad as "robbing the mail."

In the hall of White's Club hangs a carved wooden copy of the whimsical old coat of arms of the Club—the original painting of which is at Arthur's. This was painted by Dick Edgecumbe after the design had been concocted one wet day at Strawberry Hill by the painter, George Selwyn, George (known as Gilly) Williams, and their host Horace Walpole, who had the arms engraved.

The original arms were as follows:—

"Vert (for a card-table); between three parolis, proper, on a chevron sable, two rouleaux in saltire between two dice, proper. In a canton sable, a ball (for election), argent. Supporters, an old knave of clubs on the dexter, a young knave on the sinister side; both accoutred proper. Crest, issuing out of an earl's coronet (Lord Darlington's) an arm shaking a dice-box, all proper. Motto alluding to the crest '*Cogit amor nummi*'.[5] The arms encircled with a claret bottle ticket by way of order."

The old betting-book at White's contains many curious entries, the first of which dates from 1743. A number of the earliest wagers are concerned with the probabilities of the birth of children to well-known ladies of the day, the duration of life to be enjoyed by certain individuals, and the like.

On 21st March 1746, Mr. John Jeffries bets Mr. Dayrolle five guineas that Lady Kildare has a child born alive before Lady Catherine Petersham. A note is appended "miscarriages go for nothing."

On the 8th of October in the same year Lord Montfort bets Mr. Greville one hundred guineas that Mr. Nash is alive on the same day four years to come.

The Lord Montfort in question was a typical gamester of the time. In the betting-book at White's no less than sixty wagers, amounting to £5500, are recorded against his name. Most of these were about births, marriages, and deaths. On sporting wagers, the nobleman in question seems to have been content to risk only small sums. A true gambler, he preferred to hazard his fortune, and, as it turned out, his life, on the unforeseen.

On the 4th of November 1754, is entered the following: "Lord Montfort wagers Sir John Bland one hundred guineas that Mr. Nash outlives Mr. Cibber." This refers to two very old men, Colley Cibber, the actor, and Beau Nash, the "King of Bath." Below the entry in the betting-book, written in another handwriting, is the significant note: "Both Lord M. and Sir John Bland put an end to their own lives before the bet was decided."

The first of these tragedies took place on New Year's Day of 1755. Lord Montfort's death and the circumstances of it attracted great attention. He was considered one of the shrewdest men of his time, and, as Walpole said, "would have betted any man in England against himself for self-murder." Lord Montfort was of course eventually ruined—at White's alone he lost a fortune at hazard. As a last resource, he then eagerly applied (much to the surprise of the dilatory Duke of Newcastle) for the Governorship of Virginia or the Royal hounds. He got neither, and after spending the last evening of the year 1754 at White's, where he sat up at whist till one o'clock, went home in a strange mood, and shot himself next morning.

A tragic fate likewise befell Sir John Bland, who dissipated his entire fortune at hazard. At a single sitting he at one time lost as much as £32,000, though he recovered a portion of it before play was ended. Sir John shot himself on the road from Calais to Paris.

Some of the wagers chronicled in the betting-book are decidedly vague, the following for instance: "Mr. Talbot bets a certain gentleman a certain sum that a certain event does not take place within a certain time."

During the Napoleonic era several bets were made as to the chances of the Emperor getting back to Paris at the close of the Russian campaign, about ten to one being wagered on such an event happening.

A curious bet, dated February 14, 1813, is the following: "Lord Alvanley bets Sir Joseph Copley five guineas that a certain Baronet understood between them is very much embarrassed in his circumstances in three years from the date hereof; if one of his bills is dishonoured, or he is observed to borrow small change of the chairmen or waiters, Sir Joseph is to be reckoned to lose."

In 1797, hazard seems to have been allowed at White's, but it was expressly laid down that no member should be permitted to keep a faro bank. This rule was doubtless made to avoid the state of things which had lately prevailed across the way at Brooks's.

As time went on gambling became a thing of the past within the walls of White's, and the survivors of a reckless era in its history sobered down into grave and somewhat crotchety old men, who, from the stronghold of an accustomed seat, eyed younger members with a freezing gaze. When the question of smoking in the morning-room was raised their indignation knew no bounds, and even infirm old members—fossils who Alfred Montgomery declared had come from Kensal Green—tottered into the Club to oppose it. So given were these relics of the past to wrapping themselves in a cloak of exclusiveness that at one time the Club came almost to a standstill. Within recent years, however, White's has taken a new lease of life, and after an existence of one hundred and seventy-three years is now in as flourishing a state as ever. The Club-house has been enlarged and various alterations made—always, let it be said, with due regard for the traditions of the past. Unfortunately, in the course of time much connected with its former history has disappeared—it does not, for instance, possess a set of old gaming counters, which have a certain historic interest in these more sober days. The Club is particularly anxious to acquire any relics connected with its past, and also any representations of the Club-house (at the present time under repair) as it existed before the alterations of 1853, when a new façade replaced the old front.

Lower down St. James's Street, on the other side of the road, another Club, in old days notorious for high play, still exists. This is the Cocoa Tree, where very large sums once changed hands. During the year 1780 no less than £180,000 was lost here in a single week. In the same year Mr. O'Birne, an Irish gamester, won £100,000 at hazard of a young Mr. Harvey of Chigwell, a midshipman, who, by his elder brother's death, had suddenly come into a good estate. "You can never pay me," said O'Birne. "I will sell my estate to do so," replied the young man. "No," was the not ungenerous reply, "I will win ten thousand and you shall throw for the odd ninety." The dice were cast and Harvey won—still the evening cost him £10,000.

After Waterloo there appears to have been a revival of gaming in the West End, many officers returning to England with long arrears of pay at their command. This wave of gaming ruined Brummell. At first he was not particularly devoted to play, and had extraordinary luck when he indulged in it. At one sitting at whist at White's he won £10,000 from George Harley Drummond, the banker. It is said that this was the first game Drummond ever played at a Club; it was probably his last, for it led to his withdrawal from the banking business. But Brummell was not a man of large property, and when later he began to play habitually, a few reverses were sufficient to ruin a man of small means who matched his fortune against the much longer purses of his friends.

Brummell had no illusions as to the ultimate fate of a gambler, and once tied himself up against play, receiving a ten-pound note from Pemberton Mills on condition that he should forfeit a thousand if he played again at White's for a month. Nevertheless, a fortnight later he was playing again. His friend did not claim the thousand but merely said: "Well, Brummell, you may at least give me back my ten pounds." Playing at hazard one night with Alderman Combe, whom he playfully called "Mash-tub" because he was a brewer, the Beau, having won a considerable sum, said, pocketing the cash: "Thank you, Alderman; in future I shall never drink any porter but yours." "I wish, sir," was the reply, "that every blackguard in London would tell me the same."

In the end Brummell went under, owing, he declared, with all the superstition of a gambler, to the loss of a lucky sixpence with a hole in it, which he had picked up in the small hours of the morning in Berkeley Square. He gave it away, by mistake, to a cabman, and used to say that he supposed "that rascal Rothschild, or some of his set, had got hold of it."

One of the greatest gamblers in the early part of the nineteenth century was Lord Rivers, whose dashing play at Parisian tables had earned for him the name of "Le Wellington des Joueurs."

During a portion of his career this nobleman was said to have won nearly a hundred thousand pounds by gambling. As a card-player he was cool and skilful, whilst at the same time quick to seize the moment for exchanging caution for dash. At times, however, he was careless—he once lost £3400 at whist by not remembering that the seven of hearts was still in.

Crockford's eventually ruined him as it did many others—some it could not ruin. Lord Sefton, for instance, is said to have lost no less than £200,000 there. After his death the proprietor presented an acceptance for £40,000 to his son, which was paid. At the beginning of the nineteenth century young men-about-town were exposed to every sort of dangerous temptation.

In 1813 a youthful commoner, heir to large estates, was unpleasantly initiated into the mysteries of fashionable play by losing nearly £20,000 at hazard at a West-End Club, it being the first time he had ever played. His single antagonist was a noble Lord of considerable experience, who by mere chance held the box so luckily as to throw in seven times successively. A remark being made upon so extraordinary a run of the dice, his Lordship insisted upon having them cut up, to manifest that his success had been perfectly honourable—and the bones, on dissection, were found perfectly innocent.

Gambling flourished at all the fashionable clubs. Brooks's in particular was noted for unlimited gambling during the first forty years of its existence. The prevalence of gambling there is shown by one of the old rules, which prohibited "gaming in the 'eating-room' except tossing up for reckonings." The penalty for a breach of this regulation was paying the whole bill of the members present.

Though a rule existed which forbade the members to stake upon credit, it was more or less treated as a dead letter, Mr. Brooks being generally ready to make any advance which the members might desire. The result of such confidence in the solvency of his clientele appears to have been disappointing, for after eight years Mr. Brooks withdrew from the Mastership of the Club and died in very poor circumstances. All things considered this was not surprising, for he was a man

Who, nursed in clubs, disdains a vulgar trade,
Exults to trust, and blushes to be paid.

During the gaming period losses and winnings amounting to five, ten, or fifteen thousand pounds were not at all uncommon. Lord Stavordale, before he was of age, having lost £11,000 one night, struck a good run at hazard and got it all back. This, however, did not satisfy his Lordship, who swore a great oath, saying, "Now if I had been playing deep I might have won millions."

One member, Mr Thynne, retired in disgust in March 1772. According to a note written opposite his name in the Club books this was because he had "won only £12,000 during the last two months, and that he may never return is the ardent wish of members."

At Brooks's, Charles James Fox found himself amidst the most congenial facilities for ruin, and he did not let them pass. Fox, who joined Brooks's when he was sixteen, once sat in the Club playing at hazard for twenty-two hours in succession, when he lost £11,000. At twenty-five he was a ruined man, though his father had paid £140,000 for him out of his own property.

In 1793 his friends raised £70,000 to pay his debts and buy him an annuity—a proof of the affection this curious character inspired.

It was at Brooks's that Lord Robert Spencer is said at one stroke to have recovered his considerable fortune lost at play. General Fitzpatrick and Lord Robert, having both come to their last shilling, contrived to raise a sufficient sum of money to keep a faro bank, which proved an extraordinarily lucky one. Lord Robert's share was no less than £100,000, with which he retired from the gambling-table for ever, and never played again.

Another well-known man of fashion lost at Brooks's £70,000 and everything else which he possessed, including his carriage and horses, which was his last stake. Charles Fox, who was present, and partook of the spoils, moved that an annuity of £50 per annum should be settled upon the unfortunate gentleman, to be paid out of the general fund, which motion was agreed to *nem. con.*, and a resolution was entered into at the instance of the same gentleman, that every member who should be completely ruined in that house should be allowed a similar annuity out of the same fund, on condition that they are never to be admitted as sporting members; as in that case the society would be playing against their own money.

The old betting-book at Brooks's is a most curious record. A certain member, for instance, bets another five hundred guineas to ten that none of the Cabinet will be beheaded within the following three years. Another wagers fifty guineas that Mademoiselle Heinel will not dance at the opera next year. The whole volume is most characteristic of an age when all fashionable London lived in a vortex of speculation.

THE GAMBLING-ROOM AT BROOKS'S.
From a Water-colour Drawing in the possession of the Club.

Faro, quinze, and macao were the favourite games at Brooks's, but at one time whist for high stakes came into great favour. Two of the best players at this were a couple of characters known as Tippoo Smith and "Neptune"—the latter an old gentleman who had gained his nickname owing to his having once thrown himself into the sea under the false impression that he could no longer keep his head above water.

At Brooks's are preserved a number of relics of the old gambling days, including the faro table at which Fox played. This has a portion cut away, in order, it is said, to give room for his portly form. A complete set of the old gaming counters—the highest inscribed 500 guineas—is also here, whilst several prints and pictures (one of them reproduced in these pages by the courtesy of the Committee) give a good idea of a vanished day.

Brooks's was much frequented by a famous whist-player, General Scott, the father-in-law of George Canning and the Duke of Portland, who is said to have won about £200,000 at the game, of which he was a past master.

The General, indeed, was a very shrewd man where all forms of speculation were concerned, and once won a large wager at Newmarket in the following way. Just as his horse was about to start for a sweepstake, Mr. Panton called out to him, "General, I'll lay you a thousand pounds your horse is neither first nor last." The General accepted the bet and immediately gave directions to his rider; his horse came in last, and he claimed the money. Mr. Panton objected to payment, because the General had spoken to his rider; but the Jockey Club held that the bet was laid not upon the chance of the place in which the horse would come, if the rider was uninformed of it, but upon the opinion, that he had not speed enough to be first, nor tractability enough to be brought in last.

Nevertheless, the General, like most gamblers, had his moments of generosity. He was playing one evening with the Count d'Artois and the Duc de Chartres, at Paris, when a petition was brought up from the widow of a French officer, stating her various misfortunes, and praying relief. A plate was handed round, and each put in one, two, or three louis d'or, but when it was held to the General, who was going to throw for a stake of five hundred louis d'or, he said, "Stop a moment, if you please, sir: here goes for the widow!" The throw was successful, and he instantly swept the whole into the plate, and sent it down to her.

General Scott was an excellent whist-player, and lived in a most careful manner, which gave him a great advantage over his contemporaries, many of whom were reckless to a degree, tossing their money about in all directions, and borrowing from any one when short of cash.

General Scott followed a regime which assisted him to keep all his faculties in the very best condition for getting the most out of his cards. His dinner usually consisted of a boiled chicken, washed down with toast and water. His memory, coolness, and judgment were remarkable. With players such as these, whist became almost a religious function of a singularly profitable kind.

At the present day, when whist has fallen from its ancient high estate, and rendered practically obsolete owing to the popularity of bridge, it is difficult to realise the place which the game held in the estimation of many of our forefathers.

At the beginning of the nineteenth century almost as large sums were lost and won at whist as at the hazard-table, which was chiefly the resort of those who, like Fox, complained that games of skill afforded no excitement.

Many who were not entirely devoted to high play found their only relaxation in whist. Such a one was Lord Camden's brother, Mr. Edward Pratt, connected with the East India Company, whose sole bond with humanity is said to have lain in whist.

By no means an avaricious man, Mr. Pratt spent little upon his personal comfort, always living in the upper floor of a house owing to its tranquillity, and regularly dining in a room by himself at a tavern every day of the year, his only companion a solitary bottle of port.

He was seldom heard to speak, but no circumstance, however urgent, could prevail on him to break silence at whist, the favourite amusement, or rather occupation of his life; and, at the conclusion of each rubber, he could correctly call over the cards in the exact order in which they were played, as well as the persons from whose hands they fell, and enumerate various instances of error or dexterity in his associates, with practical remarks. This extraordinary exertion of the retentive powers was often doubted, and as often ascertained by considerable wagers.

Abstinence from speech, however, was the favourite, habitual, perhaps the affected, pleasure of his life; to such a pitch did he carry this eccentricity that he deliberately chose to forego many little satisfactions and comforts, rather than be at the trouble to ask for them.

In his voyages to India, Mr. Pratt might have been compared to some Eastern mystic, whose eyes and thoughts are immovably riveted by inspiration, madness, or emptiness to the region of the navel. When on voyages by sea it was his invariable custom to present the appearance of one entirely engrossed by his own thoughts, which, it was opined from his countenance, were of a peculiarly morose character. He often doubled the

Cape without having scarcely uttered a word. During one voyage, when his ship had been detained by a long and troublesome calm, the anxious and dispirited crew were at last revived by the advent of the long-wished-for breeze. Amidst general excitement, a miserably dressed seaman on the topmast being at last able to proclaim the welcome tidings of land, Mr. Pratt alone struck a discordant note, for whilst the officers and ship's company were congratulating each other on the approaching joys of being on shore, though his features were observed to alter and somewhat unbend, no sound escaped his lips. "I knew you would enjoy the sight of land," at length said the first officer. "I saw it an hour before the careless ragamuffin aloft," were the first, the last, and the only words Mr. Pratt uttered during the voyage.

"A clear fire, a clean hearth, and the rigour of the game," was the sole earthly aim of Mr. Pratt, as it was of the old lady who declared that next to her devotions she loved a good game of whist. Players of this sort were not lukewarm gamesters or half-and-half players who have no objection to take a hand if one is wanted to make up a rubber; affirming that they have no pleasure in winning, or that they like to win one game and lose another. Keen antagonists, they never desired an adversary who had slipped a wrong card, to take it up and play another. They loved a thorough-paced partner and a determined enemy. They took and gave no concessions; they hated favours, never made a revoke, or passed it over in an adversary without exacting the utmost penalty. They never introduced or connived at miscellaneous conversation during the progress of a game, for, as they emphatically observed, cards were cards. Whist was their business and duty—the thing which they had come into the world to do—and they did it.

In the early days of the nineteenth century a great deal of gambling went on at Wattier's Club, No. 81 Piccadilly (now a private house), which made a speciality of macao. This game is said to have been introduced into England by French *émigrés.*

Wattier's was kept by an old *maître d'hôtel* of George IV., who, quite a character in his way, prided himself upon the excellence of his cuisine and wines.

The life of Wattier's was a short and merry one, for it only lasted some twelve years, being closed in 1819, when for a time it became a sort of common gambling-house. Byron, Beau Brummell, and many other men of fashion frequented the Club, and, occasionally, says tradition, solaced themselves for their losses by throwing bottles of wine out of the window into the yard of the house just across the way.

Some sixteen years later there was a good deal of high play at whist at Graham's Club, and a scandal occurred. Lord de Ros being charged with unfair play by the *Satirist* newspaper, against which he brought an action for libel. Much curious evidence was given during the trial, one witness admitting that he had won no less than £35,000 in fifteen years at whist. Another—Captain Alexander—estimated his winnings at about £1600 a year. Asked by Counsel how long he had played on a certain occasion, he replied: "All night." "After a slight dinner I suppose?" "As good a dinner as I can get." "A small boiled chicken and a glass of lemonade perhaps?" The witness for some reason considered this insulting and excitedly said: "I deny the lemonade altogether—I never take lemonade"—a disavowal which plunged the court into laughter. Considerable amusement was also created by another witness who, being asked whether he had ever seen anything suspicious about the prosecutor's play replied: "Yes." "What course did you take?" "I always backed him," was the answer.

In the end the peer, who was Premier Baron of England, lost his case. He did not long survive the disgrace, and on his death in 1837 the following line was suggested by Theodore Hook as an epitaph—

> Here lies England's Premier Baron patiently awaiting the last trump.

Towards the middle of the nineteenth century gambling in Clubs began to decline, though, as is always the case, intermittent fits of private gambling were frequent at the West End. In the late 'seventies and early 'eighties, however, of the last century there was some revival of gaming-clubs, or rather places called clubs.

A considerable number of these, started merely for the purposes of play, sprang up in the West End; and the proprietors in many cases realised large sums by cashing the cheques of players, a certain percentage being deducted from the amount of the sum, which was not infrequently handed over in counters. A clever proprietor would, of course, know how much any particular client was good for, and take care to run few risks. Where play was high and the members rich a plentiful harvest was reaped.

The most fashionable Club of this sort was the Park Club, Park Place, St James's, where, in 1884, there was a good deal of high play at baccarat. The existence of what was virtually a gaming-club aroused much comment, and, the matter reaching the ears of the authorities, it was not long before action was taken.

As considerable misapprehension exists as to how the English law views gaming, some account of the proceedings which followed may not be out of place.

On the 17th of January 1884, Mr. St John Wontner attended at Bow Street on behalf of Mr. Howard Vincent, the Director of the Criminal Investigation Department, to apply for process against the Park Club, Park Place, St. James's, under the provisions of the Gaming Acts.

Mr. Wontner, referring to the section of the Act under which it was proposed to proceed, said that the summons was applied for against the proprietor, the secretary, the committee, and various members of this Club, for keeping the premises as a common gambling-house, where they habitually allowed baccarat to be played.

Attention was called to the comments of the Press on gambling, and it was said that various complaints had been made to the police, in consequence of which an inspector was instructed to intimate to the proprietors of various Clubs that the practice of playing games of chance was illegal, and proceedings would be taken were it to be continued.

Play had been suspended at various Clubs, but in the ease of this particular Club, Messrs. Lewis & Lewis, Solicitors, of Ely Place, had communicated with the authorities to the effect that it was the intention of those concerned to test the question, and expressed willingness to answer any proceedings that might be instituted.

On the 1st of February 1884, at Bow Street, before Sir J. Ingham, Jenks (proprietor), Dalton (secretary), and certain members of this Club and its committee appeared to a summons charging them with a contravention of the Gaming Act.

Mr. St. John Wontner prosecuted, Mr. Charles Russell, afterwards Lord Russell of Killowen, and Mr. Poland, instructed by Mr. George Lewis, defended.

The charge against the defendants was that they were concerned in keeping a common gaming-house, and permitting a game of chance to be played called "baccarat." For the prosecution Mr. Wontner quoted some rules of the game. He said that the regulation bank at this Club was fixed at £50, an open bank at £1000. As a rule, the banks varied from £25 to £300, but were often larger. Mr. Wontner quoted a printed description of the game of baccarat, and submitted that it was purely a game of chance of a dangerous character, at which excessive gambling took place. Playing cards for amusement was not prohibited, but it was contended that excessive gambling was punishable by law.

Sir J. Ingham inquired as to the definition of the word "excessive." Mr. Wontner submitted that the Legislature had defined excessive gambling as criminal, while moderate gaming was not. So the proprietor of a place where excessive gaming was allowed, and who received the profits, was guilty of the offence at common law of keeping a gaming-house, and habitual users of the house were also liable.

An ordinary Club-house, where the profits went to the members, would be equally a gaming-house if excessive and habitual play were allowed.

Mr. Wontner quoted several decisions, and referred to various Acts dealing with gaming, dating from the reign of Henry VIII., when all games except archery were declared illegal. A subsequent Act repealed that Act, as far as games of skill went, but the old enactment still held as to games, and he contended that whether unlawful gaming went on in a house, the proprietor of which admitted members on payment of subscription, or whether it took place in an ordinary Club, the offence was just the same.

Inspector Swansen, of Scotland Yard, had had interviews with Jenks as to particulars respecting the Club. Jenks told him the Club was open in 1882, and he had bought the lease of the premises. He explained the game of baccarat. After two o'clock the banks were put up to auction. Each bank paid one per cent, and each player five shillings for card-money up to 2 A.M. After that time, five shillings until 5 A.M., when £1 an hour was charged, in order to make the game prohibitory. The profits so derived went to the proprietor. One per cent was also charged for cashing cheques. The rules of the Club prohibited the introduction of any stranger to the card-room. The profits realised were from the subscriptions and the card-money. The kitchen had been a loss, and wine and cigars were sold at cost price. On a subsequent occasion, Mr. Jenks told witness that members' cheques were cashed, and one per cent was charged as an insurance against bad cheques. He stated that he did not cash cheques beyond a reasonable amount, which he estimated at £300. In cross-examination by Mr. Russell, witness admitted that Jenks had given all information freely. The Club, of which he was the proprietor, consisted of from 200 to 300 members, comprising gentlemen well-known in society.

The night steward of the Park Club was called, and gave evidence as to the play in the card-room. Baccarat was not played there until Mr. Jenks took possession of the Club. Play began about 4.30 in the afternoon, and a break would be made about half-past seven for dinner, after which play was resumed and kept up till two, three, four, and sometimes eight o'clock in the morning. The average bank would be about £100.

After further evidence had been taken, and speeches made for and against the defendants, Sir James Ingham, in giving his decision on the summons, said that Jenks was substantially charged with keeping a house for unlawful gaming, and the other gentlemen were substantially charged with aiding and assisting him in doing so. The first question to determine was why and for what purpose Jenks kept this house open. Was it an ordinary Club at which gambling was casually introduced, or was it substantially a gaming-house? The question could be answered by the evidence, as the profits arising from the wines, spirits, and tobacco were admitted to be trifling, while the profits from food were absolutely nothing, the kitchen being carried on at a loss. The subscriptions received from 250 members at six guineas per year produced annually £1711, which was subjected to very large deductions for rent, taxes, etc. It must be clear to everybody that as a Club for social purposes, the business would not be worth the care and attention which it would require. What was the case with respect to gambling? Jenks received one per cent upon all banks, and contributions from all players who stayed after certain hours. Without going into particulars he calculated on consideration of the number of games that would be played ordinarily in the course of an evening, that Jenks must realise from £45 to £50 per night, and that his annual profits must be £10,000 to £12,000, or perhaps many thousands more. Therefore, no one could doubt that the house had been kept and used for the purpose of gambling, for its character as a social Club was absolutely ancillary to its business as a gambling-house. The statute, however, required that there should not only be gambling, but gambling at an unlawful game, and the main question was whether the game of baccarat was an unlawful game. It must be admitted that although a great many games had been prohibited by the Legislature, baccarat had not, and whether it was unlawful or not, must depend on other considerations. Baccarat appeared to be a game of chance, tempered by a certain amount of skill and judgment. Many games of mixed chance and skill might be innocently played. It was important to glance at the state of the old law. Sir J. Ingham then quoted from Baker's abridgment on the subject of gaming for recreation and common gaming-houses, "which promote cheating and other corrupt practices, and incite to idleness and avariciousness persons whose time might otherwise be employed to the general good of the community."

The principle to be extracted was that gaming productive of the above evils ought to be considered unlawful, and he (Sir James) considered that the game of baccarat was not "a game played for recreation, whereby a person is fitted for the ordinary duties of life." A great deal had been said upon the subject of large and excessive gambling, and the argument had been advanced that games which would be large and risky and excessive for a man who was in the position of a shop-keeper, would be nothing, trifles infinitesimal, in the eyes of a man of large property. Granted that was so, still there might be cases in which the law could be easily applied, and he thought this was one. Referring to the rules of the Park Club, which was to consist of noblemen, members of the learned professions, officers of the Army and Navy, and gentlemen, Sir James observed that a man at the game in question might lose, with consistent bad luck, £1000 before dinner, and a considerable sum in addition afterwards. Would there be any difficulty in saying that that was large and excessive gambling in the case of members of the learned professions, clergymen, bishops, great leading counsel of the day, or even judges with the largest salaries, physicians, and so forth? Gaming such as had been proved to exist would be large and excessive for any of those classes of men, and still more so for officers of the Army and Navy. He had no hesitation in saying, with reference to the gentlemen composing the Club at Mr. Jenks's house, that gaming had been large and excessive, and that it came within the principle of the law laid down by Chief Justice Abbot in the case of "King *v.* Rosier." But he considered the case did not stop there, and proceeded to refer at great length to the Act of Queen Anne, limiting gambling.

In conclusion, the learned Magistrate held that all the parties, with the exception of Mr. Dalton (secretary), had been guilty of gaming. He fined Mr. Jenks £500, the members of the committee £500, and each of the players £100.

Notice of appeal was given.

The appeal was brought on May 26 and 27, and in giving judgment, Sir Henry Hawkins (afterwards Lord Brampton), after saying that the facts were undisputed—there was no profit except on the gaming, though from the admirable printed rules one might well conclude that the Club was a sociable Club, where a gentleman might dine and have his rubber at whist, whilst not on any account allowed to gamble. The rules in question were, however, nightly disregarded, and looking at the nightly doings, it was impossible for any man in his senses to doubt that the house was really opened and kept for the purpose of gaming at the game of baccarat as its main and principal object.

He now had to consider the illegality of the gaming and not merely the illegality of the game—the common law did not prohibit the playing at cards and dice, which were not unlawful games, but the keeping of a common gaming-house was at common law an indictable offence.

Sir Henry Hawkins, after some comments on what constituted a gaming-house, went on to say that in his judgment it was not necessary for a gaming-house to be a public nuisance, which the Park Club was not:—a common gaming-house being itself a nuisance, though the gaming there was limited to the subscribers and members of the Club. The keeper of such a house could always admit or exclude whom he chose, and the committee elected whom they pleased, provided the list of members did not exceed 500. It might be 5000 and yet still not be a public, but a common gaming-house.

As to unlawful games—no games had been in so many words declared by name unlawful, though the Legislature intended to cover some games which, being lawful in themselves, were only unlawful when played in particular places or by particular persons. The Act of 1845 enacted that a house is proved to be a common gaming-house which is kept for playing any unlawful games and a bank is kept by one or more of the players, exclusively of the others, or where the chances of any game played are not alike favourable to all the players.

He divided unlawful games into two classes:

First, those absolutely forbidden by name, to the gaming at which a penalty is attached. This class included "ace of hearts," "pharaoh or faro," "basset," and "hazard," and any other game with a die or dice except backgammon.

Second, a number of games not altogether prohibited under penal consequences, nor declared to be altogether illegal, but which, nevertheless, have been declared unlawful by the Legislature, because the keeping of houses for playing them, and the play in them therein by anybody, were rendered illegal.

The unlawful games of the Acts of Henry VIII. were "bowls," "quoits," "dicing," "tennis," and "carding," most of which would seem to have been games of mere skill. The Acts in question were all repealed by 8 and 9 Vic.

The present unlawful games, then, were "ace of hearts," "faro," "basset," "hazard," "passage," "roulette," and every game of dice except backgammon, and every game of cards which was not a game of "mere skill." He was inclined to add any other game of "mere chance."

The question was, did "baccarat" come within this category?—the description of the game given by Mr. Russell satisfied him that it did.

Baccarat was a game of cards—a game of chance—and though, as in most other things, experience and judgment might make one player or banker more successful than another, it would be a perversion of words to say it was in any sense a game of mere skill. It was, therefore, in his opinion an unlawful game within the meaning of the statute.

It was said that it was a modern game—assuming it to be so, it was just what the Legislature intended to include in the phraseology of one unrepealed section of the law of Henry VIII., which mentioned "any new unlawful game hereafter to be invented."

With regard to excessive gaming since the repeal of the statutes of Anne and George II., he did not think excessive gaming at any game would in itself render the game unlawful, for excessive gaming *per se* was not any longer a legal offence. Nevertheless, though excessive gaming was no longer *per se* unlawful, the fact that it was habitually carried on in a house kept for the purpose of gaming was a cogent piece of evidence to be offered to a jury or other tribunal called on to determine whether a house was a common gaming-house so as to make the keeper of it liable to be indicted for a nuisance at common law.

Seeing that Mr. Jenks was the occupier and kept the house open for the purpose of gaming, at, amongst other games, baccarat, an unlawful game within the meaning of the Statute, he was of opinion that he was properly convicted.

As to the four members of the committee, the only question was whether these appellants had the care or management of the house—he thought they had—they could not but have been cognisant of the rules and of the true character of the Club. The second rule of the Club placed its internal management in their hands—he thought there was abundance of evidence to warrant their conviction.

As to the three players, he found no evidence that they did more than play at baccarat in the house, by which it might be that they somewhat enhanced the profits, but they took no part in the management. Adding to the profits was not a legal offence, as assistance in conducting the establishment was—the conviction with respect to the three players ought to be quashed.

Mr. Justice Smith followed, and his summing up entirely coincided with that of Sir Henry Hawkins. This lucid judgment is of considerable interest as affecting games played in English Clubs, and did much to clear up all ambiguity as to how far a Club might allow gambling. It put an end to all open baccarat, though the game was shortly afterwards played for a time at "The Field Club," near St. James's Street, an establishment which much resembled the defunct Park Club in its diversions, members, and methods, but the police soon interfered, and with its demise Club gambling at games of chance has become a thing of the past, except in the low dens of Soho, where faro intermittently calls for the intervention of the authorities. Police raids upon bogus Clubs mainly frequented by foreigners of a low class are often reported in the newspapers.

As regards respectable Clubs, a certain amount of bridge, usually for very moderate stakes, is indulged in, but gambling for high stakes is strongly discountenanced. Members inclined to indulge any tendencies in this direction generally do so elsewhere than in a Club. From time to time small Clubs in which there is some high play have sprung up and had a brief existence. When bridge first began to capture London, a bridge Club was started in the West End where very high stakes were the rule. It lasted but a short time, owing chiefly to the fact that a young and not very astute member lost a very large sum, which created considerable scandal and broke up the Club.

High bridge is now played in London mostly by wealthy people, well able to take care of themselves. The outcry raised some time ago about young girls being compelled to join in playing for large stakes is not based upon any solid foundation of truth, for as a rule high players are not fond of running the chance of drawing a novice as a partner. A bad player spoils the game.

Though there is practically no gambling in West-End Clubs, a good deal of baccarat and poker is occasionally played in private houses, ladies being not infrequently amongst the players, and here gaming assumes its most undesirable form. Temper as well as money is generally lost, whilst the winners are exposed to a by no means remote probability of never being paid. Private gambling is especially dangerous to young men, and without doubt a thousand times more harm is done by play of this sort than by all the properly conducted public tables in the world.

FOOTNOTES:

[5] The love of money compels.

V

Talleyrand whilst at cards announces the death of the Duc d'Enghien—"The curse of Scotland"—Wilberforce at faro—Successful gamblers—The Rev. Caleb Colton—Colonel Panton—Dennis O'Kelly—Richard Rigby—Anecdotes—Strange incidents at play—Aged gamesters—A duel with death—General Wade and the poor officer—Anecdote of a caprice of Fortune—Stock Exchange speculation—A man who profited by tips.

The history of card-playing is connected with many dramatic incidents. If the story be true, one of the most striking of these was when Talleyrand, who had been playing very late at "*la bouillotte*" with the Duchesse de Luynes, suddenly laid down his cards, and in his cold, impassive voice asked, "Has the Prince de Condé any other grandchildren than the Duc d'Enghien?" Receiving an answer in the negative he calmly said, "Then the house of Condé has come to an end."

At that very moment the ill-fated Duc was being led out to be shot at the château of Vincennes.

A grim historical interest is also generally supposed to be connected with the nine of diamonds, which is known as "the curse of Scotland," the reason assigned being that the Duke of Cumberland wrote his sanguinary orders on the back of such a card in 1746. Notwithstanding this popular tradition, the nine of diamonds had been known as "the curse of Scotland" as far back as thirty years before Culloden—perhaps because a somewhat similar design formed the arms of Colonel Packer, who was on the scaffold when Charles I. was executed. Another reason given is that there were nine lozenges resembling diamonds in the arms of the Earl of Stair who made the Union.

Cards have at times attracted the most saintly persons. The first time the philanthropic Wilberforce was at Brooks's he joined in playing faro—according to his own account—from mere shyness. A friend of his, very much surprised, called out to him, "What, Wilberforce, is that you?" George Selwyn, who was keeping the bank, resented the interference, and said in his most expressive tones, "Oh, sir, don't interrupt Mr. Wilberforce, he could not be better employed."

Oddly enough, one of the most remarkable instances of a really successful gambler was an English clergyman, the Reverend Caleb Colton. A man of considerable learning, he was originally a fellow of King's College, Cambridge, and curate of Tiverton. In 1812 he created some slight stir with two poems entitled "Hypocrisy" and "Napoleon." His literary reputation was further enhanced in 1818, when the author had become Vicar of Kew, by the publication of a volume of maxims called *Lacon: or Many Things in Few Words*. This work, however, was not absolutely original, being in a great measure founded upon Lord Bacon's *Essays*, Burdon's *Materials for Thinking*, and the well-known aphorisms of La Rochefoucauld.

LA BOUILLOTTE.
From a scarce print after Bosio.

About this time Mr. Colton began to speculate, and, having dabbled rather recklessly in Spanish bonds, his affairs became involved. This frightened the reverend gentleman, and, though there appears to have been no pressing reason for taking such a step, he absconded.

His affairs were subsequently put in order, after which Mr. Colton for a time betook himself to America, eventually returning to Europe and settling down in Paris. Here he took up his abode in the Palais Royal, at that time the head-quarters of dissipation and amusement—surely the queerest spot ever selected by an English clergyman for his abode.

Colton now began to make an exhaustive study of the intricacies and mysteries of the gaming-table, every facility for putting theory into practice being at his very door. Unlike most searchers after infallible methods of winning, he was completely successful, and in the course of a year or two won over £25,000 by some method of staking, of which no reliable record seems to exist. More wonderful still, the Reverend Caleb kept his winnings, part of which he devoted to the purchase of pictures. He was a cultivated man, and published an ode, which was privately circulated, on the death of Lord Byron.

The end of Mr. Colton was a tragic one, for in 1832 he blew out his brains at the house of a friend living at Fontainebleau. The act in question was, of course, attributed to the effect of gambling losses. A thrilling story was told which described how the unfortunate clergyman, after ruinous losses at Frascati's, had blown his brains out in the forest of St. Germain, and, as always follows in such cases, an outcry arose, demanding the suppression of the tables in the Palais Royal and at Frascati's. Gambling, however, was in no way responsible for Colton's end, the real cause of his suicide having been a disease necessitating a painful operation, to which the successful gambler preferred death.

A very fortunate gamester was Colonel Panton, who in the early part of the eighteenth century suddenly realised a considerable fortune by keeping a gaming-house in Piccadilly. Though by nature a confirmed gambler he then exhibited extraordinary common sense, and, having invested his winnings in house property and land, entirely abandoned the card-table and the dice-box. His name is still preserved in Panton Street, Haymarket.

Another sporting character who amassed a large fortune by gambling and the Turf was Colonel Dennis O'Kelly,[6] the owner of the famous race-horse Eclipse.

The rank of Colonel which this Irishman was entitled to assume was procured by him in a characteristically curious way. In 1760, when the county of Middlesex was very backward in raising sufficient men for its militia, a well-known Scotch adventurer, MacGregor by name, whose family had suffered a good deal for the Stuarts in 1745, seeing a good opportunity of making some money, set about raising a regiment in Westminster which the Government promised to recognise as soon as three-fourths of the commissions should be filled up. He found, however, difficulty in obtaining officers and had to ransack the town and hold out commissions to all sorts of people, amongst whom was O'Kelly, who became an ensign, in due course of time rising to be Lieutenant-Colonel. O'Kelly, though totally ignorant of discipline, is said to have presented the most soldierly appearance of any officer in the regiment. This was not saying much, for the third captain was a tea-dealer, the fourth a tailor, and the fifth a boatswain's mate who had bought an ale-house with prize-money and could just sign his name. The most junior officer was a crippled creature of foreign extraction.

When O'Kelly became a major, he is described as having put his regiment through certain military evolutions to the entire satisfaction of the King and his staff, whilst his Lieutenant-Colonelcy was celebrated by a splendid entertainment which many of the aristocracy of Leicestershire attended. O'Kelly was sometimes known as Count O'Kelly, a title which was supposed to have been conferred upon him by his fellow-prisoners during a sojourn in the "Fleet" when he was a young man. Here he met Catherine Hayes, who lived as his faithful companion through life. Though she was never married to him, her position was more or less recognised, and O'Kelly left her an annuity which she continued to enjoy till she died, in the second decade of the nineteenth century, at the age of eighty-five.

Among many racing successes O'Kelly won the Derby twice—in 1781 with Young Eclipse by Eclipse, and three years later again with Sergeant by Eclipse out of Aspasia.

His racing colours were scarlet and black cap.

Whilst there is no doubt but that O'Kelly was very lucky in much that he undertook, his originality and penetration were largely responsible for a success which, however, never gained him admission into fashionable circles.

Though a hospitable man of a certain genial humour, O'Kelly was not very open-handed to dependents. In spite of his affluence he was even mean enough to keep jockeys of the poorer class out of their money, season after season, being sometimes even sued by them in the law courts, and personally dunned on the race-course stands. In such a place, on one disgraceful occasion, an old sportsman made the Captain look extremely small by apostrophising him as a mean, low-lived, waiter-bred skunk. In spite of these failings O'Kelly achieved a certain popularity by the good dinners and excellent wines which he provided at his house at Epsom, his dry and truly Irish facetiousness affording the highest zest to those entertainments. At his country house he would never allow any betting or gambling. A constant subject of jest amongst his familiars was the tone in which at dinner he used to say, "John, bring the aaples," meaning the pines, and the whimsicality with which he would apostrophise his servant on certain occasions. The latter having announced the non-arrival of fish, "Begorra," said his master, "and if you can't get any fish, bring herrings." O'Kelly was a gentlemanly and even graceful man in behaviour, a strong contrast to his bear-like figure, dark and saturnine visage, with the accompaniment of his rough striped coat and old round hat. A quite peaceable man, though a true-bred Milesian, O'Kelly never had the smallest appetite for fighting with any weapon whatever. He was a great contrast in this respect to the bullying Dick England, with whom he once became involved in a law-suit. He was ambitious of honour and distinction, a proof of which was his successful pretension to military rank. In the darling object of his life, however, capricious fortune left him in the lurch; the

Jockey Club, whose action in this matter was generally approved, steadily refusing to admit among them a parvenu, not, perhaps, of unequivocal character. This O'Kelly, so much of a philosopher in other things, did not possess philosophy enough to forgive, but, in revenge, never failed to characterise the honourable body which refused to admit him by the very hardest professional names which his wit and bitterness could devise.

Very much aggrieved at not being admitted into certain of the Clubs at Newmarket and in London, which were frequented by aristocratic sportsmen, he never lost an opportunity of retaliating on those whom he deemed responsible for his exclusion.

On one occasion, when making an arrangement to retain the services of a certain jockey, he told him he had no objection to his riding for any other person provided he had no horse running in the same race; adding, however, that he would be prepared to double his terms provided he would enter into an arrangement and bind himself under a penalty never to ride for any of the black-legged fraternity. The consenting jockey saying that he did not quite understand who the Captain meant by the black-legged fraternity, the latter instantly replied with his usual energy, "Oh, by ——, my dear, and I'll soon make you understand who I mean by the black-legged fraternity:—there's the Duke of G., the Duke of D., Lord A., Lord D., Lord G., Lord C., Lord F., the Right Hon. A.B.C.D., and C.I.F., and all the set of thaves that belong to their humbug societies and bug-a-boo Clubs, where they can meet and rob one another without detection."

This curious definition of the black-legged fraternity is a sufficiently clear demonstration of how severely O'Kelly felt himself affected by his rejection. He made a point of embracing every opportunity of saying anything to excite the irascibility of the sporting aristocracy, whilst shirking no difficulty or expense to obtain that pre-eminence upon the Turf which he eventually enjoyed. Dining at the stewards' ordinary at Burford races, in the year 1775, Lord Robert Spencer in the chair, Lord Abingdon and many other noblemen being present, matches and sweepstakes as usual, after dinner, were proposed and entered into for the following year—amongst the rest, one between Lord A. and Mr. Baily, of Rambridge, in Hampshire, for 300 gs. h. ft., when the Captain was once or twice appealed to by Mr. B. in adjusting the terms, and Lord A. happened to exclaim that he and the gentleman on his side the table ran for honour, the Captain and his friends for profit. The match was at length agreed upon in terms not conformable to the Captain's opinion, and consequently, when he was applied to by B. to stand half, he vociferously replied, "No, but if the match had been made cross and jostle, as I proposed, I would have not only stood all the money, but have brought a spalpeen from Newmarket, no higher than a twopenny loaf, that should (by ——!) have driven his Lordship's horse and jockey into the furzes, and have kept him there for three weeks."

His support of and attachment to Ascot was strikingly conspicuous. During the races there he ran a horse each day for years, whilst his presence and his pocket enlivened the hazard-table at night.

Here it was that, seeing him turning over a quire of bank-notes, a gentleman asked him what he was in want of, when he replied he was looking for a little one. The inquirer said he could accommodate him, and desired to know for what sum. Upon which he answered, a "fifty, or something of that sort, just to set the caster." At this time it was supposed he had seven or eight thousand pounds in his hand, but not a note for less than a hundred. He always threw with great success, and when he held the box, was seldom known to refuse throwing for any sum that the company chose to set him; and when "out" was always as liberal in setting the caster, and preventing a stagnation of trade at the table. On the other hand, his large capital and good luck not infrequently captured the last guinea of the bank.

It was O'Kelly's usual custom to carry a great number of bank-notes in his waistcoat pocket, wisped up together with the greatest indifference. Playing at a hazard-table at Windsor during the races, as a standing better (every chair being full), a strange hand was observed by those on the opposite side of the table, furtively drawing two notes out of his pocket. The alarm was given, and the hand as instantaneously withdrawn, the notes being left more than half out of the pocket. The company were eager for the offender to be taken before a magistrate, and many attempted to secure him for that purpose, but the Captain very philosophically seizing the thief by the collar, merely kicked him downstairs with the exultant exclamation that "'twas a sufficient punishment to be deprived of the pleasure of keeping company with jontlemen."

On one occasion, when at Newmarket, O'Kelly offered to bet a considerable sum with a gentleman who knew nothing about the redoubtable Irishman. The stranger, half suspecting that the challenge came from one of the black-legged fraternity, begged to know what security he would give for so large a sum, if he should lose, and where his estates lay. "O! Begorra, my dear creature, I have the map of them about me, and here it is, sure enough," said O'Kelly, pulling out a pocket-book, and giving unequivocal proofs of his property, by producing bank-notes far exceeding in value the amount of the wager.

Besides having been owner of the equine wonder Eclipse, old O'Kelly was in his last years the possessor of a wonderful parrot said to have been purchased at Bristol, where it had been bred—the only parrot of this kind ever born in England. This extraordinary bird died at a great age in the early years of the nineteenth century. It was of moderate size, chiefly green in colour, with some grey and red, and spoke with a clear and distinct articulation, and with so little inferiority to the female human voice divine, that when its tones were heard outside in the street, people would dispute as to whether the voice was that of a woman or a parrot.

After O'Kelly's death it became the property of his nephew and heir, Colonel Andrew O'Kelly, who lived in Half-Moon Street, which quiet thoroughfare was very much enlivened by the performances of the parrot at a window. When pressed to sing by passers-by, lively Poll would swear and laugh at them, all the time spreading and fluttering its wings in triumph. The bird's favours were divided between an old lady and the Colonel, with both of whom it would converse on a variety of topics. When the latter was returning home. Poll, if at the window, would espy him across the street, upon which it would instantly clap its wings, and set up an impatient squalling—"The Colonel! the Colonel is coming! open the door!" If in a bad mood and asked to talk, Poll would sometimes reply sullenly, "I'll see you damn'd first!" At times, especially if not near the window, with the sash up below its cage—which was the bird's favourite place—being asked, "How d'ye do to-day, Poll?" the parrot would curtly answer, "Why, I don't know," "Middling," or "What's that to you?"

Colonel O'Kelly was very proud of his bird and had regular "parrot concerts," on which occasions Half-Moon Street was filled with carriages and an admiring crowd, to such a degree as to be scarcely passable. Although solicited by many distinguished people, the Colonel did not permit his parrot to leave his home and pay visits. So great became the parrot's renown that his owner was once offered a very large sum, by a well-known caterer of amusements, to allow Poll to appear in public, the bird's life to be heavily insured.

Colonel O'Kelly, it should be added, had profited by the good English and French education which his uncle had bestowed upon him. He was Lieutenant-Colonel in the Middlesex Militia, and pursued the Turf with some spirit.

Another gambler who achieved prosperity was Mr. Richard Rigby, who rose to affluence owing to an incident on a race-course.

Having at an early age inherited a comfortable fortune, young Mr. Rigby proceeded to squander it whilst yet incapable of appreciating the value of money. Gaming, racing, and other forms of getting into difficulties occupied his time, with the result that most of his inheritance soon passed into the hands of lawyers and money-lenders. He would probably have sunk into a state of abject destitution had not the Turf, which had so largely contributed to diminish his fortune, also been the means of restoring him to opulence.

The Duke of Bedford of that day had given great offence to the gentlemen in the neighbourhood of Litchfield, by an improper and unfair interference at their races; and as at the end of the eighteenth century it was by no means safe or easy effectually to punish a man fortified by rank, privilege, and wealth, they at last determined to bestow on this illustrious offender manual correction. The overbearing conduct of the Duke in some matter relating to the starting of their horses, and their weights, in which he had no kind of right to interfere, soon afforded the confederates an opportunity of executing their purpose. He was in one moment separated from his attendants, surrounded by the party, hustled and unmercifully horsewhipped by an exasperated country attorney, with a keen sense of his wrongs and a muscular arm. The lawyer persevered in this severe discipline without being interrupted by his Grace's outcries and repeated declarations that he was the Duke of Bedford, an assertion which Mr. Humphries, the assailant, positively denied, adding that a peer of the realm would never have conducted himself in so scandalous a manner. The matter soon circulated over the course, and reaching Mr. Rigby's ear, the latter with a generous, if perhaps calculated gallantry, burst through the crowd, rescued the distressed noble, completely thrashed his antagonist, and conveyed the Duke to a place of safety.

The result of this affair was most fortunate for the spendthrift, who, as a consequence, eventually amassed a huge fortune.

The Russell family were very grateful for the singular service which Mr. Rigby had rendered to the Duke, whose rescuer was loaded with favours. These eventually culminated in his obtaining the most lucrative office in the gift of the Crown, that of Paymaster-General; the emoluments arising from which, during the American War, amounted annually to £50,000.

In 1782, on Lord North's retirement, Mr. Rigby lost his post, and was also called upon to refund a large sum declared to be public money which should have been accounted for. Under these circumstances Rigby applied to Thomas Rumbold, who, originally a waiter at White's, had risen to be Governor of Madras. Whilst fulfilling his duties in St. James's Street, the latter had often advanced Rigby, who was a desperate punter, small sums, and on this occasion his services were once more sought. The ex-waiter had returned to England with immense wealth, procured, it was declared, by very doubtful means. Public indignation having been aroused, a bill to strip the Anglo-Indian of his ill-gotten gains had been introduced in the House of Commons.

Under these circumstances an arrangement was effected, which settled his own difficulties and at the same time saved the fortune of his old friend from White's.

The latter advanced Rigby a large sum, which enabled him to adjust matters regarding the missing money, whilst the bill of confiscation was dropped, its introducer being an intimate friend of the former Paymaster.

Rigby's nephew and heir soon after married Rumbold's daughter, so all ended happily owing, as it was said, to Rigby's former devotion to hazard.

Mr. Rigby appears to have been a generous man, as the following anecdote shows. Being one evening at a hazard-table in Dublin he was very successful; and having won a considerable sum, he was putting it in his purse when a person behind said in a low voice to himself, "Had I that sum, what a happy man should I be!" Mr. Rigby, without looking back, put the purse over his shoulder, saying, "Take it, my friend, and be happy." The stranger made no reply, but accepted it, and retired. Every one present was astonished at Mr. Rigby's uncommon beneficence, whilst he derived additional pleasure from being informed that the person who had received the benefit was a half-pay officer in great distress. Some years after, a gentleman waited upon him in his own equipage, and being introduced to Mr. Rigby, acquainted him that he came to acquit a debt that he had contracted with him in Dublin. Mr. Rigby was greatly surprised at this declaration, as he was an entire stranger. "Yes, sir," continued the visitor, "you assisted me with above a hundred pounds at a time that I was in the utmost indigence, without knowing or even seeing me"; and then related the affair at the gaming-table. "With that money," continued the stranger, "I was enabled to pay some debts and fit myself out for India, where I have been so fortunate as to make an ample fortune." Mr. Rigby declined to take the money, but, through the pressing solicitations of the gentleman, accepted a valuable diamond ring.

The strange incidents which arose at the old hazard-tables, frequented as they were by all sorts and conditions of men, often produced strange changes in men's lives.

General Wade had so great a propensity to gaming, that he frequented places of every description where play was going forward, without considering the low company he met there. At one of these places, one night, in the eagerness of his diversion, he pulled out an exceedingly valuable gold snuff-box, richly set with diamonds, took a pinch, and passed it round, keeping the dice-box four or five mains before he was "out," when recollecting something of the circumstances, and not perceiving the snuff-box, he swore vehemently no man should stir till it was produced, and a general search should ensue. On his right sat a person dressed as an officer, very shabby, who from time to time, with great humility, had begged the honour of going a shilling with him, and had by that means picked up four or five; on him the suspicion fell, and it was proposed to search him first. Begging leave to be heard, he said, "I know the General well; not he, nor all the powers upon earth, shall subject me to a search while I have life to oppose it. I declare, on the honour of a soldier, I know nothing of the snuff-box, and hope that will satisfy all suspicions: follow me into the next room, where I will defend that honour, or perish!" The eyes of all were now turned on the General for an answer, who, clapping his hand eagerly down for his sword, felt the snuff-box (supposed to have been lost, and put there from habit) in a secret side-pocket of his breeches, made for that purpose. The injustice of his suspicions greatly affected the General, who naturally felt a good deal of compassion for his poor fellow-soldier. Overcome with remorse, he at once left the room, having said, "Sir, I here, with great reason, ask your pardon, and I hope to find it granted by your breakfasting with me, and hereafter ranking me among your friends." As may be easily supposed the invitation was complied with, and when, after some conversation, the General conjured the officer to say what could be the true reason that he should object to being searched: "Why, General," was the answer, "being upon half-pay, and friendless, I am obliged to husband every penny; I had that day very little appetite, and as I could not eat what I had paid for, nor afford to lose it, the leg and wing of a fowl were then wrapped up in a piece of paper in my pocket; the thought of which coming to light, appeared ten times more terrible than fighting every one in the room." "Enough! my dear boy, you have said enough! Let us dine together to-morrow; we must prevent your being subjected again to such a dilemma." They met the next day, and the General then gave him a captain's commission, together with a purse of guineas to enable him to join his regiment.

Whilst fortune as a rule seems to delight in favouring novices at play, and is somewhat pitiless to those who have wooed her for years, there have been certain old gamblers who, by making a study of some particular game, have attained to such perfection in playing it as seldom to lose. With some of these play endures as a dominant passion after almost all the other faculties have become impaired.

Not very many years ago a well-known figure in a certain Parisian Club, existing mainly for the purposes of play, was an old gentleman who, paralysed below the waist, was most afternoons carried upstairs in an invalid chair, placed in a fauteuil, and propped up with cushions in order that he might hold a bank at his favourite écarté, a game at which he was an expert of the highest kind.

Up to within a day or two of his death he continued to indulge in a game which was practically his only link with the living world, his faculties, though usually somewhat clouded, recovering all their old vitality as far as concerned the purposes of the card-table.

A case of much the same sort was described by Brillat Savarin, who, in the country where he resided, knew an old guardsman who had served under Louis XV. and Louis XVI.

This aged individual, rather below than above the average of ordinary men in general intelligence, possessed an extraordinary aptitude for games—an expert at all the old ones, he would master any novelty in this line after having played it once or twice.

With the advent of old age he had become paralysed—two faculties alone remaining unimpaired—that of digestion and that of play. Every day for twenty years he had been in the habit of frequenting a house where he was made welcome. Here he would sit in a semi-comatose condition, hidden away in a corner, seemingly indifferent to anything that was done or said. When, however, the card-table was drawn out, he immediately revived, and having dragged himself to a seat, soon demonstrated that his powers as a gamester were as brilliant as in the long dead past when he was a dashing officer at Versailles.

One day there came down into this part of France a Parisian banker who was soon discovered to be a passionate votary of piquet, a game which he declared himself ready to play with any one for very large stakes. A council of war was held, and eventually it was decided that the old guardsman should champion country against town, a war fund being raised by general subscription, winnings or losings to be allocated according to the size of the different shares.

When the banker sat down to the card-table to find himself confronted by a grim, gaunt, twisted figure, he at first believed himself the victim of a joke, but when he saw this spectre take the cards, shuffle and deal with the air of a professor, he began to divine that no unworthy antagonist was pitted against him. This conclusion was before long considerably strengthened, for the unfortunate Parisian was outmatched in play to such an extent that he eventually retired the loser of a very substantial sum. Before setting out for his return journey to Paris, the banker in question, whilst thanking all he had met for their hospitality, declared that there was only one thing he had to deplore, which was having been so bold as to pit himself against a corpse at cards.

There is an awful story told of a gambler who refused to die, and who, when *in extremis*, had the card-table drawn up to his bedside with strong meats and drinks, and held the cards against Death himself; but the grim tyrant held all the trumps, and soon snatched his prey.

Utter absorption to extraneous influences brands gamblers as with a hot iron, and so great is the fascination which play exercises over certain natures, that there exist people who fully believe that there is only one thing less pleasant than winning—which is to lose. The originator of the maxim in question was Lieutenant-Colonel Aubrey, one of the boldest and most adventurous men that England has ever known, who lived on into the twentieth century.

Piquet and hazard, particularly the former, were the games in which the Colonel was known to excel, and on which he adventured greater sums than any man living in his time. The Duke of York, George IV., Colonel Fitzpatrick, Alderman Combe, and other distinguished personages were his antagonists and associates at play, and he was always considered an "honourable" man.

The domination exercised by gambling sometimes amounts almost to insanity, all sense of decency and proportion being lost. This was the case with a certain English Colonel, who was so addicted to gambling, that having one night lost all the money he could command, determined to stake his wife's diamond ear-rings, and going straight home, asked her to lend them to him. She took them from her ears, saying that she knew for what purpose he wanted them, and that he was welcome. The jewels in question proved lucky, and the Colonel won largely, gaining back all that he had lost that night. In the warmth of his gratitude to his wife, he, at her desire, took an oath that he would never more play at any game with cards or dice. Some time afterwards he was found in a hay-yard with a friend, drawing straws out of the hay-rick, and betting upon which should be the longest! As might be expected, he lived in alternate extravagance and distress, sometimes surrounded with every sort of luxury, and sometimes in dire want of half a crown. Nevertheless, he continued gambling all his life. Bewailing a run of ill-luck to a serious friend one day, the soldier in question said, "Is it not astonishing how I always lose?" "That's not what surprises me," was the reply, "so much as where you get the money to pay." As a matter of fact too many gamblers have taken much the same point of view as was adopted by a certain Italian gamester who, after an intolerable run of ill-luck, apostrophised Fortune, calling her a vixenish jade.

"Thou mayest," said he, "indeed cause me to lose millions, but I defy thy utmost power to make me pay them."

In certain rare instances fortune seems to delight in suddenly showering her gifts upon some one who is not a gambler.

A remarkable exemplification of this occurred in Australia not so many years ago, when what was probably the biggest stake ever played for was lost and won. A curious feature of the game having been that neither winner nor loser knew that they were playing for anything but an insignificant stake.

A young Englishman, who had gone out to Australia with a slender capital, was one day standing at the door of his hut, wondering if fortune would ever smile upon him, when two travel-stained men, having much the appearance of tramps, appeared and, saying that they had come a long way, begged that they might be allowed to rest for the night. In accordance with the traditions of Colonial hospitality, the young man at once proceeded to do all he could to make his rough-looking guests comfortable, and in due course sat down with them to the best dinner which his slender resources could provide. The meal over, pipes were lit, and conversation (always limited in remote regions), being exhausted, one of the men pulled out of his pocket an old greasy-looking pack of cards and proposed a game. To make a long story short the young man, who, it must be added, was no gambler, eventually consented to hold a small bank at écarté against his two visitors. He stipulated, however, that when either he or his opponents should have chanced to lose such money as they had in their pockets, the game should come to an end. For a time fortune wavered, but a sudden run in favour of the host swept all the modest capital of his antagonists to his side of the table.

A discussion now ensued, the guests being anxious to continue the game, declaring that any losings should be promptly remitted on their arrival at the nearest town. The Englishman, however, was obdurate. "We agreed to play for ready money only, and ready money it shall be," said he, "your losses after all are trifling. We are all tired and had better turn in."

This was not at all to the taste of the losers, who argued and entreated, with, however, complete lack of success, when suddenly one of them said: "Bill, where's that bit of paper we got up country, perhaps he'll play us for that." A well-thumbed document was then produced which appeared to be the title to some plots of land up country. The owners did not seem to attach any great importance to it, for after some discussion it was eventually agreed that the document, which the host considered a very flimsy security, should be estimated as worth something like ten pounds; the game was resumed, and luck continuing in the same direction, the Englishman went to bed with the slip of paper in his pocket-book. The next morning the men proceeded on their way, having, at the request of their host, given an address so that, should any question arise as to the title of the land, they might be referred to.

About a week after this the Englishman, who had forgotten all about the slip of paper, which he had sent, with some other securities, to the bank, was once more standing in front of his hut, when a mounted stranger appeared, and saying that he had come a long way, begged for a night's entertainment and lodging. The new arrival, though roughly-dressed, was a man who, it was easy to see, enjoyed the command of a certain amount of money. He was, he declared, anxious to purchase plots of land for which he professed himself ready to give a liberal price. Particularly persistent in inquiring of his host if he knew of any claims likely to be sold, he eventually elicited from him the story of the bit of paper, over which he seemed to be very much amused. "I expect," said he, "that it's worth nothing at all, but I've taken a fancy to you and I daresay you won't be sorry to take a tenner for it." The Englishman, however, said he would rather do nothing till he had had another look at the paper in the bank. "Besides," he added, "I've a fancy to keep it."

"Well," replied the stranger, "that's queer. I'm a man of fancies too, and though you may think me a flat, I'll give you another chance—£20 for the paper!"

This offer and yet others of £30, £40, and at last of £50, having met with no better success than the first, the stranger eventually dropped the subject, and the next morning rode off, apparently very much amused at what he called the pigheadedness of his host.

About ten days passed and once more the same horseman appeared, this time in a more serious mood. A veritable craving for the little bit of paper, he said, had seized him, and as the thing was positively getting on his mind he had ridden out to say that, to end the matter and do his young friend a good turn, he was ready to give £200 (which he had brought in cash) for it.

The Englishman now began to think that the document was really valuable, and bluntly told his visitor that no offer whatever would be accepted.

His estimate was correct. The bit of paper, won in the Australian hut from two wandering miners, eventually gave its possessor a fortune of something not very far short of a million pounds, for, owing to the title which it conveyed, he became the largest shareholder in one of the richest mines in all Australia. The lucky winner is alive to-day, and makes no secret of the origin of his wealth, which came to him as if by the stroke of some magic wand. It is only fair to say that in due course he provided handsomely for the two miners who had played with him what was almost certainly the highest game of écarté on record.

The would-be purchaser, it afterwards appeared, was a speculator in mines, who, having by some means or other learnt the value of the piece of paper, had traced it with the intention of thus acquiring a highly valuable property.

The modern English view of gambling is a sadly confused one, the card-table and the race-course being bitterly denounced, whilst speculation in stocks and shares is considered an entirely legitimate method of attempting to make money. As a matter of fact, in a great number of instances, this amounts to no more or less than backing a stock to either rise or fall in value. Outside brokers exist, it is even said, who do not always actually buy or sell any shares at all, but simply, as it were, allow their clients to bet with them on a selected stock rising or falling in price. These are to all purpose and effect mere bookmakers, though, for some unknown reason, their calling is not regarded with the same odium which British austerity is generally ready to affix to members of the Ring.

For those who are not versed in the intricacies of City matters speculation almost invariably results in loss, the odds being about 99 to 1 against the ordinary individual proving successful.

Speculation on the Stock Exchange, gambling generally, and betting on the Turf are exactly similar from the point of view of the moralist; there is no difference between all three.

During the recent debates upon the Budget a member stated in the House of Commons that ninety per cent of the business of the London Stock Exchange was of a gambling description, and represented only purchases made with a view to a rise in prices. He wished to see such transactions taxed.

The Chancellor of the Exchequer replied that were this done it might stop such transactions altogether.

Another member—Mr. Markham—supported such a tax, adding that he did not wish to appear in a false light, and would admit that he gambled himself, and, like most fools, always lost money—a remark which excited considerable merriment.

Unimpeachable information about stocks and shares has ruined many a man—nothing indeed is more fatal, as a rule, than so-called good tips about the rise and fall of stocks, which, when originating from an inspired quarter, are so much sought after by speculators.

There have, of course, been instances where tips have made people a fortune.

A few years ago an author, who, though fairly successful, had made no particular stir in the literary world, and whose books did not seem likely to have had a very enormous sale, suddenly purchased a nice estate in which was included a luxurious country house, where he began to entertain. An old friend of his on a visit frankly expressed himself surprised at this sudden accession of prosperity, and alone one wet day with his host in the smoking-room bluntly asked:

"However did you make so much money, surely not by your books?"

"No," was the reply, "by speculating in the City."

"An experience as rare as it was pleasant—I suppose you were given some good tips."

"Yes, not taking them was the secret of my success!"

The host then proceeded to explain that, chancing to know a number of men in the City who were in the best possible position to have sound information as to the rise and fall of stocks and shares, the thought one day struck him that he might profit by such opportunities. Accordingly he let it be known that he had a certain amount of money which it was his intention to try and increase by careful speculation.

Tips poured in upon him—he was entreated to become a bear of this and a bull of that—people appeared anxious to put him into all sorts of ventures, and he became the recipient of much "exclusive" information.

His idea of speculation, however, was original. Told to buy a certain stock he invariably sold it; warned of a coming fall, he speculated for a rise; in fact it became his practice to act in a manner exactly contrary to that indicated by his many advisers, whom, meanwhile, he kept in ignorance of what he was doing.

By this curious and original method in a comparatively short time he accumulated a comfortable fortune, and then decided to abandon speculation and spend the rest of his days in prosperous ease.

As this shrewd and fortunate speculator explained to his friend, human nature must be reckoned with in all things, and in a vast number of cases those who give tips are interested in the particular stocks which they not unnaturally seek to bolster up—a really good thing does not need much puffing.

On the other hand, regular schemes to depress certain stocks are often engineered in a most clever manner, adverse rumours being spread as to a probable fall in order to facilitate large purchases at a small figure; these having been made, the stock rises with startling rapidity. The best maxim for speculators, not well versed in City matters, is to take plenty of advice, and in the vast majority of cases to operate in an exactly contrary way.

FOOTNOTES:

[6] An excellent account of this adventurer is given by that gifted writer Mr. Theodore Andrea Cook, in *Eclipse and O'Kelly*, published two years ago.

VI

Colonel Mellish—His early life and accomplishments—His equipage—A great gambler—£40,000 at a throw!—Posting—Mellish's racing career—His duel—In the Peninsula—Rural retirement and death—Colonel John Mordaunt—His youthful freaks—An ardent card-player—Becomes aide-de-camp to the Nawab of Oude—Anecdotes—Death from a duel—Zoffany in India and his picture of Mordaunt's cock-fight—Anecdotes of cock-fighting.

Amongst the sporting characters of the past who flung their fortunes to the winds at the gaming-table or on the race-course there were not a few who were possessed of considerable intelligence and charm. Such a one was the handsome, gallant, and accomplished Colonel Mellish, beyond all doubt the Admirable Crichton of his day.

The son of Mr. Charles Mellish, of Blyth Hall, near Doncaster, a gentleman devoted to antiquarian research and obviously of very different disposition from his son, Henry Mellish was born in 1780, and coming into his kingdom after a long minority, plunged at once with infinite zest into every form of patrician dissipation. It has been said that he was at Eton, but his name does not appear in the school lists. At any rate, whatever his school, he seems to have distinguished himself at it by a variety of escapades, which culminated in his running away and flatly refusing to return. In his seventeenth year he joined the 11th Light Dragoons, from which he exchanged into the 10th Hussars, the smartest light cavalry regiment of the day, with the Prince of Wales for its colonel. There is a tradition that Mellish was granted perpetual leave lest his extravagance should corrupt the young officers; but his subsequent career proves that he must at least have seen enough of soldiering to have learned his duty. After he had left the 10th Hussars, his name appears in the army list as an officer of the 87th Royal Irish Regiment, and also as a major of the Sicilian Legion, in which many Englishmen held honorary commissions. At the same time, his name figures in the list of Lieutenant-Colonels. Mellish was no mere fashionable spendthrift. He was a man of many accomplishments. Nature, indeed, seemed to have qualified him for taking the lead, and to have given him a temperament so ardent, as made it almost impossible for him ever "to come in second."

He understood music, and could draw, and paint in oil colours. As a companion he was always in high spirits, and talked with animation on every subject; whilst his conversation, if not abounding in wit, was ever full of interesting information founded on fact and experience. He had a manner of telling and acting a story that was perfectly dramatic. He was at home with all classes, and could talk with the gentleman and associate with the farmer.

In Mellish culminated all the best of these various qualities which were considered the appanage of a patrician sportsman of his day. A most expert whip, no man drove four-in-hand with more skill and with less labour than he did; and to display that skill he often selected very difficult horses to drive, satisfied if they were goers. As a rider he was equally eminent: for years after his death his memory lingered in many a hunt, where he had led all the light weights of Leicestershire, Rutlandshire, and Yorkshire, when he was himself riding fourteen stone. His was the art of making a horse do more than other riders, and he accustomed them, like himself, "to go at everything."

The following stanza, one of those in a famous hunting song composed when Lord Darlington, afterwards Duke of Cleveland, hunted the Badsworth country, commemorates the young sportsman, who was well-known as a daring rider with these hounds:—

Behold Harry Mellish, as wild as the wind,
On Lancaster mounted, leave numbers behind;
But lately returned from democrat France,
Where, forgetting to bet, he's been learning to dance.

A melancholy occurrence once gave him an opportunity of displaying, not only his filial affection, but also his determination as a horseman. Having heard the alarming intelligence of his mother's illness, he mounted one of his barouche-horses to proceed to London, and actually rode from Brighton to East Grinstead, a distance of twenty miles, in an hour and twenty minutes; the strain of this feat was so severe that on arrival at his destination the gallant horse which had carried him fell dead.

As a runner he was by no means to be despised. He beat Lord Frederick Bentinck (renowned for fleetness of foot) in a running match on Newmarket Heath. For everything connected with sport Colonel Mellish possessed a natural aptitude, as was universally recognised.

In appearance he was a big man, who even as a youth weighed some twelve stone. Nearly six feet high and admirably proportioned, the pallor of his complexion was rendered more noticeable by his black hair and brilliant eyes. In dress he had a great fondness for light hues and usually wore a white "boat hat,"[7] white trousers, and silk stockings of the same colour. When he arrived on the course at Newmarket his barouche, which he drove himself, was drawn by four beautiful white horses, whilst two out-riders in crimson liveries, also mounted on white steeds, preceded this brilliant turn-out. Behind rode another groom leading a thoroughbred hack, whilst yet another waited at the rubbing post with a spare horse in case of accidents.

At that time he had thirty-eight race-horses in training, seventeen coach-horses, twelve hunters, four chargers, and a number of ordinary hacks. The expenses of his establishment were enormous. Besides these he lost very large sums at the gaming-table, where he once staked £40,000 at a single throw and lost it. At his own home he gambled away vast sums, and a table was formerly preserved at Blyth on which its former owner had once lost £40,000 to the Prince Regent. At one sitting at a London Club—it is said at Brooks's, though Mellish's name does not appear in the list of former members—he rose the loser of £97,000, and was leaving the Club-house, when he met the Duke of Sussex, who, hearing what had happened, persuaded him to return and try his luck once more. This he did, and in two or three hours won £100,000 off the Duke, who paid as much of this sum as he could, promising to settle the rest by a life annuity of £4000. It would, however, seem somewhat doubtful whether the entire debt was ever liquidated.

As a matter of fact such large sums were often lost at hazard that it was no infrequent thing for losers to compromise their debt by paying an annuity to fortunate opponents. The impression that in old days all gambling liabilities were scrupulously discharged on the spot is not based upon any very solid foundation, and winners sometimes had the greatest difficulty in getting their money. Under such circumstances defaulters were occasionally posted.

The expression "posting a man" for not having paid a debt of honour is now more or less figurative, but, as recently as the beginning of the nineteenth century, defaulters were publicly posted.

In September 1824, for instance, all Brighton was surprised to find the following placard posted up at Lucombe's Library and other places of the same sort:—

> BRIGHTON, *September 8, 1824.*
>
> Twice have I applied to the Earl of S. for the settlement of a bet, and twice, having given him the offer of a reference, I was under the necessity of requesting the satisfaction of a gentleman, which he refused. As such, I post the Earl of S.

as a man who constantly refuses to pay his debts of honour, and a coward.

W.T.

The above placard is said to have been induced by the refusal of a certain Peer to answer a demand of £2000, for which no satisfactory claim could be produced.

To guard against the possibility of a duel, warrants were issued against the nobleman and Mr. W.T. by the local magistrates. The Earl was easily found, and bound in a recognisance of the peace. Mr. W.T., however, could not be discovered, it being declared that he feared criminal proceedings being taken.

Most of the gamblers of a century ago were men of careless disposition, and Colonel Mellish in particular lived in such a whirl of excitement and gambled in such tremendous sums that a few thousands more or less were at this time very little to him. His life was devoted to frolics of every kind. On one occasion after a ball at Doncaster, Mellish and the Duke of Clarence sallied out for a lark and assisted in the arrest of a man who had been fighting in the street. When the party reached the prison, Mellish locked the Royal Duke in a cell and went off with the key, which he delivered to his brother the Prince of Wales. The Duke on his liberation took the joke very good-humouredly.

It may be added that, like most born gamblers, Colonel Mellish lost his money with the greatest coolness, ever accepting ill-luck with imperturbable equanimity. The hazardous joys of racing were to him an irresistible lure, and no more ardent supporter of the Turf than he ever lived. His career as an owner of racers only extended over about seven years, from 1801 to 1808, when financial difficulties obliged him to abandon the sport to which he was devoted. The greatest financial reverse he suffered was when Mr. Clifton's Fyldener won the St. Leger in 1806. Over a million guineas are said to have changed hands over this race, and Colonel Mellish lost an enormous sum. Nevertheless, as a judge of racing there was no man held to be his equal. If indeed judgment in such matters could preserve any one from ruin, then Mellish should have kept his fortune. Endowed with mental qualities far above those possessed by most sporting men, the owner of Blyth soon attained a remarkable knowledge of the intricacies of the Turf, and the best judges used to declare that they never knew a man who was better able to gauge the powers, the qualities, and capabilities of the racer, as well as the exact weights he could carry, and the precise distances he could run. Unfortunately there was one side of the Turf life of his day which he could not master, that was the rascality of those who took care not to leave to accident the chances which made ultimate success certain.

Colonel Mellish was not only a most excellent judge of a race-horse, but well acquainted with all the intricacies of managing a racing-stable. He was universally admitted to be possessed of an extraordinary capacity for making matches, and as a handicapper was declared to be supreme. A careful investigation, however, of the old Racing Calendars from 1805 to 1807 hardly confirms such an estimate of the Colonel's abilities in this direction. In those three years he won 38 and received forfeit for 15 matches, losing 57 and paying forfeit for 31; that is, he won £11,505 and lost £18,600 in stakes. In addition to this he must, of course, have lost very large sums in bets.

The most famous of all his matches was that between his Sancho and Lord Darlington's Pavilion. There were really three matches. In the New Claret Stakes at the Newmarket first Spring Meeting, 1805, Pavilion beat Sancho and some other horses (6 to 4 Sancho, 7 to 1 Pavilion). Mellish then challenged Lord Darlington, and a match was run in the summer at Lewes—four miles for three thousand guineas, Buckle riding Sancho and Chifney Pavilion. Sancho (the non-favourite, 2 to 1) won easily. Another match was run over the same distance on the same course for two thousand guineas, 6 to 4 on Sancho, who broke down badly. Mellish on this occasion lost altogether five thousand guineas, though at one moment before the race he had been offered twelve hundred to have it off. A third match for two thousand guineas over a mile at Brighton was made in the same year, but Sancho had to pay forfeit. Colonel Mellish's colours were white with crimson sleeves. His trainer was Bartle Atkinson, who from the time of entering his service in 1802, till 1807, turned out what was probably a greater number of winners than any other private trainer for one owner has ever done in the same period of time. In 1804 and 1805 he won the St. Leger with Sancho and Staveley, and trained many winners besides. In spite of all these successes, racing proved most disastrous to the Colonel's fortune, and like the vast majority of racing-men of this stamp, he left the Turf a ruined man. In his palmy days it is said that he never opened his mouth to make a bet under £500.

He wanted to be everything at once, and as the saying went, he was "at all in the ring"; till by deep play, by racing and expenses of every kind, and in every place, he found it necessary to part with his estate in order to satisfy the demands which obsessed him on all sides.

Though the most popular of men, Colonel Mellish once had a serious altercation with the Honourable Martin Hawke, and the result was a duel, when the following conversation is said to have occurred—it shows the light-hearted spirit of the combatants.

Mellish. "Take care of yourself, Hawke, for by —— I shall hit you."

Hawke. "I will, my lad, and let me recommend you to take care of your own canister!"

The seconds, on hearing this, agreed that they should not take aim, but fire by signal, which was done. The Colonel missed, but Hawke's shot took effect, by passing round the rim of his opponent's stomach, and eventually penetrating his left arm; on which Mellish exclaimed, "Hawke, you have winged me! Lend me your neckcloth to tie up the broken pinion!" This was immediately complied with, and the arm being bound up, they both returned in the same chaise, as good friends as ever!

This duel was fought in 1807 in a field by the roadside, and originated in a quarrel about the Yorkshire election, from which both duellists were returning in their drags.

Mellish would appear to have run a great risk of being killed, for the Honourable Martin Hawke was a singularly gifted man and could do incredible things with a pistol. Indeed his skill in that direction was probably never equalled. His nerve and courage were of the highest order.

Mr. Hawke once fought a duel near Brussels with a certain Baron Smieten. Whilst the seconds were measuring out the distance, he amused himself by drawing a mail-coach with his stick on the bank of a sandy ditch. One of the seconds, a guardsman, came up just as the finishing touches were being put to the coachman's whip, and said "All's ready," to which Hawke replied, "Just let me put the lash to this fellow's whip." Having touched off this, he instantly proceeded to touch up his antagonist, mentioning that as he had put him to so much trouble (they fought over the frontiers) he must give him a touch, but would content himself with spoiling his waltzing for a little; naming where and how he would operate—and this he did to a hairbreadth.

At one time the patron of all the superior pugilists, Colonel Mellish first brought many of them into notice. He arranged the first battle ever fought by the famous Tom Cribb, who was matched by the Colonel against Nicholl, who beat him. Unfortunately for his gallant backer, Cribb on this occasion entered the ring very drunk, and, of course, fell an easy prey to an antagonist whom in future days the champion of England would have beaten in ten minutes. Colonel Mellish likewise made the match betwixt Gully and the Game Chicken; the former of whom he caused to "give in," much against his inclination. The Colonel's humanity on this occasion cost him a large sum, as he had backed Gully heavily. Nevertheless, he insisted upon his yielding, the man being reduced to such a state of weakness that his supporter was afraid of an accidental blow proving fatal.

At the time of the Peninsular campaign a regular crisis occurred in Mellish's affairs, and Sir Rowland Ferguson appointed him his aide-de-camp, and he went out to Spain. Previous to the battle of Vimeiro, as the general officers were dining together, one of them observed to Sir Rowland Ferguson that if the thing were not impossible, he should have declared that an officer he had seen was a gentleman whom he had left a week or two ago in the cockpit at York, with cocks engaged in the main there—his name he had understood was Mr. Mellish. "The very same man," returned Sir Rowland, "he is now my aide-de-camp, and I think you will say, when you have the opportunity of knowing more of him, a better officer will not be found," and this proved to be the case. On many different occasions, indeed, the Duke of Wellington declared that a better aide-de-camp than Mellish he had never observed. The undaunted manner with which he encountered danger, the quickness with which he rode, and the precision with which he delivered his orders, never making any mistake in any moment of hurry or confusion, were circumstances which excited much favourable comment from friend and foe alike.

After the battle of Busaco, Colonel Mellish was sent with a flag of truce to the French head-quarters, on a message respecting some prisoners. On his arrival at Leiria, Massena invited him to dinner, and treated him with great attention and respect.

After remaining some time with the army abroad, Colonel Mellish returned home, and after that period engaged no more in military duties. According to rumour his return was owing to the resumption of his former habits of play, which the Duke of Wellington had forbidden; but this is not certain.

The Prince Regent, who was so often accused of forgetting those who had served him, certainly did not justify this reproach in the case of Colonel Mellish; for on his having obtained a small appointment abroad in one of the conquered islands, the Prince made him his equerry, in order to enable him to enjoy the emoluments of it whilst remaining at home.

In addition to this the uncles of the Colonel, who had undertaken the management of his property when he was abroad, enabled him, by their arrangements, to take up his abode at Hodsock Priory, where he had occasionally lived before, and where at a comparatively early age he ended his days. On his way to this farm he had to pass the magnificent mansion and domain of Blyth, the seat of his ancestors and formerly his own, which the vicissitudes of a Turf career had obliged him to sell.

Colonel Mellish, however, accepted his lot with considerable equanimity, and lived at his somewhat modest abode without any mortifying regrets. Having married one of the daughters of the Marchioness of Lansdowne,[8] who brought him a very handsome fortune, his circumstances again became easy, and he was enabled to indulge in those rural pursuits which appear early and late to have been congenial to his disposition. He took to coursing and established a fine stud of greyhounds. He also bred cattle with great success, winning many prizes at northern cattle shows, and obtaining high prices for his stock, and more fortunate than most men of his disposition and tastes, ended his life in comfort and peace. His death, however, occurred at a comparatively early age, for he fell a victim to dropsy in his thirty-seventh year.

Another gallant sporting man, though of quite another description, was the Anglo-Indian Colonel John Mordaunt, a natural son of the Earl of Peterborough.

John Mordaunt, as a boy, was too wild to learn much at school, his whole time being devoted to playing the truant; as he often said, "one half of his days were spent in being flogged for the other half." Devoted to cards from youth, he received many a castigation in consequence. "You may shuffle, Mordaunt, but I can cut," was the remark made to him by his schoolmaster on more than one occasion.

In consequence of this unsatisfactory behaviour, when the boy left school he was about as learned as when he first was sent there. His guardians were very much annoyed at this and blamed his master, upon which young Mordaunt very handsomely stepped forward to exculpate the latter, whose attention he declared to have been unparalleled. Slipping off his clothes, he exhibited the earnestness of the good man's endeavours; humorously observing, that as nothing could be got into his brains, his master had done his best to impress his instructions on the opposite seat of learning.

When the moment came for the youth to pass muster before the India directors he could not be found, and it was nearly too late when he was at last discovered playing marbles in Dean's Yard. No time, however, was wasted in driving him up to Leadenhall Street, where, more bent on frivolity than on answering the grave questions put by his examiners, he was near being rejected as an idiot, when one of the quorum, who understood such a disposition well and who probably wished to see John appointed, asked him if he understood cribbage. In an instant young Mordaunt's attention was thoroughly roused, his eyes glistened, and regardless of every matter relative to his appointment, he pulled out a pack of cards, so greasy as scarcely to be distinguished, and offered "to play the gentleman *for any sum he chose*!"

The youth now felt himself at home, and speedily convinced his examiners that, however ignorant he might be of the classics, he was a match for any of them at cards! He was passed, and despatched to Portsmouth to embark on an Indiaman ready to sail with the first fair wind; but as there seemed no likelihood of this for some days, the person who had charge of him put him on board and returned to town. Needless to say, Mordaunt at once got away to shore, where he played a number of pranks before the ship eventually set sail.

On arriving at Madras young Mordaunt was received with open arms by all his countrymen; but General Sir John Clavering, who was then Commander-in-Chief in India, and who was, accordingly, second on the council at Calcutta, having promised to provide for him, Mordaunt went on to Bengal, where he was appointed an honorary aide-de-camp to that officer, still retaining his rank on the Madras establishment. In consequence of this he was afterwards subjected to much ill-will.

The young soldier unfortunately was quite uneducated, not being able even to write an ordinary letter without making many mistakes. Study was little to his taste, and he made scarcely any effort to remedy this disadvantage or improve himself. Nevertheless, he excelled in most things which he undertook entirely by natural intuition. His ignorance of writing was the more remarkable as he spoke English with an excellent diction and even refinement of phrase, though he could not write two lines of it correctly. He spoke the Hindoo language fluently, and was a tolerable Persian scholar. Mordaunt's weakness as a writer was once strikingly demonstrated on an occasion where a friend, having borrowed a horse from him for a day or two, wrote to ask if he might keep it a little longer. The Colonel's reply was, "You may kip the hos as long as you lick."

Subjected to a good deal of chaff on account of this failing, which he himself realised, Mordaunt was generally very good-tempered, though quick with an answer when any one he did not care for attempted to make him a butt. On one occasion a very worthy young gentleman of the name of James P——, who was rather of the more silly order of beings, thinking he could take the liberty of playing with, or rather upon him, called out to Mordaunt, before a large party, desiring him to say what was the Latin for a goose. The answer was brief. "I don't know the *Latin* for it, but the *English* is *James P——*."

It should be mentioned that the above question was put to Mordaunt in consequence of his having, in a note sent to a person who had offended him, required "an immediate *anser* by the bearer." The gentleman addressed, wishing to terminate the matter amicably, construed the word literally, and sent a *goose* by the bearer; stating also that he would partake of it the next day. This, to a man of Mordaunt's disposition, was the high road to reconciliation; though to nine persons in ten, and especially to those labouring under such a desperate deficiency in point of orthography, it would have appeared highly insulting!

In addition to his almost complete ignorance of calligraphy, Colonel Mordaunt knew absolutely nothing of the ordinary rules of arithmetic. He kept no books, but all his accounts were done on scraps of paper in such an eccentric manner that the figures were only intelligible to himself. It was necessary for him at times to register large financial transactions, and he had immense losses and gains to register in the I.O.U. way. Yet even the most intricate cases never puzzled him; and, at settling times, he was rarely, if ever, found to be in error. This was one of the points in which he was apt to be peremptory; for no sooner did he hear a claim stated, which did not tally with his own peculiar mode of calculation, than he condemned it, in round terms, and would scarcely hear the attempt to substantiate that which he so decidedly denied.

He was a man of most masterful disposition, very impatient of contradiction, especially from his brother Harry, who was in India at the same time. The latter possessed little social charm or originality, but John always treated him with particular consideration. When, however, Harry tried to oppose or argue with him, the Colonel would soon check him with, "Hold your tongue, Harry, you are a puny little fool, and fit for nothing but to be a lord."

Excelling at most things which he attempted, Mordaunt was so much master of his racket, and was so vigorous, that he would always wager on hitting the line from the over-all, a distance of thirty yards, once in three times. As a matter of fact he could beat most people with a common round ruler.

Card-playing, however, was the Colonel's particular passion. He was an expert at most games, being besides acquainted with all the ordinary tricks in the shuffling, cutting, and dealing way. The following is an instance of his skill. On a certain occasion Mordaunt observed that one of his adversaries at whist was remarkably fortunate in his own deals; and, as he was rather a doubtful character, thought it needful to watch him. When Mordaunt came to deal, he gave himself thirteen trumps! This excited the curiosity of all, but particularly of the gentleman in question, who was very pointed in his observations on the singularity of the case. Mordaunt briefly said, "Sir, this was to show you that you should not have all the fun to yourself," and rising from his seat, left the blackleg to ruminate on the obvious necessity of quitting India! Here, however, Mordaunt's goodness of heart showed itself, for he obtained a promise from the whole party to keep the secret, provided the offender instantly left the country; which he did by the first conveyance.

It was well known that the Colonel could arrange the cards according to his pleasure, yet such was the universal opinion of his honour, that no one hesitated to play with him, sober or otherwise, for their usual stakes. His decision, in cases of differences, was generally accepted as final, and many references were made to him, by letter, from very distant places, regarding doubtful points connected with gaming.

It may readily be supposed that Mordaunt was more ornamental than useful in General Clavering's office; however, the latter could not help esteeming him, and had he lived, would probably have effected Mordaunt's removal from the Madras to the Bengal army. The Madras officers never failed to comment, sometimes, indeed, in rather harsh terms, upon the injustice of having on their rolls an officer who never joined his regiment for nearly twenty years, and whose whole time was passed in the lap of dissipation.

Being on a party of pleasure to the northward, and near to Lucknow, the capital of Oude, and the residence of the Nawab of Oude, Asoph ud Doulah, the young soldier was naturally curious to see this potentate and his Court. The free, open temper of Asoph pleased Mordaunt, whose figure and manner made a great impression on his illustrious host, who was devoted to most forms of gambling and sport.

The Nawab in question was an original character. Being desirous of becoming a highly efficient swordsman, he determined to get the best practice possible and exercise his arm to some purpose. For some time he used daily to order from his stables five horses and a couple of bullocks, which he would cut down; the same fate befell five tigers, the same number of bears, and two or three nylgaus.

In a short time Mordaunt became such a favourite, that he was retained by the Nawab at his Court, in the capacity of aide-de-camp, though he never attended at the Palace except when in the mood to do so, or for the purpose of shooting or gambling with its ruler. During this period the various sarcastic attacks directed against Mordaunt, as an absentee from his corps for so many years—amusing himself a good two thousand miles away—were disregarded both by himself and by the supreme Government, of which all the members were personally attached to the Colonel.

Mordaunt was now in the receipt of a handsome salary, and possessed many distinguished privileges under the patronage of the Nawab, who often used to refer Europeans to him on occasions requiring his advice; this he not infrequently did when he needed an excuse for not complying with some demand.

Mordaunt's influence, it should be added, was generally used in a very kindly manner. Old Zoffany, who had come out to India and resided at Lucknow as Court Painter to the Nawab, once, in a humorous moment, painted a full-length picture of that potentate in high caricature. Zoffany lived at Colonel Martine's, whose house was frequented by immense numbers of natives, a number of whom, when the Nawab wanted money, took his jewels to the Colonel's to be pledged. The picture, of course, was seen by some of these men, and it was not long before the Nawab was informed of the joke. The latter, in the first moments of irritation, was disposed to shorten the painter by a head, and to dismiss the Colonel, who was his chief engineer, and had the charge of his arsenal. He was, however, unwilling to do anything without his "dear friend Mordaunt" to whom a message was despatched, requiring his immediate attendance, on "matters of the utmost importance." This being a very usual mode of summoning his favourite, who would attend, or rather visit, only when it pleased himself. As a matter of fact the message would probably have been disregarded, had not the bearer stated that the Nawab was incensed against Martine and Zoffany. Accordingly the Colonel betook himself to the Palace, where he found the Nawab foaming with rage, and about to proceed with a host of rabble attendants to the Colonel's. Mordaunt, however, having got the story out of the Nawab as well as he could, argued him into a state of calmness, sufficient to let his sinister purpose be suspended until the next day, and retired as soon as he could prudently do so; he then, as privately as possible, sent a note to Zoffany warning him of the intended visit.

The bold painter lost no time, and the laughable caricature was in a few hours changed by his gifted hand into a superb portrait of a most decorative kind, bearing far more resemblance to the Nawab than any hitherto painted at regular sittings. Next day the potentate arrived, his mind full of anxiety for the honour of his dignified person. He was attended by Mordaunt, whose feelings for his friend's fate were speedily dissipated, when, on entering the portrait-chamber, the picture in question shone forth so superbly as to astonish and delight the Nawab, who, beaming with pleasure, hurried the picture home, gave Zoffany ten thousand rupees for it, and ordered the person who had informed him of the supposed caricature to have his nose and ears cut off. Mordaunt, however, again interposed, and was equally successful in obtaining the poor fellow's pardon; and as the Nawab declined to keep him as a servant, very generously made him one of his own pensioners.

At another time, the barber who cut the Nawab's hair happened by a slip to draw blood. This was considered an offence of the highest atrocity, because at that time crowned heads throughout India became degraded if one drop of their blood were spilt by a barber. A drawn sword was always held above a barber performing his duty, to remind him of his fate in case of the slightest incision.

In consequence of this prejudice the barber had been condemned to be baked to death in an oven, when Mordaunt applied for his pardon. He could only obtain it conditionally, and certainly the condition was both ludicrous and whimsical. Balloons were just invented when this happened, and Colonel Martine being very ingenious, had made one which had taken up a considerable weight for short distances.

The Nawab changed suddenly from great wrath to a wild hilarity, which continued so long as to alarm Mordaunt; who at last was relieved to hear that instead of being baked, the barber was to mount in the balloon, and to brush through the air according as chance might direct him.

In due course the balloon was sent up in front of the palace, and the barber carried through the air more dead than alive at a prodigious rate. The poor man, however, sustained no injury, the balloon finally descending to earth some five miles from the city of Lucknow.

Mordaunt never allowed the Nawab to treat him with the least disrespect or with hauteur; indeed, such was the estimation in which he was held by that prince, that, in all probability, the latter never showed any sign of wishing to exert his authority. Mordaunt's independence is shown by the following anecdote. The Nawab wanted some alterations to be made in the howdah of his state elephant, and asked Mordaunt's opinion as to the best mode of securing it; the latter very laconically told the Nawab he understood nothing of the matter, he having been born and bred a gentleman, but that probably his blacksmith (pointing to Colonel Martine) could inform him how the howdah ought to be fastened.

This sneer, no doubt, gratified Mordaunt, who, though extremely intimate with Martine, and in the habit of addressing him by various ludicrous but sarcastic nicknames, seemed not to relish that fondness for money, and other doubtful practices, of which he was said to be guilty.

Lord Cornwallis was either unwilling to compel Mordaunt to return to the Madras establishment, or was prevailed on by the Nawab to let him remain on his staff. The Marquis, one day, seeing Mordaunt at his levee, asked him if he did not long to join his regiment. "No, my Lord," answered Mordaunt, "not in the least." "But," continued he, "your services may perhaps be wanted." "Indeed, my Lord," rejoined Mordaunt, "I cannot do you half the service there, that I can in keeping the Nawab amused, while you ease him of his money."

As a bon-vivant, as a master of the revels, or at the head of his own table, few could give greater variety or more complete satisfaction than Mordaunt. He had the best of wines, and spared no expense, though he would take very little personal trouble in providing whatever was choice or rare. He stood on little ceremony, especially at his own house, and, at his friends', never allowed anything to incommode him from a bashful reserve. Whatever was in his opinion wrong, he did not hesitate to condemn.

These observations were very quick, and generally not devoid of humour. His old friend, Captain Waugh, dining with him one day, made such a hole in a fine goose as to excite the attention of Mordaunt, who, turning to his head servant, ordered aloud that whenever Captain Waugh dined at his house, there should always be two geese on the table, one for the Captain, the other for the company.

Colonel Mordaunt was an excellent pistol shot, who could hit the head of a small nail at fifteen yards. Nevertheless when he and a friend engaged in a quarrel of a very serious nature with a third, whom they had accused of some improper conduct at cards, he missed his adversary, who, on the other hand, wounded both Mordaunt and his friend desperately. This was not owing to agitation, but, as Mordaunt expressed in very curious terms at the moment of missing, to the pistol being too highly charged.

The Colonel never entirely recovered from the effects of the pistol shot which he had received in his breast, and though possessed of a vigorous constitution, seemed to descend, as it were, down a precipice into his grave. A very Rochester of his day, inordinately fond of women, he seemed, when at length stricken down, to regret his condition chiefly as depriving him of their society. For some time before this, actuated by that mistaken pride which so often urges men who have done wonders not to allow their decrease of vigour to be noticed or suspected, he had attempted to continue his usual mode of life, and neglecting the warnings given him by one or two serious attacks on his liver, had thus hastened his approach to a most untimely end.

He died in the fortieth year of his age, beloved and regretted by a number of friends to whom his many genuine qualities were known.

An especial reason for the influence enjoyed by Mordaunt over the Nawab was the latter's intimate knowledge of everything connected with the branch of barbarity known as cock-fighting. So devoted was the Prince in question to this form of sport that he often neglected to attend to important business with the residents at his Court in order to indulge in a "main" with him whom he called his "dear friend Mordaunt."

The well-known print representing Colonel Mordaunt's cock-fight depicts a famous battle fought at Lucknow in 1786. Amongst the figures are the Nawab, Colonel Mordaunt, and Colonel Martine, who founded the Martine colleges at Lucknow, Calcutta, and Lyons, and Zoffany himself. The picture, which was painted for Warren Hastings, was carefully preserved in the Palace at Lucknow, but most unfortunately met with a disastrous fate during the Mutiny, when with others of great value it was destroyed.

A water-colour drawing of "The Cock-fight" was, however, made under the last King of Oude in 1853, by "Masawar Khan," a Court miniature-painter, and other copies also exist. The mezzotint of this picture, together with the scarce engraved key published in May 1794, are here reproduced.

Zoffany was a great favourite of Royalty. After the establishment of his reputation in England, he passed many years of his life in India, though in spite of the favour of the Nawab he does not seem to have returned from Lucknow in very opulent circumstances, his industry not having equalled either his reputation or his ability. An excessive devotion to women, and to the Asiatic customs and luxuries, totally precluded the execution of many works which would have brought this painter prosperity. Many of his pictures, however, achieved great popularity. This was especially the case with the "Water Cress Girl," which is engraved. The model, it may not be generally known, was a girl of about sixteen who had achieved a certain notoriety by having been one of a group of nymphs, who ran from the fields of Paddington, to their lodgings in the vicinity of St. Giles's, at noonday, unencumbered with one single habiliment or rag, from head to foot. It was in the summer season, and they had been bathing in a pond, when some wicked wag bundled up and made off with the whole of their clothes.

"The Cock-fight" was certainly one of the most successful works ever executed by Zoffany; the portrait of Mordaunt in particular, according to those who knew him, giving an excellent idea of his manly and elegant appearance.

THE COCK-FIGHT AT LUCKNOW.
Engraved by R. Earlom, after Zoffany.
From a Print in the possession of Messrs. Robson & Co., 23 Coventry Street, W.

KEY TO THE COCK-FIGHT.

The Colonel is represented as in the act of handing a cock, which he has backed heavily, in opposition to a bird belonging to the Nawab, who is portrayed in a loose undress on the opposite side of the pit.

Colonel Mordaunt's taste for cock-fighting had, of course, originally been acquired in England, where this somewhat brutal sport would appear to have been most popular towards the middle of the eighteenth century. At that time it was no unusual circumstance to insert clauses in the leases of farms and cottages, which ensured the right of walking a certain number of game-cocks. As the century waned the cockpit began rather to fall into disrepute, but about the years 1793-1794 a revival occurred. Great patrons of cock-fighting were Lord Lonsdale (when Sir James Lowther); the Duke of Northumberland, who fought regular annual mains against Mr. Fenwick at Alnwick and Hexham, as did Lord Mexborough with Sir P. Warburton and Mr. Halton at Manchester; the Duke of Hamilton with Sir H.G. Liddell at Newcastle, and Lord Derby with Mr. Wharton at Preston.

Amongst other lovers of cock-fighting were Colonel Lowther, Mr. Holford, Mr. Bullock, Captain Dennisthorpe, and Mr. George Onslow, out-ranger[9] of Windsor Forest, who was known as "Cocking George."

In 1793 the Cock Pit Royal, St. James's Park, was the scene of more subscription matches than had occurred for some years before, an extra battle, fought on the 13th of December between two red cocks belonging to Colonel Lowther and Vauxhall Clarke for forty guineas, causing particular excitement. Throughout this combat the odds were constantly varying, till Colonel Lowther's cock was suddenly struck down dead at a moment when odds of four and five to one were being laid upon his opponent.

One of the most horrible anecdotes connected with cock-fighting was that of a certain Mr. Ardesoif, the son of a rich cheesemonger, who was at one time well-known in the streets of London, it having been his peculiar hobby to drive his phaeton through those thoroughfares which were the most crowded with traffic. Mr. Ardesoif lived at Tottenham, where he kept a number of game-cocks. One of these birds having refused to fight, the cruel owner savagely had him roasted to death, whilst entertaining his friends. The company, alarmed by the dreadful shrieks of the poor victim, interfered, but were resisted by Ardesoif, who threatened death to any who should oppose him; and in a storm of raging and vindictive delirium, and uttering the most horrid imprecations, he dropped down dead.

A cockpit was a scene not easily matched. On a race or a prize-fight, the betting is nearly finished when the sport begins; but the same state of affairs did not prevail at a cock-fight, where no one backed a cock till he had had a good look at him. In consequence of this all the betting had to be done in a short time, and the noise and apparent confusion of layers and backers were quite bewildering. The betting changed with considerable rapidity—in many a battle the odds would veer round from 100 to 1 on one cock, to 40 to 1 against the same.

The issue of a cock-fight is never quite certain till a cock is actually killed, an apparently moribund bird sometimes proving the unexpected winner.

A very striking instance of this once occurred at Mr. Loftus's cockpit at Newcastle, where a gentleman, on a cock being pounded, betted ten guineas to a crown, which he lost in nearly the space of a minute, as the pounded cock, while his antagonist was pecking in triumph, rose, and after a stroke or two, laid him dead. As luck would have it, while the same gentleman was going from the cockpit to the race-course in his carriage, accompanied by some other gentlemen, one of them observed the absurdity of buying money so dear, to which the other replied, he would bet the same on anything, if he thought he could win; the former gentleman said he would take it. "Done," says the gentleman, "I will bet £10 to a crown that my carriage does not break down on 'going or returning from the race-course.'" The bet was accepted; and after going about 100 yards farther, down came the carriage. And thus, in the course of the same day, he lost his two bets of £10 to 5s. In the course of this week's fighting, there were several guineas betted to shillings, and lost, on the various battles.

Cock-fights as a rule took place in the evening, seven having been the usual hour appointed for the sport to commence.

In the palmy days of cock-fighting there were several celebrated pits in London, the chief of which, of course, was the Cock Pit Royal, which had been much frequented by Charles II. and his courtiers. Another well-known cockpit existed at Moss Alley, Bankside, Southwark, where great battles were contested. At the New Pit, Hoxton, in January, 1794, a number of spirited mains were fought, the gentlemen of Islington having challenged the gentlemen of Hackney for five guineas a battle and fifty guineas the odd battle. Hackney easily proved victorious.

The Royal Cockpit in St. James's Park was taken down in 1810, never again to be rebuilt. The Governors and Trustees of Christ's Hospital, to whom the ground belonged, met on the spot, the very day the lease expired; and, as might naturally be expected from the patrons of such an institution, gave directions for the immediate demolition of the building.

A curious custom which was long ago sometimes enforced at cock-fights prescribed that any one indulging in foul play or not paying his bets should be put into a large basket and drawn up to the roof of the cockpit. This was called being basketed. A man well-known to the sporting world, being once in this predicament, and notwithstanding that he had no money in his pocket and could not expect his bets to be taken, had the fever of betting so strong upon him that in spite of his situation in the basket, he could not help vociferating, as the odds varied, "I'll lay six to four—two to one—five to two—three to one—four to one—five to one—a guinea to a shilling—the long odds, ten pounds to a crown," to the no small diversion of the auditors and spectators, who, at length, commiserating his case and attributing his imprudence to an insurmountable passion for play, shortened his punishment; and when a gentleman present gave him a small sum he took the long odds all the way through, went off with a hundred guineas in his pocket, and from this source alone became a very distinguished character on the Turf.

In Hogarth's print of the cockpit, published in 1759, a shadow of mysterious contour is thrown upon the floor of the pit, the origin of which may be seen to be a gambler who, having been basketed for not paying his debts, is vainly offering his watch as a pledge so that he may be let down and allowed to take his place among the somewhat ill-favoured crowd which is watching the battle. The principal figure in this print represents a nobleman (Lord Bertie) who, though stone-blind, was a zealous patron of cock-fighting, though it is difficult to see how, under these unfavourable circumstances, the sport could have had any attraction for him.

The Preston race-meetings used to be a great rendezvous for cock-fighters. Lord Derby long held a distinguished place among the patrons of the sod, and was reckoned one of the best judges of a cock in England. The excellent walks which his Lordship owned on his own estates, and the number of cocks he bred, ensured him a plentiful supply of fine young birds; consequently his birds never had a feather wrong; this, joined to their true blood, which made them show fight to the last, and the skill of Paul Potter, his feeder, caused Lord Derby to be the winner of many a Preston main.

The following is a specimen of a challenge to a cock match:—

CHALLENGE

> The gentlemen of Windsor Forest having lost their annual opponent (who is gone to reside in Somersetshire), wish to show thirty-one in the main for five guineas a battle, and twenty the odds. Adding 10 byes at two guineas a battle for two days' play, to fight at Wokingham, Berks, between the present day and Whitsuntide. Any acceptance of the terms may be made through the medium of this communication, which shall be instantly acceded to and the necessary regulations made in proper form.
>
> C.W.T. & M.
>
> *February 22nd, 1794.*

Though cock-fighting is now forbidden by law in England, a certain amount of it still goes on in secret, whilst the sport flourishes openly in the North of France and in Spain.

In former days there were regular families of cock-feeders or trainers. The greatest authority on cock-fighting is said to have been Joe Gilliver, who fought cocks for George III. and George IV. in the Royal Cockpit at Windsor. He it was who fought the famous main at Lincoln in 1815. On the occasion there were seven battles for five thousand guineas the main and a thousand guineas a battle. Five battles were won by Gilliver's birds.

The great-nephew of old Joe Gilliver still lives—the last of the cock-fighters—at Cockspur, Polesworth. Over sixty years ago this veteran[10] fought and won a main against Lord Berkeley in Battersea fields, and within the last two decades he vindicated the honour of the English game-cock at Lille, where some birds he took over proved victorious—a particularly fine cock after a successful battle leaping upon the body of its conquered opponent and emitting a series of lusty crows.

Game-cocks are extraordinarily bold birds, and records exist of their having even attacked men. A gentleman, for instance, passing down Park Street was once surprised to find something fluttering about his head, and turning round, received the spur of a game-cock in his cheek. He beat off his antagonist, who, however, instantly returned to the charge, and wounded him again in the shoulder. Another gentleman, passing by at the same time, was also attacked by this feathered desperado.

A game-cock bred by Mr. Hunt of Compton Pauncefoot, Somerset, in 1814, displayed extraordinary courage when three years old. A fox having seized a hen, her cries drew the attention of the cock, who, discovering the fox in the act of carrying off his prey, flew at reynard, and at one blow killed him on the spot, and saved the life of the hen. In 1820 this cock fought a gallant battle at Epsom Races, and won at high odds against him.

The high spirit of the game-cock was once strikingly manifested in a naval action.

By some mistake or other a particularly fine bird was sold with a number of other fowls to Captain Berkeley of the *Marlborough*, 74, for his sea-stock. The purchase was made previous to the departure of the British fleet that sailed under the gallant Lord Howe, in the month of May 1794, about which time the cock was deposited in the coops on board, for the purpose of being brought to table. On the glorious 1st of June, the fate of the above ship, the intrepid bravery of whose crew led her into the hottest scene of action, hung in the balance. The enemy's shot had destroyed all the convenience made on her poop for keeping the live stock, and the fowls were flying about in different parts of the ship. Some time after the engagement had commenced, all her masts were shot away by the board, and smoke, hurry, and alarm were general. When the main-mast went, broken off about eight feet from the deck, the cock immediately flew to the stump, where he began to flutter his wings, and to crow with all the exultation so commonly observed in a conquering bird; a circumstance so singular in its nature, that the tars who were viewing it conceived a noble resolution from the example, and actually maintained the same sense of triumph as did the cock, until victory and glory crowned the gallant contest.

The spirit of the noble bird became the subject of much observation when the ship arrived in the Hamoaze, and many curious spectators came from different parts of the country to see the feathered hero who had so proudly vindicated the conquering spirit of Old England.

Some time after a silver medal was struck by the orders of Admiral Berkeley; it was hung upon the neck of the old game-cock, who in the parks and around the princely halls of Goodwood passed the remainder of his downy days in honoured ease.

FOOTNOTES:

[7] He is described in contemporary sporting records as wearing this, though the author has been unable to discover exactly what a "boat hat" was. The French still make use of a similar expression, calling a particular kind of straw hat a "*canotier*."

[8] This lady's first husband had been Sir Duke Giffard, and Mrs. Mellish was one of several daughters she had by him. The writer is indebted to Mr. Henry Mellish of Hodsock Priory for this and other interesting details of his ancestor's career.

[9] The outrangership of Windsor Forest was originally instituted for the protection of the deer between Windsor Park and the river Wey, but in 1641 it was decided that no part of Surrey except Guildford Park (afterwards granted away) belonged to the Forest, and the post became a sinecure, keeping a salary of £500 a year. About the time of the American War, however, when votes were valuable, this was increased to £900.

[10] An interesting interview with William Gilliver appeared in *Fry's Magazine* for March 1909.

VII

Prevalence of wagering in the eighteenth century—Riding a horse backwards—Lord Orford's eccentric bet—Travelling piquet—The building of Bagatelle—Matches against time—"Old Q." and his chaise match—Buck Whalley's journey to Jerusalem—Buck English—Irish sportsmen—Jumping the wall of Hyde Park in 1792—Undressing in the water—Colonel Thornton—A cruel wager—Walking on stilts—A wonderful leap—Eccentric wagers—Lloyd's walking match—Squire Osbaldiston's ride—Captain Barclay—Jim Selby's drive—Mr. Bulpett's remarkable feats.

In the eighteenth century the bloods of the day bet on anything and everything. A well-known spendthrift, for instance, made a practice of backing one raindrop to roll down a window quicker than another—a practice which gave rise to the following lines:—

The bucks had dined, and deep in council sat,
Their wine was brilliant, but their wit grew flat:
Up starts his Lordship, to the window flies,
And lo! "A race!—a race!" in rapture cries;
"Where?" quoth Sir John. "Why, see the drops of rain
Start from the summit of the crystal pane—
A thousand pounds! which drop with nimblest force,
Performs its current down the slippery course!"
The bets were fix'd—in dire suspense they wait
For vict'ry pendent on the nod of fate.
Now down the sash, unconscious of the prize,
The bubbles roll—like pearls from Chloe's eyes,
But ah! the glittering charms of life are short!
How oft two jostling steeds have spoiled the sport.
Lo! thus attraction, by coercive laws,
Th' approaching drops into one bubble draws—
Each curs'd his fate, that thus their project cross'd;
How hard their lot, who neither won nor lost!

Besides the huge sums which were lost at games (in 1793, £22,000 changed hands in a single day between two players at some billiard-rooms in St. James's Street), a great deal of money was frittered away in matches of an eccentric kind.

In 1722, for instance, a number of young men subscribed for a piece of plate, which was run for in Tyburn Road by six asses, ridden by chimney-sweepers. Two boys rode two asses on Hampstead Heath for a wooden spoon, attended by above five hundred persons on horse-back. Women running for Holland smocks was not uncommon; and a match was even projected for a race between women, to be dressed in hooped petticoats. Considerable sums of money are said to have changed hands over these events, whilst a wager of £1000 depended on a match between the Earl of Lichfield and Mr. Gage that the latter's chaise and pair should outrun the Earl's chariot and four. The ground was from Tyburn to Hayes, and Mr. Gage lost through some accident.

In 1735, Count de Buckeburg, a well-known German author, on a visit to England, laid a considerable wager, that he would ride a horse from London to Edinburgh backwards, that is, with the horse's head turned towards Edinburgh, and the Count's face towards London; and in this manner he actually rode the journey in less than four days.

At the end of the eighteenth century an officer trotted fifteen miles from Chelmsford to Dunmow in one hour and nine minutes with his face to the tail.

The eccentric wager made by George, Lord Orford, an ancestor of the present writer, is well known. The latter, in 1740, bet another nobleman a large sum that a drove of geese would beat an equal number of turkeys in a race from Norwich to London. The event proved the justness of his Lordship's expectations, for the geese kept on the road with a steady pace, but the turkeys, as every evening approached, flew to roost in the trees adjoining the road, from which the drivers found it very difficult to dislodge them. In consequence of this, the geese arrived at their destination two days before the turkeys.

This nobleman, who, by his eccentricities, had acquired the name of the mad Lord Orford, trained three red deer to draw him in a light phaeton, and in this uncommon equipage he frequently made excursions to some distance, in Norfolk and Suffolk, till a singular adventure taught him the danger of the practice.

One morning in winter, when the scent lay well on the ground, he was taking one of his common drives towards Newmarket; his way was over the heath. It happened that a pack of hounds, being out for a chase, took scent of the deer, opened and followed in full cry. The deer caught the death sound, took the alarm, and set off at full speed. It was in vain his Lordship endeavoured to pull them in; fear of death was greater than fear of their lord, and they dashed off towards Newmarket, a place they were well accustomed to. The dogs were at their heels, but the deer were sufficiently in advance to reach the inn they were accustomed to put up at, when they dashed into the yard, with their terrified lord close at their heels, and the hounds not far behind them; the ostlers, however, exerted themselves to get the gates fastened before the hounds came up, when the whipper-in called them off.

In 1758, Miss Pond, daughter of the compiler and publisher of *Ponds Racing Calendar*, wagered a thousand guineas that she would ride a thousand miles in a thousand hours. This feat she accomplished (it is said on one horse) by the 3rd of May, having begun in April. A few weeks later Mr. Pond rode the same horse in two-thirds of the time.

Even the most trivial things were utilised for losing or winning money.

A Yorkshire sportsman won a considerable bet on the extreme extent to which a pound of cotton could be drawn in a thread by one of the Manchester spinning jennies; the loser betted that it would not reach two miles in length; but, upon measurement, it was found to exceed twenty-three.

A young man of the name of Drayton undertook for a considerable sum to pull in a pound weight at the distance of a mile, that is, the weight had to be attached to a string a mile in length, and Drayton to stand still and pull it to himself. The time allowed for this singular performance was two hours and a half. The odds were against him, but he won his wager.

A printer at Chester for a wager picked up 100 stones each a yard apart, returning every time with them to a basket at one end of the line, in 44½ minutes, it having been betted that he would not complete his task within 47 minutes.

So great was the love of betting amongst sporting men that when they were on a journey they would wager as to what they might meet with next. This method of gambling was afterwards made into a regular game which was called "Travelling Piquet." This was defined as a mode of amusing themselves, practised by two persons riding in a carriage, each reckoning towards his game the persons, or animals, that passed by on the side next them, according to the following estimation:—

A parson riding on a grey horse	Game
An old woman under a hedge	do.
A cat looking out of a window	60

A man, woman, and child in a buggy	40
A man riding with a woman behind him	30
A flock of sheep	20
A flock of geese	10
A post-chaise	5
A horseman	2
A man or woman walking	1

Death itself was not infrequently made the subject of a wager. Just before two unfortunate men, hung at the Old Bailey, were *dropped off*, a young nobleman present betted a hundred guineas to twenty "that the shorter of the two would give the last kick!" The wager was taken, and he won; for the other died almost instantly, whilst the shorter man was convulsed for nearly six minutes.

So great was the mania for wagers at this epoch, that even the clergy were affected by the prevailing craze. A young divine, in the vicinity of Edinburgh, declared himself ready to undertake for a wager of a hundred guineas to read six chapters from the Bible every hour for six weeks. The betting was ten to one against him.

In France matters were much the same as in England.

The Duc de Chartres, the Duc de Lauzun, and the Marquis de FitzJames once competed in a foot-race from Paris to Versailles for two hundred livres; this was won by the Marquis de FitzJames.

The Duc de Chartres bet a considerable sum with the Comte de Genlis that the latter would not go from Paris to Fontainebleau and back before he (the Duc de Chartres) had pricked 500,000 pinholes in a piece of paper. The Comte de Genlis was the winner by several hours.

The wager of the Comte d'Artois as to the building of Bagatelle is historical. He bet Marie Antoinette 100,000 livres that he would erect a palace on a certain site in the Bois de Boulogne in six weeks.

Nine hundred workmen were employed night and day, whilst patrols of the Swiss Guard seized any building materials which might be of use on the roads in the vicinity—these, it must, however, be added, were paid for. At the end of the six weeks the Comte d'Artois entertained Marie Antoinette at a splendid fête in the completed house.

Matches against time were common. In 1745 Mr. Cooper Thornhill rode three times between Stilton and Shoreditch—two hundred and thirteen miles—in eleven hours and thirty-four minutes on fourteen different horses. Six years later, Captain Shafto won £16,000 by winning a wager that he would cover fifty miles in two hours. He was allowed as many horses as he pleased.

Not a few of these matches against time were carried out under most whimsical conditions.

On 22nd August 1774, for instance, Anthony Thorpe, a journeyman baker, at the Artillery Ground, ran a mile tied up in a sack, in eleven minutes and a half.

In 1773 a London to York match was run, the winner, a mare, taking forty hours and thirty-five minutes to complete the journey.

A sensational match of a more sporting description was the ride of George IV., when Prince of Wales, to Brighton and back, a journey of one hundred and twelve miles, which the Royal sportsman is said to have performed on one horse in ten hours.

A wonderful ride was that performed in 1786 by a featherweight jockey at Newmarket, who rode one horse twenty-three miles in two or three minutes under the hour.

The Duke of Queensberry ("Old Q.") was at one time fond of sporting matches, in which he generally came off victorious, for he was a shrewd man. In 1789, during the Newmarket October Meeting, he and Sir John Lade, mounted on a brace of mules, rode from the Ditch in for £1000. This ludicrous race, which was very anxiously and obstinately contested, terminated in favour of the Duke.

Mr. Thomas Dale was also the hero of a donkey match at Newmarket, where he rode one hundred miles in twenty-two hours and a half on an ass; £100 to £10 was laid against this being done within twenty-four hours.

Old Q., when Earl of March, for a wager, sent a letter fifty miles within an hour by hand, which was cleverly effected by the missive in question being enclosed in a cricket ball and thrown from one to the other by twenty-four expert cricketers.

On another occasion Old Q. made a bet of a thousand guineas that he would produce a man who would eat more at a meal than any one Sir John

Lade could find. The bet being accepted, the time was appointed, but his Grace, not being able to attend the exhibition, wrote to his agent to know what success, and accordingly received the following note:—

> MY LORD,—I have not time to state particulars, but merely to acquaint your Grace that your man beat his antagonist by a *pig and apple-pye.*(Signed) J.P.

A curious wager which led to litigation was one between Old Q., when Lord March, and Mr. William Pigot. The latter and Mr. Codrington being together at Newmarket, it was proposed to run their fathers against each other. Mr. Pigot's father was upwards of seventy, and Mr. Codrington's father little more than fifty. The chances were calculated, and Mr. Codrington, thinking them disadvantageous to him, declined the bet, whereupon Lord March agreed to stand in his place, and mutual notes were interchanged. Mr. Pigot's note was:—

> I promise to pay to the Earl of March 500 guineas if my father dies before Sir William Codrington.
>
> WILLIAM PIGOT.

The Earl's was:—

> I promise to pay to Mr. Pigot 1600 guineas in case Sir William Codrington does not survive Mr. Pigot's father.
>
> MARCH.

The fact was that Mr. Pigot's father was then actually dead, but that was wholly unknown to the parties.

It was contended on the part of Mr. Pigot, that, as he could not possibly win, he ought not to lose, and it was compared to a ship insurance. If the policy upon a ship had not the words "lost or not lost" inserted, and the ship should be actually lost at the time of making that policy, it would be void.

For the plaintiff it was argued that the contract was good, because the fact being wholly unknown to the parties, it could not influence either.

The wager was held to be good, and the plaintiff obtained a verdict of £500, the amount of his wager.

The most important match made by the "evergreen votary of Venus," as Old Q. was called, was in 1750, when, as Lord March, he bet Count O'Taafe, an Irish gentleman notorious for eccentricity, one thousand guineas that a carriage with four wheels could be devised capable of being drawn at not less than nineteen miles within an hour.

Wright of Long Acre exhausted all the resources of his craft to diminish weight and friction; the harness was made of silk combined with leather. Four thoroughbreds, with two clever light-weight grooms, were selected, and several trials, causing the death of some horses, were run. On August 29, 1750, the match came off over a course of a mile at Newcastle, many thousands of pounds being wagered on the result, which was favourable to Lord March, the carriage being drawn over the appointed distance well within the hour. Three of the four horses which drew the machine had won plates. The leaders carried about eight stone each, the wheelers about seven, and the chaise, with a boy in it, about twenty-four. The time was 53 minutes 27 seconds.

The print (here reproduced) was published in 1788 by J. Rodger, after the original painting by Seymour, which is now, I believe, in the possession of Lord Rosebery.

Large sums were laid upon very trivial and useless performances, and a certain number of individuals, well-known for their physical strength, used to undertake to carry out all sorts of queer tasks.

In 1789 a man called Shadbolt, a respectable innkeeper at Ware, called Goliath on account of his great muscular powers, undertook, for a considerable wager, to run and push his cart from Ware to Shoreditch Church (a distance of twenty-one miles) in ten hours, which he easily performed within the space of six hours and a few seconds, without the least appearance of fatigue. Great sums were won and lost on the occasion.

All sorts of curious wagers were laid in Ireland. The celebrated Buck Whalley, for instance, once jumped over a carrier's cart on horse-back for a bet. This he did from an upper story of a house, quantities of straw being laid on the other side of the cart.

Thomas Whalley, known as Jerusalem Whalley, owing to the journey which he made for a wager to Jerusalem, was the son of a gentleman of very considerable property in the north of Ireland. His father, when advanced in years, married a lady much younger than himself, and left her a widow with seven children.

THE CHAISE MATCH.

Thomas Whalley was the eldest son of this family, and had a property of £10,000 per annum left him by his father. At the age of sixteen he was sent to Paris to learn the French language and perfect himself in dancing, fencing, and other elegant accomplishments. The tutor selected to accompany him was not able or desirous of checking young Whalley's extravagance. The latter purchased horses and hounds, took a house in Paris, and another in the country, each of which was open for the reception of his friends. His finances, ample as they were, were found inadequate to the support of his extraordinary expenses, and, with the hope of supplying his deficiencies, he had recourse to the gaming-tables, which only increased his embarrassments. In one night he lost upwards of £14,000. The bill which he drew upon his banker, La Touche, in Dublin, for this sum was sent back protested, and it became necessary for him to quit Paris. On his return to England, however, his creditors (or rather the people who had swindled him out of this money) were glad to compound for half the sum.

Whalley then went back to Ireland and took a house in Dublin, where he lived in the most expensive manner, but quickly tiring of rural life decided to return to the Continent. While he was still hesitating as to his exact place of destination, some friends, with whom he was dining, and who had heard that he was intending to go abroad, made inquiry of him whither he was going. He hastily answered: "To Jerusalem." Upon this, certain that he had no such intention, they offered to wager him any sum he did not reach that city. As a result of this, in spite of the fact that he originally had not the faintest idea of such an expedition, he was so much stimulated by the offers made him that he accepted bets to the amount of £15,000, and at once made preparations for his journey. A few days later he set out, and having accomplished what was then an adventurous journey, eventually returned to Dublin within the appointed time, and in due course claimed and received from his astonished antagonists the reward of his most unexpected performance.

After staying some time in Dublin, Whalley again went to Paris, and was witness to the very interesting scenes which occurred in the early part of the Revolution in France. He remained in Paris till after the return of the King from Varennes; and, when it became no longer safe for a subject of the King of Great Britain to remain in France, he returned to Ireland.

Being of a very active disposition, Whalley made constant trips to England, where he frequented the gaming-houses in London, Newmarket, and Brighton, and soon dissipated a large part of his remaining fortune. He then retired to the Isle of Man, where he employed himself in cultivating and improving an estate he possessed there, and in educating his children. He at the same time drew up memoirs of his own life, which were discovered a few years ago and published under the title of *Memoirs of Buck Whalley.*

Another sporting character well known in Ireland was the celebrated Buck English, who spent the latter part of his life in litigious turmoil, and was a man who experienced infinite vicissitudes of fortune. Born to a large estate, the earlier part of his life was spent in scenes of the most unbounded dissipation; but these were curtailed when he got into the hands of a litigious attorney, who, for years, kept him out of his property. Mr. English was tried for his life, for the murder of Mr. Powell, and was with difficulty acquitted, and escaped narrowly from being torn to pieces by the mob in Cork. Previous to this, he threw a waiter out of a window, and desired him to be "charged in the bill!" In his career, he fought two duels with swords, in the streets of Dublin; was a Member of Parliament, and an excellent speaker; was thrown into a loathsome prison for debt, where his constitution was totally destroyed. He died almost immediately after his liberation, just as he recovered his fortune.

In October 1791, at the Curragh Meeting in Ireland, Mr. Wilde, a sporting gentleman, made bets to the amount of two thousand guineas, to ride against time, viz., one hundred and twenty-seven English miles in nine hours. On the 6th of October he started in a valley, near the Curragh course, where two miles were measured in a circular direction; each time he encompassed the course it was regularly marked. During the interval of changing horses, he refreshed himself with a mouthful of brandy and water, and was no more than six hours and twenty-one minutes in completing the one hundred and twenty-seven miles; of course he had two hours and thirty-nine minutes to spare.

Mr. Wilde had no more than ten horses, but they were all thoroughbreds from the stud of Mr. Daly.

Whilst on horse-back, without allowing anything for changing of horses, he rode at the rate of twenty miles an hour for six hours. He was so little fatigued with this extraordinary performance, that he was at the Turf Club-house in Kildare the same evening.

The Right Honourable Thomas Conolly also rode for a wager of five hundred guineas on the Curragh. He was allowed two hours to ride forty miles with any ten hunters of his own. He with ease rode forty-two miles in an hour and forty-four minutes on eight hunters.

At this time much money was wagered both in Ireland and England upon the leaping powers of the horse, and occasionally the methods employed were none too honourable.

A young sportsman, for instance, having boasted of the powers of a recently purchased hunter which he offered to back at jumping against any horse in the world, a friend ridiculed the idea, and said he had a blind hunter that should leap over what the other would not. A wager to no inconsiderable amount was the consequence, and day and place appointed. The time having arrived, both parties appeared on the ground with their nags; when laying down a straw at some distance, the friend put his horse forward, and at the word "over" the blind hunter made a famous leap; while neither whip nor spur could induce the other to rise at all.

A very sporting bet was decided in the most fashionable part of London in 1792. On the 24th of February in that year was accomplished the feat of leaping over the high wall of Hyde Park from Park Lane. A bet of five hundred guineas was reported to have been laid between a Royal personage and Mr. Bingham, that the latter's Irish-bred brown mare should leap over the wall of Hyde Park, opposite Grosvenor Place, which wall was six feet and a half high on the inside, and eight on the out. Mr. Bingham having sold his mare to Mr. Jones, the bet, of course, became void. Mr. Jones offered bets to any amount that the mare should do it, but his offers were not accepted. Mr. Bingham, to show the possibility of its being done, led his beautiful bay horse, Deserter, to the same place, who performed this standing leap twice without any difficulty, except that, in returning, his hind feet brushed the bricks off the top of the wall. As the height from which he was to descend into the road was so considerable, he was received on a bed of long dung. The Duke of York, Prince William of Gloucester, the Earl of Derby, and a number of the nobility joined the vast concourse of impatient spectators, who were pretty well tired out before the jumping began.

Another remarkable feat was the leap over a dinner-table with dishes, decanters, and lighted candelabra, performed by Mr. Manning, a sporting farmer, on a barebacked steed in the Rochester Room at the White Hart Inn, at Aylesbury, during the steeplechases in 1851.

Wagers entailing considerable risk and endurance were popular in the past. Two gentlemen at a coffee-house near Temple Bar once made an extraordinary bet of this nature. One of them was to jump into seven feet of water, with his clothes on, and to entirely undress himself in the water, which he did within the appointed time.

The present writer, when an undergraduate at Cambridge, witnessed a somewhat similar exploit performed in the Cam on a particularly cold winter's day.

On this occasion, however, the undergraduate, a man of herculean frame, who had wagered that he would undress in the water, was allowed to cancel his bet after he had discarded everything but one sock. As he appeared to be much exhausted, all bets were declared off by mutual consent. The layer of the wager was in a terrible state on leaving the water, but entirely recovered the next day.

Those fond of shooting frequently wagered on their powers as shots.

In 1800 the celebrated Colonel Thornton made a bet that he killed 400 head of game at 400 shots. The result was, he bagged 417 head of game (consisting of partridges, pheasants, hares, snipes, and woodcocks) at 411 shots. Amongst these were a black wild duck and a white pheasant cock; and at the last point he killed a brace of cock pheasants, one with each barrel. On the leg of the last killed (an amazing fine bird) was found a ring, proving that he had been taken by Colonel Thornton when hawking, and turned loose again in 1792.

Colonel Thornton could not bear to hear that any one had outdone him at anything. On one occasion a foreigner was boasting of the sporting powers of the Comte d'Artois, afterwards Charles X., and asserted that the Prince in question was, without doubt, considered the greatest shot in Europe. On hearing this the Colonel looked highly offended, when the foreign sportsman added, "except Colonel *Tornton*" (thus pronounced), "who is acknowledged to be the longest shot in the world." There was a great deal of bitter-sweet in this, but the Colonel wisely interpreted the phrase in a sense complimentary to himself.

Colonel Thornton, though his name has come down to us as a great sporting character, was not by any means universally popular in his own day. Notwithstanding that he was of quite respectable descent, and had inherited a comfortable fortune, he was never on familiar terms with the aristocratic sportsmen of his age, with whom it was his darling passion to be able to associate. A well-known member of the Jockey Club, when the

Colonel's name was mentioned, once said: "Oh! Thornton, never let us hear that fellow named; we don't know him."

The Colonel provoked much ridicule by his overwhelming ambition to excel everybody in everything—a notable instance of which was his taking Thornville Royal, a palatial house of which his family and suite could only occupy one corner, his means being inadequate to keep up the house and domain in proper style. Incapable of restraining an innate tendency to exaggeration, Colonel Thornton was known to many as "Lying Thornton," a nickname which was in some degree justified by the palpably mendacious accounts of his exploits, which his craving for notoriety prompted him to disseminate. His conceit was gigantic. He once actually sent an apology for not being present at a Royal Levee, which absurd conduct caused a great personage many a hearty laugh.

The Colonel's extravagance, and the lawsuits in which he indulged, often reduced him to great straits for ready money. Nevertheless, he was always possessed of considerable property. Colonel Thornton undoubtedly deserves to be remembered as a sportsman, though his reputation as such would have been greater had he not sought to excel all men in bodily activity and physical exertion, as well as eclipse them in the extent and variety of land and water sports, which was naturally an impossible feat.

Much given to litigation in life. Colonel Thornton gave the lawyers employment even after his death. By his will he bequeathed all his remaining property to an illegitimate daughter by Priscilla Druins, leaving his wife, Mrs. Thornton, nothing, and his son by her only £100. The will was disputed by the lawyers both in France and England. In the English Courts it was decided that the Colonel had never ceased to be a British subject, and that, therefore, the will must be valid. The French Court, passing a contrary judgment, decreed that the Colonel had petitioned in 1817, and obtained a complete naturalisation; that his real domicile being therefore in France, the will must be decided by its laws; and that the property having been willed to a child born in adultery, and otherwise contrary to the laws of France, the will was null and void; and they adjudged accordingly, with costs in favour of Mrs. Thornton, the lawful wife. The Colonel's real property appeared to be very little. He inhabited the Château de Chambord only as a tenant, but he had purchased the domain of Pont le Roi, and the vendors sued the Colonel's legatees for the purchase money.

At the dawn of the nineteenth century long-distance matches continued to be in vogue. The distance between Burton, on the Humber, and Bishopsgate, in the City of London, one hundred and seventy-two miles, was covered in something like eight hours and a half by a sportsman in

1802, who had bet that, with the fourteen horses allowed him, he would accomplish the journey in ten hours.

In April 1806 a very singular bet, or agreement, was made at Brighton between Lieutenant-General Lennox and Henry Hunter, Esq. The former, after some remarks on the prevalent winds at Brighton, proposed to give to the latter, during the space of twenty-eight days, whenever the wind blew from the south-west, one guinea per diem, provided the other would forfeit to him the same sum, during the same period, every day that the wind should blow from the north-east, which proposal was instantly accepted. For the ensuing thirteen days the wind lay mostly in the south-west quarter, upon which Mr. Hunter remarked that, in spite of south-west gales not being to every one's taste, this was merely another proof of the old adage that "It is an ill wind that blows nobody good."

In 1807, Captain Bennet, of the Loyal Ongar Hundred Volunteers, engaged to trundle a hoop from Whitechapel Church to Ongar, in Essex, in three hours and a half, a distance of twenty-two miles, for the wager of one hundred guineas.

He started on Saturday morning, November 21, precisely at six o'clock, with the wind very much in his favour, and the odds about two to one against him. Notwithstanding the early hour, the singularity of the match brought together a numerous assemblage. The hoop used by Captain Bennet on the occasion was heavier than those trundled by boys in general, and was selected by him conformably to the terms of the wager. The first ten miles Captain Bennet performed in one hour and twenty minutes, which changed the odds considerably in his favour.

He accomplished the whole distance considerably within the given time, as the Ongar coachman met him only five miles and a half from Ongar, when he had a full hour in hand.

A cruel wager was the following, made in December of the same year, when a Mr. Arnold, a sporting man who resided at Pentonville, bet Mr. Mawbey, a factor of the Fulham Road, twenty guineas that the former did not produce a dog, which should be thrown over Westminster Bridge at dark, and find its way home again in six hours, as proposed by Arnold. The inhuman experiment was tried in the evening, when a spaniel bitch, the property of a groom in Tottenham Court Road, was produced and thrown over from the centre of the bridge. The dog arrived at the house of her master in two hours after the experiment had been made.

Little consideration was shown for animals in those days.

On a Saturday evening in August 1808, a crowd of people assembled at Hyde Park Corner to watch the start of a pony which was, for a stake of five hundred guineas, matched to start with the Exeter Mail and be in Exeter first, with or without a rider. A man leading the pony was at liberty to take a fresh post-horse whenever he liked. The backer of the pony won the match, for though the odds were against it, the game little animal arrived at Exeter in very good condition, forty-five minutes before the Mail reached that city. Several thousands of pounds were wagered on the result.

It should be added that the pony drank ale during the journey, and several pints of port in addition.

The distance from London to Exeter is about one hundred and seventy-four miles.

In 1809 a very extraordinary wager was decided upon the road between Cambridge and Huntingdon. A gentleman of the former place had betted a considerable sum of money that he would go, a yard from the ground, upon stilts, the distance of twelve miles, within the space of four hours and a half: no stoppage was to be allowed, except merely the time taken up in exchanging one pair of stilts for another, and even then his feet were not to touch the ground. He started at the second milestone from Cambridge in the Huntingdon Road, to go six miles out and six miles in; the first he performed in one hour and fifty minutes, and did the distance back in two hours and three minutes, so that he went the whole in three hours and fifty-three minutes, having thirty-seven minutes to spare within the time allowed him.

In the winter of 1810-1811 a bet of £500 was made by the Duke of Richmond, then Lord-Lieutenant of Ireland, with Sir Edward Crofton (who afterwards committed suicide), that the latter should not produce a horse who would leap, in fair Irish sporting style (which allows just touching with the hind feet), a wall seven feet high. Sir Edward brought forward a cocktail horse, called Turnip, being got by Turnip, a thoroughbred son of old Pot8o's (a horse imported, like the celebrated Diamond, into Ireland by Colonel Hyde), out of a common Irish mare.

On the day appointed, a gate was removed from its place in a very high park wall, near the Phœnix Park, and, men and stones being ready, was built up to the required and specified height, in the presence of his Grace. While this was being expeditiously accomplished by men used to building up such fences. Turnip was kept walking about, by a common groom in jacket and cap. When all was ready, and the signal given, over he went, but had so little run that the Duke, thinking the rider was going to turn him round and give him a race at it, turned his head at the moment, and did not see the leap; to reassure him, however, the horse was put over it again. He was a slow horse, and died afterwards from the effects of a severe run with the Kildare hounds in an open country, where, though the fences would in England be reckoned severe, they were nothing to the walls of Roscommon and Galway.

About 1811 there appears to have been a recrudescence of the craze for eccentric wagers. A good deal of interest was excited in January of that year by the strange performance of a soldier in the Guards, who had betted two guineas that he would mark a cross on every tree in St. James's Park, that was within his reach, in an hour and ten minutes. He started at ten o'clock in the morning from the first tree in Birdcage Walk, and completed his task in three minutes less than the time allowed him. A great number of bets depended upon the result.

In the same year a French cook, in the employ of Lord Gwydir, wagered a considerable sum in the neighbourhood of Lincoln, that he could roll a round piece of wood like a trencher from Grimsthorpe to Bourn, a distance of nearly four miles, church-steeple road, at one hundred starts. The bet having been accepted, the Frenchman had a groove formed round the edge of the wood, and, with the aid of a piece of cord, he accomplished his task in ninety-nine starts.

In the same year an ostler of the Dragoon Inn, at Harrowgate, undertook, for a wager of one guinea, to drag a heavy phaeton three times round the race-course there, being nearly four miles, in six hours. He started at six in the evening, and at fifteen minutes to nine he had performed his singular task.

In 1812 Scrope Davis, then a Fellow of King's College, Cambridge, betted five thousand guineas that he would swim from Eaglehurst, the seat of Lord Cavan, near Southampton Water, to the Isle of Wight. This feat, however, he did not attempt, as he received seven hundred and fifty guineas forfeit from the sporting gentleman with whom he made the wager.

Scrope Davis was a particularly cultivated man, who for a time frequented the gaming-table with considerable success. Eventually, however, like the great majority of gamblers, he found himself with little to live upon except his Cambridge fellowship. He retired to Paris and bore his altered fortunes with the greatest philosophy, whilst occupying himself in writing a diary which has unfortunately disappeared.

In 1813 another literary man of sporting tendencies—a Mr. Thacker, who had been an assistant master at Rugby—undertook at Lincoln, for a wager of £5, to make two thousand pens in ten hours; this he performed nearly two hours within the time. It was stipulated that they should be well made; and a person was appointed umpire who examined every pen as he made it. The pens were afterwards sold by auction at the Green Dragon, where the bet had been decided.

In 1814 a somewhat novel wager was decided in a tavern in the City.

Two gentlemen undertook to drink against one another, one to drink wine, and the other water, glass for glass, and he that gave in was to be the loser. They drank the contents of a bottle and a half each, but the wine-drinker was triumphant. The unfortunate water-drinker was afterwards taken ill, being confined to his bed with an attack of the gout.

In February 1815 a journeyman baker performed a wonderful feat of winning a bet of fifty pounds to ten laid him by a gentleman that he would not stand upon one leg for twelve hours. A square piece of carpet was nailed in the centre of the room, and the time fixed was three o'clock in the afternoon, when the baker made his appearance without shoes, coat, or hat, and proceeded to take up his position upon his right leg. After standing eight hours and a half, before a great number of people, the gentleman, seeing the agony which the baker appeared to be in, offered him one-half of the wager to relinquish the bet; but, to the great astonishment of the spectators, the man refused, saying he would have the whole, or at least try for it; the perspiration was then running off him like rain, but he still persisted, when the bets were fifty to one against him. Nevertheless he performed what was in its way a wonderful feat, remaining on the one leg three minutes longer than the stipulated time, when he was put into a chair, and carried home.

In May of the same year, a novel bet of £500 was laid in a coffee-room in Bond Street. The wager in question stipulated that a gentleman should go from London to Dover, and back, in any mode he chose, while another made a million of dots with a pen and ink upon a sheet of writing-paper.

In 1826, Lloyd, the celebrated pedestrian, started, on Monday the 19th March, at eight in the morning, to perform thirty miles *backwards* in nine successive hours, including stoppages, at Bagshot, Surrey. He went on during the morning at the rate of four miles an hour, although the ground was much against him, and finished his task with apparent ease fourteen minutes within the time. He immediately mounted a friends horse, and proceeded to Hartford Bridge, where he took up his quarters for the night, and walked on to Odiham the next morning (Tuesday), where he undertook to walk twenty miles backwards in five hours and a half, which, with the advantage of a good road, he again accomplished seven minutes and a half within his time.

The same year a gentleman made a bet that he would cause all the bells of a well-frequented tavern in Glasgow to ring at the same period without touching one of them, or even leaving the room. This he accomplished by turning the stop-cock of the main gas-pipe, and involving the whole inmates in instant darkness. In a short period the clangor of bells rang from every room and box in the house, which gained him his bet amidst the general laughter and applause even of the losers.

As the nineteenth century crept on, life grew more strenuous, and the eccentric wagers, once so popular, went out of fashion; sporting matches, however, were occasionally made.

In 1831, Squire Osbaldiston, of historic sporting memory, when forty-four years old and over eleven stone in weight, won a thousand guineas by riding two hundred miles in eight hours and thirty-nine minutes, the conditions of the wager stipulating that he should go the distance in ten hours. No less than twenty-eight horses were utilised in this historic match.

At 3.15 A.M., July 13, 1809, at Newmarket, Captain Barclay, the famous pedestrian, successfully ended a walk of a thousand miles in a thousand successive hours at the rate of a mile in each and every hour. This great walker had three-quarters of an hour to spare and completed his task with great ease, 100 to 1 being offered upon him on the last morning of his walk. About £100,000 depended upon this match, of which £16,000 was won by Barclay himself.

Seventeen years later Captain Polhill easily accomplished the task of walking, driving, and riding fifty miles in twenty-four consecutive hours, the whole distance of a hundred and fifty being negotiated with five hours to spare.

Jim Selby's coaching feat of driving to Brighton and back in eight hours is still fresh in the memory of many. A thousand pounds to five hundred was laid at the Ascot meeting of 1888 against such a performance. Selby started from the White Horse Cellar, Piccadilly, at 10 in the morning of July 13, and reached the Old Ship at Brighton at 1.56. Immediately starting on the return journey, he arrived at the White Horse Cellars at 5.50, and thus won the bet by ten minutes. In the same year an extraordinary sporting feat was performed by a friend of the writer, Mr. Charles Bulpett (thirty-seven years old at the time), who took £500 to £200 that he would ride a mile, run a mile, and walk a mile—three miles in all—within sixteen minutes and a half. This he was successful in doing, the exact time occupied being sixteen minutes and seven seconds. It should be added that the extraordinary athletic powers displayed on this occasion were greatly enhanced by the fact that Mr. Bulpett was suffering from a game leg.

The same gentleman also won another sporting match of an original kind. Dining one evening at the Ship at Greenwich (formerly a great resort and the scene of an annual ministerial fish dinner) with some friends, the subject of swimming came under discussion, and in the course of the conversation some one, pointing across the river, spoke of the difficulty of swimming the Thames at this spot in ordinary clothes.

"I will," said Mr. Bulpett, "lay you £100 to £25 that I do it." The bet was taken and the next day, according to the terms of the wager, Mr. Bulpett entered the water at the Ship dressed in a frock coat, top hat, with a cane in his hand. A boat with his friends in it followed his progress. He reached the opposite shore with the greatest ease, though he was carried a mile and a quarter down by the tide, and when he got there offered to lay the same bet that he would then and there swim back to the other shore, but there were no takers. Had the wager been repeated, there is little doubt but that another £25 would have found its way into the pockets of this redoubtable athlete.

A feat of a somewhat similar kind to Mr. Bulpett's was performed in 1891 by Mr. J.B. Radcliffe, who within the space of fifteen minutes rowed, swam, ran, cycled, and rode a horse the distance of a quarter of a mile, successfully covering the mile and a half in the appointed time.

VIII

Gambling in Paris—Henry IV. and Sully—Cardinal Mazarin's love of play—Louis XIV. attempts to suppress gaming—John Law—Anecdotes—Institution of public tables in 1775—Biribi—Gambling during the Revolution—Fouché—The tables of the Palais Royal—The Galeries de Bois—Account of gaming-rooms—Passe-dix and Craps—Frascati's and the Salon des Étrangers—Anecdotes—Public gaming ended in Paris—Last evenings of play—Decadence of the Palais Royal—Its restaurants—Gaming in Paris at the present day.

There has always been much gambling in Paris, and up to the middle of the last century that city was the stronghold of public gaming, the Goddess of Chance wielding absolute sway in the Palais Royal, where licensed gaming-tables existed.

The toleration of public gaming in Paris dated as far back as the reign of Henri IV. In 1617 there were forty-seven "Brelans" frequented by any one who cared to play, each of which paid a daily tribute of one pistole to the Lieutenant Civil, who held an office in a great measure corresponding with that of the modern Prefect of Police. Henri IV. himself was much addicted to gaming, and the celebrated Sully attempted to reform him. The King in question having once lost an immense sum of money at play, Sully let his royal master send to him for it several times without taking any notice; at last, however, he brought it and spread the coins before him upon a table. The King fixed his eyes upon the vast sum—said to have been enough to have bought Amiens from the Spaniards—and at last cried out to Sully, "I am corrected, I will never again lose my money at gaming while I live."

The gaming-resorts of old Paris were filled with people whose reputations for probity were generally a good deal more than doubtful. In one of the best of these *tripots* a gentleman, whose turn to hold the hand had come, delayed the game by insisting on searching for a few pieces of gold which he had dropped on the floor. The other players, eager to pursue their game, remonstrated with him saying, "You know we are all honest people here." "I know that," was the reply, "honest people, one of whom gets hung every week when the law is in a mood to do its duty."

Scandals of the most disgraceful kind were of constant occurrence, and in consequence of the numerous quarrels relating to unpaid wagers, Francis the First once proposed to create a special court of jurisdiction to deal with such cases. A list of judges and officials was even drawn up, but the scheme was never actually put into execution.

Whilst the ordinary folk flocked to more or less obscure gaming-houses, the *noblesse* in the seventeenth century were great patrons of the tennis-court known as the "Tripot de la Sphère," in the Marais. A considerable amount of etiquette prevailed, and not a few careers were wrecked owing to the overbearing demeanour of some of the great nobles.

Cardinal Mazarin, however, introduced games of chance at the Court of Louis XIV. in 1648, and having initiated the King and the Queen Regent into the pleasures of the gaming-table, as an indirect consequence caused the decadence of tennis, mail (pall mall), and billiards.

Games involving strength, skill, and exercise became neglected, and the population somewhat demoralised.

Gaming spread from the Court to Paris, and from thence to provincial towns, in many cases producing a very disastrous effect.

Louis the Fourteenth was fond of backgammon, at which one day he had a doubtful throw. A dispute arose, and the surrounding courtiers all remained silent. The Count de Gramont happened to come in at that instant. "Decide the matter," said the King to him. "Sire," said the Count, "your Majesty is in the wrong." "How," replied the King, "can you thus decide without knowing the question?" "Because," said the Count, "had the matter been doubtful, all these gentlemen present would have given it for your Majesty."

Cardinal Mazarin himself was generally ready to bet about anything. He was driving in the country one day with a certain Count, when the latter proposed that they should wager on the number of sheep they should pass in the fields on each side of the road, one taking the right and the other the left side. The Cardinal was a heavy loser over this, as, much to his surprise, both going and returning the side selected by his companion simply swarmed with sheep, whilst very few were to be seen on the other.

As a matter of fact, as he afterwards genially hinted, the Count had taken measures not to lose his bet, but the Cardinal, who was good-natured in such matters, bore him no ill-will.

Another great ecclesiastic who was equally good-humoured about losses at play was the Cardinal d'Este, who, one day entertaining at dinner a brother prince of the Church, the Cardinal de Medici, played with him afterwards, and quite carelessly allowed the latter to win a stake of some ten thousand crowns, because, as he told an onlooker, he did not wish his guest to go away in a bad humour, or feel that he had been made to pay for his dinner.

Hoca was a very popular game about this time. Certain Italians who had come into France in the train of Cardinal Mazarin contrived to obtain a concession from the King which enabled them to establish places in which this game might be played, and as they took care always to keep the bank themselves, they soon began to attract unfavourable notice owing to the large sums which fell into their maw. The game in question was prodigiously favourable to the bank, the players having only twenty-eight chances against thirty. In consequence of the public scandal which resulted, the Parliament of Paris stepped in and threatened severe punishment against these men, whilst it was made punishable by death to play hoca at all. Nevertheless, it continued to be in high favour at the Court, where many were ruined by gambling.

In 1691, Louis XIV. determined to put a stop to the evil, and issued an order that no one should engage at faro, basset, and other games of chance on any consideration; every offender was to be fined 1000 livres, and the person at whose house any such game was played incurred a penalty of 6000 livres for each offence. Gamblers were also to be imprisoned for six months. The order in question, however, appears to have effected nothing, for some years later the same prince published a still severer edict, by which he forbade, on pain of death, any gaming in the French cavalry, and sentenced every commanding officer or governor who should presume to set up a hazard-table to be cashiered, and all concerned to be immediately and rigorously imprisoned.

About the commencement of the Regency all Paris went mad over gaming; many of the houses of the great nobles were virtually *tripots*, special lights outside announcing this to passers-by. Horace Walpole declared that at least a hundred and fifty people of the highest quality lived on the play which took place in their houses, which any one wishing to gamble could enter at all hours. At the mansion of the Duc de Gevres persons desirous of taking the bank paid about twelve guineas a night. Such proceedings were deemed to be no disgrace to the nobles.

Soon the gambling fever assumed a far more dangerous form than cards or dice, owing to the wild speculation brought into fashion by Law. This man, who was born in 1688, was the son of a lawyer at Edinburgh. Coming up to London he fell in love with the sister of a peer, who, disapproving of such a marriage with an adventurer, challenged Law, and fell in the duel. Law immediately escaped into Holland, and was tried, convicted, and outlawed in England. Perhaps it was in Holland he acquired that turn of mind which revels in immense calculations; anyhow he became an adept in the mysteries of exchanges and re-exchanges. From thence he proceeded to Venice and other cities, studying the nature of their banks. In 1709 he was at Paris, avid as ever of speculation.

At the close of the reign of Louis XIV., the French finances were in great disorder; and Law, having obtained an audience of that monarch, had almost convinced the bankrupt king of the feasibility of his speculative projects. He had offered to pay the national debt by establishing a company, whose paper was to be received with all possible confidence, and who were to make immense profits by their commercial transactions. The minister, Desmarest, however, took alarm and, to get rid of Law, threatened him, by one of his emissaries, with the Bastille. Law quitted Paris, and became a wanderer through Italy. He then addressed himself to the King of Sardinia, who refused the adventurer's assistance, curtly declaring that he was not powerful enough to ruin himself!

At the death of Louis XIV., the Duke of Orleans was Regent. Law saw his chance and ventured again to Paris, where he found the Regent docile enough. The latter, indeed, was placed in a most trying situation: the finances were all confusion, and no one appeared competent to settle them. At first the Regent listened somewhat reluctantly to Law, doubtful as to what consequences must follow such colossal schemes as those in which the adventurer dealt. Matters, however, going from bad to worse, the numerical quack was called in to relieve, by his powerful remedy, the disorder which no one else would even attempt to cure.

Law commenced with most brilliant prospects. He established his bank, was chosen director of the East India Company, and soon gave his scheme that vital credit which produced real specie. In that distracted time, every one buried or otherwise concealed his valuables; but, when the spells of Law began to operate, every coffer was opened, while the proprietors of many estates seemed to prefer his paper to the possession of their lands. All Europe appeared delighted; Law acquired millions in a morning; whilst the Regent, thoroughly duped, felicitated himself on his possession of so great an alchemist.

Law was honoured with nobility, and created Comte de Tankerville; as for marquisates, he purchased them at his will. Edinburgh, his native city, humbly presented him with her freedom, in which appears these remarkable expressions:—"The Corporation of Edinburgh presents its freedom to John Law, Count of Tankerville, etc., etc., etc., a most accomplished gentleman; the first of all bankers in Europe; the fortunate inventor of sources of commerce in all parts of the remote world; and who has deserved so well of his nation." From a Scotchman (says Voltaire) he became, by naturalisation, a Frenchman; from a Protestant, a Catholic; from an adventurer, a Prince; and from a banker, a minister of state.

Law's novel system of finance was perhaps most aptly defined by a dissipated and spendthrift member of the French *noblesse*, the Marquis de

Cavillac, who, much to the Scotchman's disgust, bluntly accused him of plagiarising from his own methods, which, as he added, consisted in drawing and giving bills which would certainly never be met.

Meanwhile a veritable rage for speculation prevailed. Fortunes were made in a month, and stock-jobbing was carried on even in the narrowest alleys of Paris. Singular anecdotes are recorded of this time. A coachman gave warning to his master, who begged at least that he would provide him with another as good as himself. "Very well," was the reply, "I have hired two this morning; take your choice, and I will have the other." A footman set up his chariot; but, going to it, got up behind, where from force of habit he remained till reminded by his own servant of the mistake. An old beggar, who had a remarkable hunch on his back, haunted the Rue Quincampoix, which was the crowded resort of all stock-jobbers; here he acquired a good fortune by lending out his hunch for five minutes at a time as a desk.

Law himself was adored; the proudest courtiers were humble reptiles before this mighty man; dukes and duchesses patiently waited in his antechamber; and Mrs. Law, a haughty beauty, when a duchess was announced, exclaimed, "Still more duchesses! There is no animal so tiresome as a duchess!"

The Court ladies never left Law alone. One morning, when he was surrounded by a body of *grandes dames*, he was going to retire. They inquired the reason, which was of such a kind as should have silenced them; but on the contrary, they said, "Oh! if it is nothing but that, let them bring here a *chaise percée* for Mr. Law." When the young king was at play, and the stakes were too high even for his Majesty, he refused to cover them all; young Law (the son of the adventurer) cried out, "If his Majesty will not cover, I will." The King's governor frowned on the boy of millions, who, perceiving his error, threw himself at the king's feet.

The infatuation ran through all classes, and even the French Academy solicited for the honour of Law becoming their associate—this Scotchman was the only speculator they ever admitted into their body.

The evil hour, however, at last arrived; the immense machine became so complicated that even the head of Law began to turn with its rapid revolutions. In 1719 he created credit; but in May 1720, uncounted millions disappeared in air. Nothing was seen but paper and bankruptcy everywhere. Law was considered as the sole origin of the public misfortune, no one blaming his own credulity. The mob broke his carriages, destroyed his houses, and tried to find the arithmetician in order to tear him to pieces. He escaped from Paris in disguise, and long wandered in Europe incognito. After some years, he found a hiding-place in Venice, where he lived, poor, obscure, yet still calculating. Montesquieu, who saw him there, said: "He is still the same man; his mind ever busied in financial schemes; his head is full of figures, of agios, and of banks. His fortune is very small, yet he loves to game high." Indeed, of all his more than princely revenues, he only saved, as a wreck, a large white diamond, which, when he had no money, he used to pawn.

Voltaire saw his widow at Brussels. She was then as humiliated, as miserable, and as obscure, as she had been triumphant and haughty at Paris.

After the collapse of Law's schemes the stream of gaming returned to its ordinary channels, and high play continued as formerly to be the pastime of the *noblesse*, some of whom kept more or less public gaming-tables.

Not, however, till 1775 were public gaming-tables, somewhat resembling those still flourishing at Monaco, licensed in Paris. In that year Sartines, the celebrated "Lieutenant of Police," began to authorise regular "maisons de jeu," the profits of which were in principle supposed to be devoted to the foundation of hospitals, but in reality failed to reach their destined goal of philanthropy. The most popular game played was called "la belle." Certain privileged ladies, it may be added, were accorded permission to preside at the twelve gaming-tables of Paris twice a week. The bankers gave these attractive sorceresses six louis at each sitting, and paid all other expenses. A third day in the seven was set aside for the benefit of the police, who, once every week, ungallantly pocketed the six golden pieces of each of the presiding goddesses, most of whom were battered baronesses and ruined marchionesses, who had petitioned for the somewhat dubious honour of presiding at these *tripots*. Amongst them were Madame de Thouvenère, la Baronne de Gancière, and la Marquise de Sainte Doubeuville. The ladies were generally represented by deputies of the fair sex, who received a fair share of the wages of iniquity. The directors of the gaming-houses in question were as a rule the valets of grand seigneurs, the best known being a man called Gombaud, who acted as cashier-general. The success of the authorised "houses" led to the establishment of rival and clandestine *tripots*. The most celebrated of these private pandemoniums, which were practically "Hells," were kept by Madame de Selle, Rue Montmartre; la Comtesse Champeiron, Rue de Cléry; and Madame de Fonteneille. Rue de l'Arsenal. It was at the last-named place that Sartines, who often visited such places as a private individual for his own pleasure, narrowly escaped the blow of a poniard, on being recognised by a ruined gambler. A good deal of crime and misery was declared to arise from the existence of these gaming-houses, and at length, in 1781, after many suicides and bankruptcies innumerable, they were temporarily prohibited. The main cause, however, was that the brother of a favourite mistress of a pet courtier, after ruining himself and robbing a friend in order to obtain funds with which to play, had put an end to his existence, by blowing out his brains, at a gaming-house kept by Madame de la Serre, Place des Victoires. After this the demon of gaming took refuge at the Court, where shady financiers and well-dressed scoundrels carried on a very lucrative traffic almost under the nose of His Most Christian Majesty. The privileged hôtels of the ambassadors, where the police had no control, became also the *sanctum sanctorum* of the vampires of that period. In addition to this, after a short lapse of time, the original Golgothas were re-licensed, the game called "biribi" displacing "la belle," and becoming the popular road to ruin of the day.

Biribi is now probably quite obsolete. It was played upon a table which contained seventy numbers, to which there were corresponding numbers enclosed in a bag.

These the banker drew out one by one, the player whose money was on the corresponding number on the table being paid a sum equivalent to sixty-four times his stake. As at roulette, there were a great number of other chances—*pair* and *impair*, *noir* and *rouge*, *du petit et du grand côté*, *la bordure du tableau*, *les terminaisons*, and the like.

There were nine columns of numbers, each of which contained eight, with the exception of the middle column, which was the banker's; this consisted of six numbers only, which were considered zeroes.

Unattractive as this game must appear to a more sophisticated generation, biribi became a regular craze.

About this time another epidemic of domestic horrors and public crimes caused the Hells to be denounced to Parliament, which cited the redoubtable lieutenant of police, Sartines, to its bar, and after a good deal of gesticulation and ultra-moral oratory—most of it from those members of the Parliament who themselves kept privileged receptacles of gaming—it was decided that the high court of peers should be convoked, in order that they might deal severely with those minor ruffians, who, in contravention of the laws, carried on clandestine play. The patrician moralists shortly after issued a decree, sanctioned by Royalty, that the bankers of unauthorised gaming-houses should be liable to the *carcan* (pillory), branding with a hot iron, and the *fout* (flogging).

After this the licensed Hells carried on their golden commerce in full security, but not entirely without competition, in spite of the aforesaid pains and penalties which were in several cases enforced. A curious and characteristic consequence of such a state of affairs was the use to which certain diplomatic representatives put their mansions, making good, or rather bad, use of the immunity from interference which their office of Envoy conferred. M. le Chevalier Zeno, the Venetian Ambassador, turned his house into a regular casino, admitting any one into it who would play. For those of the lowest degree a particular room was reserved, known to its habitués as "l'enfer." Remonstrances and representations from the authorities were powerless to effect the cessation of what became a public scandal, the Venetian Embassy continuing to be little but a gambling-hell, till the departure of the Ambassador in question.

Three other Ministers also maintained establishments of a similar kind. These were the Prussian Envoy, who resided in the Rue de Choiseul, the Envoy of Hesse-Cassel, whose house was in the Rue Poissonnière, and the Ambassador of Sweden, whose gambling establishment was on the Place du Louvre, at a house bearing the inscription "Écuries de M. l'Ambassadeur de Suède." The somewhat singular methods employed by the enterprising Diplomats in question were very freely commented upon in a report issued by the "Lieutenant de Police" in February 1781, nothing, however, being done to check the scandal. On the contrary, certain members of the *noblesse*, being struck with the pecuniary advantages to be reaped from keeping a gaming-house, followed the example of the Ambassadors, M. le Marquis and M. le Comte de Genlis presiding over establishments of this kind in the Place Vendôme and in the Rue Bergère. It became no uncommon thing for Chevaliers de St. Louis to act as bankers or croupiers. Owing to the decoration they wore they were not subject to the same jurisdiction as ordinary mortals, besides which, many of them were excellent swordsmen. This naturally gave them a great advantage in the case of any protest on the part of the players against the methods employed by the bank, a circumstance which eventually led to a royal prohibition of further gaming enterprises being undertaken by Chevaliers of this Order.

As the stormy days of '89 approached, gambling became more and more prevalent, and during the Revolution, notwithstanding the Spartan austerity which it was declared was to be a characteristic of the new era, gaming was freely tolerated by the authorities. Later, when Fouché assumed the office of Minister of Police, the privilege of keeping gambling-houses was let out as openly and as publicly as the King's Ministers had farmed out the duties upon salt, tobacco, or wine to the "fermiers généraux" of the revenue. Cards of address to gambling-houses were distributed in all parts of France in the same manner as circulars in London. The sum of money which this system of toleration brought into Fouché's pocket reached upwards of ten thousand pounds per month. The Prefect at Lyons, Vermignac, learnt, to his cost, how dangerous it was to meddle with this *lawful* income of Citizen Fouché; for, having ordered the suppression of all gambling-houses in that city, Fouché represented him in such a light to Bonaparte that he lost the honourable place of Prefect, and was sent, in disgrace, as Minister to Switzerland, a situation no Prefect's secretary would by choice accept, on account of the unsettled state of that country, and the disagreeable and difficult part a French Minister had at that time to perform there.

Besides what the farmers of the gambling-houses paid to Fouché every month, they were obliged to hire and pay 120,000 persons employed in their houses at Paris, and in the provinces, as croupiers, from half a crown to half a guinea a day; most of these 120,000 persons were also supposed to be spies for Fouché.

In 1789, Thiroux de Crosne, Lieutenant de Police, estimated that there were fifty-three houses in Paris where illegal games were played; other authorities of that time gave figures far in excess of this. *Tripots* existed in the Rue Notre Dame des Victoires, Rue des Petits Pères, Place des Petits Pères, and Rue de Cléry. No. 35 Rue Traversière, Saint Honoré, No. 18 Rue de Richelieu, and No. 10 Rue Vivienne were all well-known gaming places.

In the Palais Royal, however, thirty-one different establishments were ready to allure the votaries of fortune. At No. 33 a man named Dumoulin, who had been a lackey in the service of the Dubarry, acted as croupier; No. 50 was known as the rendezvous of Royalists; No. 113 enjoyed a bad reputation as being the cause of a great number of suicides; No. 36 was very decorously conducted, no woman being allowed to enter its doors, whilst non-alcoholic refreshments and a light beer were alone provided in order that the players should run no risk of exciting themselves.

In order to further safeguard their clients, the proprietors of No. 36 maintained a regular armed guard who effectually prevented the incursion of undesirable characters.

There existed at this period a regular gang of black-mailers, who, headed by a ruffian named Venternière, made a practice of entering gaming places and extorting money from the executive under the threat of creating such a disturbance as to cause the tables to be suppressed. The gang in question were, however, thoroughly routed in November 1793 when making a determined incursion into No. 36. They were very roughly handled, their leader being laid senseless upon the pavement.

A celebrated Parisian gamester at the time of the Revolution was Monsieur de Monville, who was a great deal in the company of the Duc d'Orléans—a Prince whose passion for play was notorious. Whilst the projected arrest of the Duc was being debated in the Convention, this gentleman was engaged in a particularly spirited gambling duel with the regicide Philippe Égalité; the players indeed were so absorbed in their game as to cause dinner to be served on the very table at which they were playing. At this moment Merlin de Douai burst into the room with the announcement of the impeachment of the Duc, who, horror-struck at such news, deplored the ingratitude of his accusers, after the many proofs of patriotism which he had given. Then turning to Monville he cried, "What do you think of such an infamy, Monville?" The latter, whilst leisurely squeezing a lemon over his sole, said in the calmest manner in the world, "It is certainly horrible. Monseigneur, but what did you expect? The rascals have got all they could out of your Highness, who is now of no more use; consequently they are going to treat you as I do this lemon." He then, in the most elegant manner in the world, threw the remains of the fruit in question into the fire-place, remarking the while, "One must never forget. Monseigneur, that a sole should be eaten quite hot."

M. de Monville was a great frequenter of the gambling-rooms over which presided the beautiful Madame de St. Amaranthe, whose tragic fate on the scaffold excited so much pity. The *tripot* over which she cast her smiles was at No. 50 in the Palais Royal, which has been mentioned before, and was the most luxurious in Paris. It was said, indeed, that it resembled nothing so much as Versailles in the days before the Revolution, and here many Royalist conspirators were wont to assemble. Denunciations of what was described as a reactionary stronghold were being constantly received by the Committee of Public Safety, and the popularity of the presiding goddess of this shrine of chance with the Royalists eventually led to her execution.

The Revolutionary authorities saw reaction in everything, even in playing-cards, and in 1792 they arrived at the conclusion that the kings were but antiquated symbols of tyranny, and attempted to substitute a card called the "pouvoir exécutif" in their place. Players using these new-fashioned cards, instead of speaking of the king of hearts or clubs, were obliged to say the "pouvoir exécutif" of hearts and so on. Citizens Dajouré and Jaume, however, improved upon this, and invented a new sort of pack in which the king became "le génie," the queen "liberty," the knave "equality," and the ace "law." Hearts, clubs, spades, and diamonds were changed into peace, war, art, and commerce. The cards in question, it may be added, made no successful appeal to gamblers, who continued to prefer the sort still in general use. They were, however, extremely prettily designed, and are now reckoned amongst the artistic curiosities produced by the Revolution.

During our war with France some French prisoners at Deal were once rather amusingly rebuked for their anti-monarchical tendencies by a private of the West Essex Militia, which regiment was then quartered at Deal. The man in question had been begged by the prisoners to procure them a pack of cards, which he did when off his duty; but before he delivered the cards, picked out the four kings. The Frenchmen, discovering the deficiency, said the pack was imperfect, having no kings in it. "Why," replied the soldier, "*if you can fight without a king, surely you can play without one*!"

The Palais Royal, called during the Revolution the Palais Égalité, soon became the most famous gambling-resort in the world—to-day it is but a pathetic shadow of its former self. Built in imitation of the Piazza San Marco at Venice by Cardinal Richelieu and bequeathed by him to Louis XIII., the palace in question was in course of time given by the Roi Soleil to his brother and thus became the property of the Orléans family. Fantastically extravagant and crippled by debts, Philippe Égalité first conceived the idea of putting the noble building raised by the great Cardinal to a commercial use, continuing to obtain a very large sum by letting out suitable parts as shops, gaming-houses, and restaurants, some of them of a rather questionable nature.

The Palais Royal, before it contained shops and gaming-tables, had been the resort of all that was most aristocratic in Paris. Walks and flower-beds abounded, whilst on the southern side was an alley of ancient chestnut trees of great antiquity, the destruction of which provoked much indignation and sorrow.

The transformation of the historic palace and grounds into a bazaar effected a great change in the habits of the Parisians, who, without distinction of rank or class, flocked to the spot which, since the stately days of Anne of Austria, had been the evening promenade of good society alone.

Louis XVI. is said, after hearing of his cousin's decision in this matter, to have remarked: "I suppose we shall now only see the Duc d'Orléans on Sundays—he has become a shop-man!"

The Prince in question, however, cared little about this as long as he was able to procure the large sums necessary for his wildly extravagant mode of living. The centre of Parisian activity, the Palais Royal was the incarnation of Paris in the eyes of all pleasure-loving Europe, the famous Galeries de Bois becoming the resort of all the profligate frivolity of a somewhat unbridled age.

The old gardens, sad and deserted to-day, have witnessed some strange scenes in their time. Here it was that one summer's day Camille Desmoulins uttered those burning words which heralded the approach of the Revolution.

It was on the Palais Royal that Philippe Égalité let his eyes linger as the tumbrel bore him through a hooting mob, past the splendid old home which he had once inhabited, to where the guillotine awaited him in the Place de la Révolution—now the Place de la Concorde. From the windows of that self-same Palais Royal, in July 1830, did the son of Égalité look hopefully yet half-fearfully expectant on another mob, yelling and triumphant, which, after storming the Louvre and sacking the Tuileries, came screeching the Marseillaise, roaring "Vive la Charte!" "Vive la République!" "Vive Lafayette!" and most portentous of all for him, "Vive Louis Philippe!" The last cry won the day; and Louis Philippe, Duke of Orleans, went forth from the Palais Royal to become the Citizen King.

Many queer characters haunted the galleries of the Palais Royal. As late as the early years of the reign of Louis Philippe there could on most days be seen there an aged individual who was pointed out as "Valois Collier." He had been the husband of the infamous Jeanne de St. Remy, "Comtesse" de la Motte, who was wont to boast (mayhap with some probability of truth) that a strain of the royal blood of the Valois ran in her veins.

On the side of the Galerie d'Orléans were the famous Galeries de Bois, the resort of all lovers of careless gaiety during the Directory, the Consulate, the First Empire, and the Restoration. In 1815 these galleries were nicknamed, owing to the extensive Muscovite patronage which they enjoyed, "Le Camp des Tartares."

The Palais Royal in its palmy days was the centre of luxury—an emporium of every alluring delight. While its brilliantly-lit piazzas were viewed with real or pretended horror by the austere, it was a very Mecca to the pleasure-seekers of the world. In England the place was often called "the Devil's Drawing-room," it being said that here a debauchee could run the whole course of his career with the greatest facility and ease.

On the first floor were cafés where his spirits could be raised to any requisite pitch; on the second, gaming-rooms where he could lose his money, and salons devoted to facile love—both, not unusually, ante-chambers to the pawnbrokers who resided above; whilst, if at the end of his tether and determined to end his troubles, he could repair to some of the shops on the ground floor, where daggers and pistols were very conveniently sold at reduced prices—every facility being thus provided for enjoying all the pleasures of life under one roof.

Besides the licensed gaming-tables there were also many forms of unsanctioned dissipation in divers subterranean chambers. A number of billiard-rooms, each containing two or three tables, provided further opportunities for passing the time. Women were everywhere, and from about midday till three o'clock in the morning, the galleries of the Palais Royal were thronged by crowds of gaily-attired nymphs ready to lend their aid in charming the dream of life. In the days of the Terror they absolutely dominated the whole place. It was an epoch when many knew that the guillotine was being made ready to receive them, and for this reason were seized with a veritable frenzy to snatch as much enjoyment as possible.

The close connection which at that time existed between illicit passion and death was well typified in the personality of one of the most popular sirens. Mademoiselle Dubois, known as "la fille Chevalier," who was a reigning favourite of the gardens. The girl in question possessed no great beauty, her chief attraction being that her father was the executioner at Dijon, who had sent numbers of people into the other world.

THE PALMY DAYS OF THE PALAIS ROYAL.
From a contemporary print.

The gaming-rooms were on the southern side of the Palais Royal. To enter them you ascended a staircase and opened the door of an ante-chamber, where several hundred hats, sticks, and great-coats, carefully ticketed, were arranged, under the charge of two or three old men, who received either one or two sous from every owner for the safe delivery of his precious deposit. No dogs were admitted into these sacred apartments, nor anything which was likely to disturb the deep attention and holy quiet which pervaded them! From this ante-chamber opened a folding-door, which led to a large, well-lighted room, in the centre of which was a table surrounded, at a moderate estimate, by two hundred and fifty or three hundred persons anxiously inspecting a game. The salons in the various establishments opened one into another, and in some there were as many as six rooms which contained tables.

At one time a curious condition was imposed upon the proprietors of the gaming-tables. They were obliged to furnish every one who entered their rooms with as much table-beer as they chose to call for. Waiters were therefore perpetually running backwards and forwards with overflowing tumblers of this refreshing beverage—six or seven crowded on a tray.

On the restoration of the Bourbons, public play in Paris continued to flourish with unabated vigour.

There were in 1818:

7	Tables of	Trente-et-un.
9	"	Roulette.
1	"	Passe-dix.
1	"	Craps.
1	"	Hazard.
1	"	Biribi.
—		
20		

These twenty tables were divided into nine houses, four of which were situated in the Palais Royal.

To serve the seven tables of trente-et-un there were:

				Francs.
28	Dealers, at	550	francs a month, making	15,400
28	Croupiers, at	380	"	10,640
42	Assistants, at	200	"	8,400

For the nine roulette tables and one passe-dix:

80	Dealers, at	275	francs a month	22,000
60	Assistants, at	150	"	9,000

"

For the service of the craps, biribi, and hazard:

12	Dealers, at	300	francs a month	3,600
12	Inspectors, at	120	" "	1,440
10	Aids, at	100	" "	1,000
6	Chefs de Partie at the principal houses, at	700	francs a month	4,200
3	Chefs de Partie for the Roulettes, at	500	francs a month	1,500
20	Secret Inspectors, at	200	francs a month	4,000
1	Inspector-General at			1,000
130	Waiters, at	75	francs a month	9,750
	Cards every month cost			1,500
	Beer and refreshments			3,000
	Lights			5,500
	The refreshments for the grand saloon, including two dinners every week, cost			12,000
				————
	The total expenses every month thus amounted to			113,930

The amount produced by the gaming-houses of Paris in 1823 was given as follows:—

	Francs.	Francs.
Rough Revenue		15,000,000
Expenses: upkeep of gaming-houses, pay of croupiers and the like	1,000,000	
Annual tax to Government	5,000,000	
Fifteen per cent for the poor	500,000	
		6,500,000
Total profits of proprietors		8,500,000

The scale of payment received by the croupiers and employés would seem to have somewhat closely approximated to that in vogue at Monte Carlo to-day. Every establishment employed the services of a functionary called *l'homme de force*, whose duties seem to have exactly corresponded with those of the less picturesquely named "chucker-out" of to-day.

The lowest stake permitted at trente-et-quarante was five francs—in certain rooms gold only was allowed—a lower limit of two francs being imposed at roulette. In this respect, matters were much the same as at German gaming-tables, which began to be put an end to after the war of 1866. The regulation now prevailing at Monte Carlo, which prescribes twenty francs at trente-et-quarante and five francs at roulette, is a very salutary one, preventing as it does a certain class of player from risking small sums which he can ill afford to lose. During the existence of the Paris gaming-tables there was at times a good deal of agitation in favour of raising the limit at roulette, the lowness of which was said to be responsible for widespread ruin amongst the working-classes. Occasionally, however, fortune was kind towards some of her humble worshippers. A cook employed at a Paris restaurant happened one day to stroll into the gaming-rooms established at No. 113 in the Palais Royal. He had no money, so amused himself looking at the people and eating oranges, a number of which he had brought with him. The rooms were hot, and a thirsty player offered to give the man six sous for one of the oranges, which the cook accepted. He then proceeded to throw the six sous on the biribi table, where he won six francs, which were increased to two hundred at roulette. At trente-et-quarante he was even more lucky, and after playing with the greatest success for some time found himself with a profit of some five hundred thousand francs. His master, the restaurant-keeper, who was a wise man, with some difficulty persuaded him to invest these large winnings in sound securities, whilst pointing out the folly of any further gambling. The cook never played again, and ended his days in affluence. He is said to have been the only man of this class who ever made a fortune at the Parisian gambling-tables.

Numbers of people who frequented the gaming-houses of the Palais Royal came there when they were already ruined, and, losing the small sums which still remained to them, afterwards created disturbance and scandal.

A GAMING TABLE IN THE PALAIS ROYAL.

A case of this sort which attracted a good deal of attention was that of an English half-pay colonel, who, having lost all his money at one of the Palais Royal Hells, determined to kill himself and every one in the place besides. With this object in view he smuggled into the place a canister full of explosive powder, which he put under the table and furtively set alight. Though players and croupiers were very unpleasantly astonished at the result, no one was hurt except the Colonel, who was very roughly handled and was thrown into prison, from which he was after a time sent over to England as a madman.

Amongst the games played were two which are now quite forgotten; these were passe-dix and craps.

Passe-dix is said to be the most ancient of all games of chance. According to tradition it was at this game that the soldiers played for the garments of Christ after the crucifixion.

There is one banker and any amount of players, each one of whom holds the box in turn. When a point under ten is thrown all the players lose their stake. If, however, a point above ten is thrown the banker pays double on all stakes. At private play every player banks in his turn, but in the Palais Royal the bank was, of course, held for the proprietors of the gaming-rooms.

The game of creps or craps mentioned in the list of tolerated games is now obsolete as a medium for any serious gambling in Europe. Curiously enough, however, it still survives in another continent, being even at the present day a favourite game in mining camps in Alaska, where it is well known in the gaming-saloons which are almost inevitable accompaniments of such settlements. The game would appear to consist of a board, something like an enlarged and glorified backgammon board, on which are emblazoned an anchor and five other emblems. The banker, when the money has been staked on these emblems, shakes out six dice, each of which bears on its facets devices corresponding with the designs on the board, the players being paid in proportion to the number of dice showing the figure they have selected. The boards used in Alaska are said to have been copied from similar ones brought by French emigrants to California during the famous gold fever in the 'forties. In some cases the identical boards exported from France are said to be still in use.

The bankers at craps claim that the odds are perfectly even as between the bank and the players, a statement which, however, would not resist the test of serious mathematical investigation.

The farmer-general of all the metropolitan houses of play at this time was Monsieur Benazet, Colonel of the Garde Nationale of Neuilly. M. Benazet, after the Revolution of 1830, was decorated by Louis Philippe with the cross of the Légion d'honneur, on account of his loyalty. Besides the officials who have been enumerated, there was a horde of attached spies, providers, pickers-up, and hangers-on, paid for doing the "dirty work" of the houses, both in and out of doors. The name, rank in life, presumed fortune, habitation, and habits of each gaming-house guest were registered; and, if they became regular customers, a sobriquet, or nickname, was given to each. By this means the constant players were, in a certain degree, known to the police. The salaried satellites of the *maisons de jeu*, when they entered upon their office, were peremptorily told that "it was their duty to regard every man who played at the tables as an enemy."

Three of the gaming-houses catered almost entirely for players of means, Frascati's and the Salon des Étrangers being well-known to all the gamblers of Europe. No. 154 in the Palais Royal, it should be mentioned, was also a favourite resort of high gamblers during the occupation of Paris by the Allies. Marshal Blücher lost very large sums there.

This rough old soldier was a most irascible player, and when he lost (which was more often than not) he would rap out volleys of German oaths whilst glaring at the croupiers. He usually played very high, and would grumble at the limit of 10,000 francs imposed as a maximum; so great was the sensation that he created, that any table at which he might be playing was always uncomfortably crowded.

In 1814 the stakes on the tables of the French gaming-houses consisted of the coins of all nations, it being not uncommon to see French napoléons and louis d'or, English guineas and crowns, Dutch ducats, Spanish doubloons, Russian roubles, as well as the various moneys of Prussia, Italy, and Germany, on the tables at the same moment. Notes were somewhat rare, though occasionally some daring gamester would stake a French one for a large amount.

The Salon and Frascati's were situated close together at that extremity of the Rue Richelieu which opens into the Boulevards; they both presented a highly aristocratic exterior, and both professed to be aristocratically exclusive and to admit no person without a suitable and satisfactory introduction. From this rule, however, Frascati's in its latter days departed; and the Cerberus who guarded the portals of that pandemonium very, very seldom refused admittance to any one whose exterior afforded evidence that he possessed any material wherewithal to feed (it were too much to say, satisfy) the devouring appetites of the bank.

Frascati's opened rather later than the other gaming-houses, its portals being only thrown open at one in the afternoon.

The Salon des Étrangers, also a favourite resort of Marshal Blücher, was frequented chiefly by that class who could afford to frequent gaming-houses, the ambassadors of foreign potentates frequently presiding at its sumptuous and magnificent entertainments.

The opening of these houses took place with nearly as great regularity as that of any bureau in Paris.

A well-known figure at the Salon was an old gentleman whose existence was bound up with that of this gaming-house. He had been completely ruined by play, and the proprietors of the Salon allowed him a pension to support him in his miserable senility—just sufficient to supply him with a wretched lodging, bread, and a change of raiment once in every three or four years! In addition to this he was allowed a supper (which was his dinner) at the gaming-house. Thither, at about eleven o'clock at night, he went. Till supper-time (two) he amused himself in watching the games and calculating the various chances, although he was destitute of the means of playing a single coup. At four he returned to his lodging, retired to bed, and lay till between nine and ten on the following night. A cup of coffee was then brought to him; and, having dressed himself, at the usual hour he again proceeded to the Salon. This had been his round of life for several years; and during all that time (except on a few mornings about midsummer) he had not beheld the sun!

Another constant frequenter of the Salon des Étrangers during the occupation of Paris by the Allies in 1814 was a Mr. Fox, a popular Secretary of the British Embassy, who was notorious for his easy-going disposition. Though usually most unfortunate at play, he once had an extraordinary run of luck, when having taken up the dice-box, he threw eleven successful throws, broke the bank, and took home some sixty thousand francs as winnings. All of this he spent in buying presents for ladies, which he declared was the only way to prevent the rascals at the Salon from getting back their money.

At the same gambling-place Lord Thanet lost enormous sums, whilst a young Irishman, Mr. Gough by name, was totally ruined there, and in consequence blew out his brains.

On the green cloth of the Salon des Étrangers also melted away the fortune of Sir Francis Vincent, who, having dissipated the whole of a fine property at play, entirely disappeared from the gay world. Frascati's—a more amusing resort—was in its palmy days regularly haunted by an aged gentleman well dowered with means, who was daily carried by his servant to the rouge-et-noir table. There he sat playing from three o'clock until five, at which hour, precisely, the servant returned and carried him (for he had entirely lost the use of his legs) back to his carriage. He was a man of large fortune, and the stakes he played were not considerable; yet he was elated by every lucky coup, and at every reverse he gnashed his teeth and struck the table in rage. No sooner, however, had the moment for his departure arrived, than he regained his equanimity, utterly regardless as to whether he had been a winner, or a loser, by the proceedings. "I have outlived all modes of excitement," said he, "save that of gaming: it is that that takes the fastest hold on the mind and retains it the longest; my blood, but for this occasional agitation, would stagnate in my veins—I should die."

Ten fêtes were given during the year at Frascati's, the sole gaming-place to which, after 1818, women were allowed admittance.

The disinclination of the Parisian authorities to throw open the public gaming-rooms to women was founded upon very substantial grounds, for at the beginning of the nineteenth century, great scandals had arisen owing to ladies becoming desperate after unsuccessful play. In 1804, for instance, a young and beautiful Hanoverian Countess, who had lost 50,000 livres, planned and executed the robbery of a fine coronet of emeralds, which she contrived to purloin at a ball given by the owner, Madame Demidoff. The youth, beauty, and high rank of the thief caused a great agitation in favour of her being pardoned, but Napoleon, who was never moved by mere sentimental considerations, refused to annul the sentence which had been passed upon her.

When they take to gambling, Frenchwomen become passionate devotees of play, as may be verified at any casino in France when baccarat and petits chevaux are in full swing. Very often they become so fascinated by the spirit of speculation that they can think of nothing else. An instance of this was the lady who, confessing to her priest, owned she was desperately fond of gambling.

The confessor, after pointing out the evils of such a passion, advanced several arguments against play, amongst which a principal one was the great loss of time which it must inevitably occasion.

"Ah," said the lady, "that's just what vexes me—so much time lost in shuffling the cards!"

Besides the licensed gaming-houses there were at this time a number of "maisons de bouillotte," which, though unlicensed, were more or less under the surveillance of the police. Here a good deal of play went on practically unchecked, an added attraction being the female society of no very rigorous morality which frequented such resorts. The favourite game played in these bouillottes was not the "bouillotte" from which they took their name, but écarté, in some ways a modification of the old French game of "la triomphe." Écarté in its present form would seem to have been first played in the early part of the nineteenth century in Paris, whence it made its way to England about 1820.

Whilst such places, together with Frascati's and the Salon des Étrangers, were the resort of the fashionable world, humbler gamblers betook themselves to half a dozen houses which were frequented by all classes of the population, the most popular being Nos. 9, 129, and 113 in the Palais Royal. Play began at twelve in the morning, except on Sundays and holidays, when one was the hour fixed; on certain Saints' Days and at Christmas all the gambling houses were compelled by law to close at midnight, except the Salon des Étrangers and No. 9 in the Palais Royal, two of those curious exceptions for which the authorities in France have always had (and still have) a liking, being made in their favour.

On January 21, the day on which the unfortunate Louis XVI. had been guillotined, a special regulation forbade any play at all. In 1819, however, no notice was taken of this, which led to a great outcry; and the following year the gambling-houses did shut their doors on the day in question, but the keepers demanded a rebate on the sum paid to the Government as compensation for their loss of profits.

The evil days of the Palais Royal as a pleasure-resort began about the time of the Revolution of 1830, when it became evident that a determined effort was going to be made to alter the character of the place entirely. In 1831, stringent measures were adopted with regard to the class of persons allowed to frequent the galleries, the amusements permitted being exposed to a rigorous censorship, whilst every effort was made to efface the traditions of light-hearted frivolity and licence which had hung about the old place since the days of the Revolution.

Numbers of the tradesmen who owned shops in the Palais Royal had called for these measures. They were imbued with the somewhat pharisaical respectability which is so often the appanage of their class, and entertained the totally fallacious idea that the purification of the gardens would cause a greater number of visitors from abroad to frequent and make purchases at their shops. It soon became evident that the fate of the gaming-tables was sealed, a great outcry being raised against the toleration of what was characterised as a public scandal, and was denounced as such in the Press. English opinion particularly was said to be bitterly hostile to the tables, and the deluded tradesmen of Paris entertained an idea that the doubtful pleasures of the Palais Royal prevented much foreign money from pouring into their pockets.

Finally in 1836, chiefly owing to the efforts of a Mr. Delessert, it was decided that the gaming-houses of Paris should be closed two years from that date, and on the 1st of January 1838 the Palais Royal ceased to offer any attractions appealing to the gambler.

At the time when the agitation for the suppression of public gaming in Paris was going on, a good deal of abuse was heaped upon the proprietors of the tables, who were denounced as vampires sucking the blood of the poor. One of them, M. Borsant by name, was exempted from censure, being noted for many favourable traits not often to be met with in those drawing their revenue from gaming. This gentleman once actually restored 17,000 francs lost by a young man to his astonished parents. The actual date of the cessation of public play in Paris was Sunday, December 31, 1837. So numerous had the visitors been during the last few weeks preceding this date, that an additional police force had been found necessary for the maintenance of order. In consequence of the excitement, the manufacturers and tradesmen of Paris had come to a general agreement not to pay their workmen's wages before twelve o'clock on Sunday night, lest the money might be carried to swell the last day's receipts of the great joint-stock company to which all the Parisian gaming-houses belonged.

On the last evening, which was a Sunday, the rooms at Frascati's were so thronged that there was scarcely a possibility of stirring in them. The tables were overladen with money. At ten o'clock such was the crowd inside that it was found necessary to shut the street doors.

Placards stuck up in all the rooms warned the gamblers that the play would not be suffered to extend a single minute beyond midnight, which was the hour specified by the law. The Salon or Cercle des Étrangers, still the most fashionable of the gambling-houses, which usually was opened only at eleven at night and closed at three or four in the morning, opened on Sunday evening at nine o'clock, a notification to such effect having been sent round to the habitual frequenters of the place. On Saturday and Sunday all the gambling-houses of Paris, especially No. 154 of the Palais Royal and Frascati's, were immensely crowded. Several dramatic incidents occurred. A workman destroyed himself on quitting No. 113, and two young men who had lost large sums disappeared entirely.

In accordance with the edict previously announced, the game ceased exactly at midnight. The gambling during the last days of the tables had been very high, and crowds flocked to witness the end. Disturbances were anticipated, and the municipal guards were in consequence posted in considerable force about the various rooms. At Frascati's an immense crowd of visitors assembled, but they dispersed peaceably, after encountering the shouts and hisses of the mob that had collected in the Rue de Richelieu outside to witness their final exit from that historic haunt of pleasure. A dramatic incident occurred, one unhappy wretch shooting himself as the doors closed for ever. He had lost heavily, and was in despair at the prospect of being unable to retrieve his losses.

In 1838 a case came on for trial before the Court of Assizes, Paris, which excited a good deal of interest. The prisoner, a clerk to a merchant, had gambled on several occasions, and had lost at Frascati's and the gaming-houses licensed by Government upwards of 100,000 francs, the property of his employer. In the course of the trial, Benazet, the lessee of these establishments, stated that in the course of a year there was thrown on the tables of the gaming-houses comprised in his licence 800,000,000 francs (£32,000,000): that, independently of the annual sum paid to Government for the licence (which was 6,000,000 francs or £240,000), the clear profit on the tables during the last year of their life, 1837, was no less a sum than 1,900,000 francs (£76,000), but that three-fourths of this sum was paid over to the city of Paris; the other fourth (£19,000) was his proportion of the gain. M. Benazet eventually declared that he would refund his part of the sum lost by the prosecutor's clerk if the city of Paris would equally pay back the three-fourths of it which had passed to its credit. The average number of gamblers admitted to those houses had been three thousand a day, another thousand having been denied entrance.

From the moment that the tables were suppressed, the prosperity of the shops in the former Palace of Cardinal Mazarin began to wane. As the years rolled on, visitors became fewer and fewer, till the place assumed the forlorn aspect which it wears to-day, when even the tourist scarcely deigns to visit its deserted galleries.

At the time of the Revolution there had been a number of first-class restaurants in the Palais Royal. The café kept by Méot, for instance, enjoyed a great reputation for its cellar. Here could be procured twenty-two sorts of red wine, twenty-seven of white, and sixteen different kinds of liqueurs, most of which had come from the cellars of the *noblesse.* Méot's was essentially a Royalist restaurant, and contained little rooms where aristocratic clients could dine in luxurious privacy.

Beauvilliers, once cook to the Prince de Condé, also kept a restaurant much frequented by adherents of the old régime, and here Rivarol Champcenetz and others used, while dining, to compose articles for the famous Royalist sheet—*Les Actes des Apôtres.*

A well-situated restaurant was Véry's, which paid no less than 196,275 livres a year as rent for No. 83. Véry's was founded in 1790: here it was that Danton gave dinners to his friends, and pointed out to them "that their turn had come to taste the delights of life; and enjoy the sumptuous mansions, exquisite dishes, rare fabrics, and beautiful women which were the legitimate spoils of the victors." This restaurant was much frequented by foreigners, with whom it had a great reputation; every Englishman of means who visited Paris made a point of dining there once or twice.

At No. 73 was the restaurant Venua, where the Girondins used to dine at ten francs a head. Robespierre also used to frequent its gaily-decorated saloons, and men alive in the middle of the last century well remembered the sinister profile and sky-blue coat of the "sea-green incorruptible" reflected in the mirrors which adorned this café.

A badly-lit, ill-appointed restaurant was that kept by Fevrier; nevertheless, its democratic lack of luxury attracted austere patriots.

Lepelletier de St. Fargeau, dining here on the 20th of January 1793, at five o'clock in the afternoon, was accosted by a young man who stabbed him to death as one who had voted for the execution of Louis XVI.

VERY'S IN 1825.

As Paris gradually recovered from the fever of the Revolution, many other first-class restaurants were established in the Palais Royal, several of which survived up to our own time.

All of these have now long disappeared from the spot which was once a shrine for the gastronomers of Europe. To-day the very name of Véfour is forgotten. Les Trois Frères Provençaux, the Café Corazza, and other resorts, once famous for their cuisine, have long ceased to make any appeal to the modern gourmet, whilst even the less pretentious cafés, which, in the early days of the third Republic, offered the passing traveller a sumptuous dinner for two or three francs, have almost, without exception, closed their doors.

From time to time schemes have been mooted which were to galvanise the Palais Royal into some semblance of life; the latest of these is a plan to pierce a street, or rather a drive, right through it, by which means the place would become a thoroughfare and regain its lost vitality.

Sad and mournful as the old gardens are to-day, it is not altogether without the bounds of possibility that they will in the future once again become the resort of the wealthy pleasure-seekers of the world.

The fine shops which formerly abounded beneath the colonnades are memories of the past, all the great shopkeepers having migrated from what has become a little city of the dead. A number of the shopkeepers in the Palais Royal lived to regret bitterly the rigorous measures for which they had once so vehemently called, and there is no doubt that the unfortunate commercial results which followed, once it had ceased to be a pleasure-resort, made a deep and lasting impression upon the mind of the Parisian tradesman, who to-day thoroughly realises that visitors to Paris are attracted by some amusement of a speculative kind.

The Parisian shop-keeper would probably welcome the revival of public gaming-tables for he is a warm supporter of French racing, where the betting is legalised and carried on by the State, well knowing the commercial benefits which indirectly accrue to the city of Paris.

During the Second Empire, Doctor Louis Véron, ex-dealer in quack medicines, ex-manager of the Grand Opéra, and ex-proprietor of the *Constitutionnel* newspaper, offered an enormous royalty to Government for the privilege of establishing a gambling-house in Paris. The Emperor Napoleon III., however, declined to consider the proposal.

At the present day, though no public tables exist, there are ample facilities for play in Paris, and baccarat flourishes in many a Club to which admission is not difficult. The great evil of the gaming-houses of the Palais Royal was that they especially appealed to a class which could not afford to lose their hard-earned money—the poor being lured to ruin. Such a state of affairs is non-existent in modern Paris, where gambling, as far as possible, is limited to those able to afford to indulge in it.

A Frenchman cares little for Clubs without play, and many a *Cercle* draws its principal support from the cagnotte at baccarat; this amounts to about ten per cent on the sum put into the bank, which goes to the highest bidder up to five hundred louis, when, if there are two or three competitors, they draw lots for it. The percentage in question, however, varies as the bank increases, and is not levied after a certain amount of renewals.

In former years the management of some of these gambling-clubs was somewhat lax, and occasionally undesirable characters entered the rooms and passed themselves off as members. At a certain well-known resort, which formerly flourished not far from the Place de l'Opéra, high gambling was the order of the day just before dinner. One fine afternoon there was as usual somewhat spirited bidding for the bank, which was eventually secured for some four hundred louis by a very distinguished-looking man whose face was new to the usual frequenters of the place. The individual in question, taking the banker's seat, the cards having been shuffled and cut, produced no money but merely told the croupier opposite, "Il y a quatre cents louis en banque," upon which that official, with all the dignity of his race, tapped a piece of red cardboard and repeated, "Quatre cents louis à la carte."

The stakes were made and the cards dealt—neuf on the right, huit on the left—both sides won. "Caissier," cried the banker to the official who exchanged money for counters and vice versa at the desk, "donnez dix mille francs." The result of this was, however, unsatisfactory, for the caissier most politely explained that he had no authority to advance money to members, and certainly not to members whom he did not know. "Well," said the banker, "if that is the case I must go and get my pocket-book from my coat; it will be the matter of an instant." This optimistic forecast, however, was hardly justified by subsequent events, for the banker never returned, and eventually the expectant and anxious players became so enraged that the management of the Club thought it best to pay them their winnings. The banker, it afterwards transpired, had been a notorious sharper.

It was at a Club of the same sort, where the membership was rather mixed, that a certain English nobleman, finding that his pocket-book, containing several thousand francs, had been taken out of his coat hanging in the hall, did not hesitate to tell the committee that it must have been purloined either by the waiters or the members, and received the reply, "We can answer for the *waiters*!"

Not very far from Paris, at the Casino of Enghein, much baccarat is played, which has rendered the resort in question very popular, so much so indeed that the criminals known as "apaches" have begun to haunt the road from Paris. Not very long ago a band of these pests contrived to stop a motor, one of them lying down in the road in front of it, and the rest attempting to rob the occupants when the car was pulled up. The miscreants were on the point of wrenching a valuable pearl necklace from a lady's neck when another car arrived and put the assailants to flight.

About a couple of years ago roulette was played—practically without let or hindrance—at St. Germain. No wheel, however, was employed, its place being supplied by a dial on which by an ingenious device the winning number and colour appeared on a croupier firing a sort of rifle. The result was the same as at ordinary roulette, and just as in the old-fashioned form of the game most people lost their money. This resort, it should be added, was eventually closed by the authorities, who were aroused by the great increase of gaming in Paris owing to the introduction of baccarat with one tableau. This will be dealt with at the end of the next chapter.

IX

Public gaming in Germany—Aix-la-Chapelle—An Italian gambler—The King of Prussia's generosity—Baden-Baden—M. de la Charme—A dishonest croupier—Wiesbaden—An eccentric Countess—Closing of the tables in 1873—Last scenes—Arrival of M. Blanc at Homburg—His attempt to defeat his own tables—Anecdotes of Garcia—His miserable end—A Spanish gambler at Ems—Roulette at Geneva and in Heligoland—Gambling at Ostend—Baccarat at French watering-places—"La Faucheuse" forbidden in France.

In former times a great deal of public gaming was carried on at Aix-la-Chapelle, where the alluring rattle of the dice-box was to be heard from morning till night. Here there were fixed hours for play, one bank opening as another shut—biribi, hazard, faro, and vingt-et-un being the favourite games. The chief banker paid a thousand louis per annum for his licence during the season; and it was said that his profit in general exceeded four thousand, and sometimes double that sum. There were two gaming-houses a mile or two from the town, and each gambling-house, each room, nay, each part of a room, had its fashionable hours. From the commencement of play to the conclusion (that is, from ten in the morning to two or three the next morning), only two hours were allotted for meals.

In 1792 a little Italian created a considerable sensation at this gaming-resort, to which he had come as an adventurer, with a few louis d'or in his pocket, determined to try the favour of fortune. His first attempt was at hazard, where he played crown stakes, which, as fortune smiled on him, were increased to half a guinea, guinea, and so on to bank-notes. In the space of twenty-four hours he had stripped the bank of upwards of four thousand pounds; and the next morning, resuming his operations, broke the bank entirely, his winnings amounting to more than nine thousand pounds. One would have imagined that a poor needy adventurer, who most probably had never seen a twentieth part of such a sum before, would at once have pocketed his winnings and returned (in his own mind a prince) to his native country. Content, however, was a stranger to his mind, and the accession of one sum only brought with it anxiety for a greater. He continued to be successful; and for several days the bankers ceased to play, so completely had he reduced them to their last stake. When a fresh supply of cash did at last arrive the little adventurer recommenced operations—for a few hours with his usual success. The luck, however, at last changed, and from being the possessor of ten thousand pounds he left the bank reduced to his very last louis. He next proceeded to negotiate a loan of about thirty pounds, and returned to the tables, much to the discomfort of the bankers, who, from the success that attended his play, had conceived no small dread of him. His usual run of good luck attended him, and from being master of only thirty pounds, he left the table with more than ten thousand. He remembered a resolution he had formed in his fit of poverty, went to an inn, ordered a carriage, and packed up his baggage. In the interim, however, one of the directors of the bank, learning his intention, set off to interview him, resolved to use all the rhetoric he was master of to persuade him to relinquish his design. His arguments were too specious not to destroy the resolution of the poor Italian, whose fortitude vanished in a moment, and instead of making for his native country he returned to the gaming-table, where, in a very few hours, he was stripped of every *soldo* he had in the world, and left to reflect on the diversity of fortune which he had known in the space of so short a time. The moment he got back to his lodgings he sold the greater part of his clothes, and by this means raised a few louis which he took to his old haunts, where he now cut a sorry figure.

ROULETTE IN THE EIGHTEENTH CENTURY.

A considerable sensation was once caused at the principal faro-table at Aix-la-Chapelle by the success of a plainly-dressed stranger, who, after playing in modest stakes for some time, suddenly challenged the bank for the whole of its capital, carelessly tossing his pocket-book to the banker, that the latter might not question his ability to pay in case he lost. The banker, surprised at the boldness of the adventurer, and no less so at his ordinary appearance, at first hesitated to accept the challenge; but on opening the book and seeing bills to a prodigious amount, and on the stranger sternly and repeatedly insisting on his complying with the laws of the game, with much reluctance he shuffled the cards in preparation for the great event. Excitement ran high, and all eyes were soon attentively riveted upon the trembling hands of the affrighted banker, who, while the gambler sat unruffled and unconcerned, turned up the card which decided his own ruin and the other's success.

The bank was broken, and the triumphant stranger, with perfect coolness and serenity of features, turned to a person who stood at his elbow, to whom he gave orders to take charge of the money. "Heavens," exclaimed an infirm old officer in the Austrian service, who had sat next the winner at the table, "if I had the twentieth part of your success this night I should be the happiest man in the universe." "If thou wouldst be this happy man," replied the stranger briskly, "then thou shalt have it"; and, without waiting for a reply, disappeared from the room. Some little time afterwards the entrance of a servant astonished the company with the extraordinary generosity of the stranger as with his peculiar good fortune, by presenting the Austrian officer with the twentieth part of the faro bank. "Take this, sir," said the servant, "my master requires no answer"; and he suddenly left him without exchanging another word.

The next morning all Aix-la-Chapelle was agog with the news that the lucky and generous stranger was no less a personage than the King of Prussia.

In more recent times Aix-la-Chapelle appeared only destined to end its gambling days as a trap for incautious travellers, many of whom, in consequence, never saw the Rhine, and returned to England with very misty ideas about Germany.

About 1840 several other German pleasure-resorts began to include gambling amongst the attractions offered to visitors. After the closing of the Parisian gaming-houses the proprietors, who found the business much too profitable to be tamely resigned, turned their gaze beyond the Rhine, where a fair field for their exertions in the pursuit of a livelihood presented itself. After many weary negotiations with the several governments, a syndicate of bankers, with M. Chabert at their head, simultaneously opened their establishments at Baden-Baden, Wiesbaden, and Ems. It was a very hard contest between the Regents and the Frenchmen before the terms were finally settled, and the latter expended much money and many promises in getting a footing. But they eventually succeeded, and a few years saw their efforts richly rewarded. As they had a monopoly, they could do pretty much as they pleased, and made very stringent and profitable regulations relative to the *refait* and other methods of gaining a pull. On the retirement of M. Chabert with an immense fortune, the company was dissolved, and M. Benazet became ostensibly sole proprietor of the rooms at Baden-Baden. The terms to which he had to subscribe were sufficient to frighten any one less enterprising than the general of an army of croupiers; he was compelled to expend 150,000 florins in decorating the rooms and embellishing the walks round the town; and an annual sum of 50,000 florins was furthermore demanded for permission to keep the establishment open for six months in the year.

At Baden-Baden a well-known figure for many years was the old ex-Elector of Hesse, who made his money by selling his soldiers to England at so much a head, like cattle, during the American War. The Prince in question was easily to be recognised by the gold-headed and coroneted rake he always had in his hand. A constant player, he was a most profitable customer to the bank. Eventually, however, the superior attractions of Homburg led him away. The Revolution of 1848 frightened or angered him to death.

At Baden the bank at roulette had two zeroes, an enormous advantage, which rendered the certainty of success in the long run, which the bank must of course possess, almost ridiculously easy. Nauheim, on the other hand, was modestly content to claim only a quarter of the *refait* at trente-et-quarante, a good deal less than that taken by the present Monte Carlo tables. The keen competition of its rivals, Wiesbaden and Homburg, was the cause of this generosity.

In the late 'sixties a gaming hero, M. Edgar de la Charme, created a great sensation at Baden, where, for a number of days together, he never left the gaming-room without carrying off a profit which usually did not fall far short of a thousand pounds in English money.

At the end of several days of almost unparalleled good fortune, M. de la Charme, reflecting that there must be an end even to the greatest run of luck, packed his portmanteau, paid his bill, and strolled down to the railway station, accompanied by some of his friends. There, however, he found the wicket closed, there being still three-quarter's of an hour before the departure of the train. "Well," he exclaimed, "I will go and play my parting game," and, taking a carriage, drove back to the Kursaal, though his friends made every effort to prevent him. Arrived at the Casino, he sat down at the trente-et-quarante, where in twenty minutes he broke the bank again. He then left, but, while getting into his cab, caught sight of the inspector of the tables walking to and fro under the arcades, and said to him in a tone of exquisite politeness, "I could not think of going away without leaving you my P.P.C."

The society at Baden was said to be as mixed as that frequenting the Paris boulevards. There was indeed a good deal of Parisian Bohemianism about this charming spot, which, since the closing of the tables, has been forced to rely upon its proximity to the Black Forest and other natural attractions—poor substitutes to the gambler for the whirl of the roulette wheel and the chanting of the croupier at trente-et-quarante.

The rooms which re-echoed to these exciting, if none too reputable sounds, to-day seem somehow to present a rather sad and almost wistful appearance. Surely, "if aught inanimate e'er grieves," the Kurhaus must sigh for the vanished days of the Second Empire, and for the gay, careless folk who thronged its halls, now so decorous and staid.

Old gamblers used to say that the croupiers at Baden were recruited from the same families who had held the rake in the gambling-rooms of the Palais Royal. Certain veterans were even pointed out as being survivors of the great days of Frascati's and the Salon.

Baden made no pretence to any particular exclusiveness. Here all men and women were equal, people sitting down cheek by jowl with any one at trente-et-quarante or roulette, a practice not much in favour at aristocratic Ems, where the fashionable lounger was more given to tossing down his stake carelessly as he or she strolled through the rooms.

Though the croupiers at Baden-Baden were generally above suspicion, the bank was swindled by its employés on more than one occasion. A notable instance was that of an official who was discovered to have carried on a system of plunder for a long time with security. He used to slip a louis d'or into his snuff-box whenever it came to his turn to preside over the money department; he was found out by another employé asking him casually for a pinch of snuff, and seeing the money gleam in the gaslight.

On the whole the croupiers at Baden were admirable, sometimes preserving their self-control under the most trying circumstances. On one occasion when a young Englishman, of high repute and bearing an honourable name, vented his rage at losing by breaking a rake over the head of the croupier, the latter merely turned round and beckoned to the attendant gendarme to remove his assailant and the pieces of the rake, and then went on with his parrot-like "*rouge gagne, couleur perd.*"

The croupiers in general seemed to unite the stoicism of the American Indian with the politeness of the Frenchman of the *ancien régime.* Impassive under all circumstances they seemed to fear neither God nor man; for when a shock of the earthquake of 1847 was felt at Wiesbaden, though all the company fled in terror, they remained grimly at their posts, preferring to go down to their patron saints with their rouleaux, as an evidence of their fidelity to their employer. It is not unlikely that they regarded the earthquake as a preconcerted scheme to rob the bank!

The public buildings of Wiesbaden were charming, especially the Kursaal, with its open "Platz," its colonnades and magnificent ball-room, its "salons de jeu," reading-rooms, restaurant, and charming gardens behind. Here were lakes, fountains, running streams, which made it as pretty a place as any of its kind on the banks of the Rhine.

Towards the last days of the gambling at Wiesbaden the majority of the players belonged to the middle and lower middle classes, leavened by a very few celebrities and persons of genuine distinction. The general run of visitors, indeed, was by no means remarkable for birth, wealth, or respectability, and it used at that time to be said that all the aged, broken-down courtesans of Paris, Vienna, and Berlin had agreed to make Wiesbaden their autumn rendezvous.

One of the well-known eccentric notabilities of Wiesbaden at that time was a certain Countess—an aged patrician of immense fortune, whose very existence seemed bound up with that of the tables. She used daily to be wheeled to her place in the "temple of chance," where she usually played for eight or nine hours with wonderful spirit and perseverance. A suite of eight domestics were in attendance upon her, and when she won, which was not often, she invariably presented each member of her retinue with—twopence! This was done, she would naively declare, "not from a feeling of generosity, but in order to propitiate Fortune." On the other hand, when she lost, none of them, save the man who wheeled her home and who received a donation of six kreuzers, got anything at all but hard words. Unlike her contemporary, a once lovely Russian Ambassadress, she did not curse the croupiers loudly for her bad luck, but, being very far advanced in years and of a tender disposition, would shed tears over her misfortunes, resting her chin on the edge of the table. This old lady was very intimate with one or two antediluvian diplomatists and warriors, whom she used to entertain with constant lamentations over her fatal passion for play, interspersed with bits of moss-grown scandal, disinterred from the social ruins of a bygone age. Radetzky, Paul Eszterhazy, Wrangel, and Blücher had been friends of her youth; and, to judge from her appearance, no one would have been surprised to hear that she had attended the Jeu du Roi in the galleries of Versailles, or played whist with Maria Theresa.

Wiesbaden boasted a financier from Amsterdam, who usually played on credit—that is to say, he pocketed his winnings, but, if he lost, borrowed money of the banker, squaring his account, which was generally a heavy one, at the end of the week. Another well-known character was an English baronet, who always brought a lozenge-box with him. When this was filled with gold he would leave the rooms. He seldom had to remain long, for he possessed his own luck, and that of some one else into the bargain.

Wiesbaden, like the other German gaming-places, was made virtuous by compulsion rather than choice. When Nassau was annexed by the astute Bismarck, the law which abolished legal gambling affected this place as it did Homburg, Ems, and other Spas. It should, however, be added that its provisions showed a scrupulous regard for vested interests.

As the fateful 1st of January 1873—the day on which all public gaming throughout the German Empire was to cease—approached, there was considerable excitement, not only amongst the usual frequenters of the tables, but also amongst the general population of the place, who fully realised the financial benefits which had accrued to them through roulette and trente-et-quarante, the impending prohibition of which they deplored.

At midnight on the 31st December 1872, after a hundred years of existence, the Kursaal clock at Wiesbaden sounded the close of play. There was considerable disorder in the rooms on the last night, the place being converted into a bear-garden. During the last week the rooms got so enormously thronged that the administration found it necessary to admit only by tickets. 1872 was a splendid financial year, for, after paying all the enormous expenses (5000 florins a day), including the yearly tax of 200,000 florins to the Prussian Government, the shareholders received interest on their capital at the rate of 107 per cent per annum. A number of the eighty or ninety croupiers were retained by M. Blanc for service at Monaco, whilst the rest it is believed went into trade.

On the last night an immense throng gathered in the rooms, eagerly crowding round the tables. The play, however, was unusually dull, and on the green cloth, which had usually been liberally sprinkled with gold, only a few spare florins were to be seen. The croupiers did their best to dispel the depression which hung over the gamesters; and as the final moment approached, shouted louder and louder, adding to their usual formula, "Faites vos jeux, Messieurs," the words "le troisième dernier!"—the third last chance; "le deuxième dernier!"—the second last; and finally "le dernier!" which seemed to sound like a death-knell. Their appeals had little effect, the moment being of such solemnity as to stifle all emotion and paralyse every movement. Here and there some small stake was noiselessly placed on the table by some timid and unfamiliar hand, but the audacious spirit of the real gambler was for the moment lulled to rest, and no one seemed eager to try a last serious struggle with the goddess of chance. The closing of the gaming-tables was a veritable convulsion of nature as regards Wiesbaden. On the 1st of January 1873 there was universal confusion in hotel and lodging-house, and the streets were thronged with departing travellers and overladen porters, while the railway stations were blocked with eager applicants for tickets. With a haste bordering on indecency the old gambling-saloons were taken possession of by the municipal authorities, and stripped of their furniture; windows and doors being thrown open to the air, and the halls, formerly devoted to chance, handed over to a host of painters, white-washers, and scrubbers. The green tables, which had caused so many emotions, were thrown out, and cast into heaps, preliminary to being carted away as old furniture. The results to the town were disastrous. Many of the hotels fell into bankruptcy and were forced to close their windows—their doors they might have left open, for there were no guests to enter them.

The shopkeepers, more especially the jewellers, who generally were pawnbrokers too, and all dealers in articles of luxury, were also great losers by the change.

The joint-stock company, which had owned the tables, dissolved, after having divided a large amount of surplus. The shareholders had indeed no cause for complaint, yet one of the two directors took the dissolution so much to heart that he soon after drank himself to death.

A few days after the cessation of play hardly a gambler remained in the place.

One exception, however, there was, who for some years was pointed out as a rare specimen of an extinct race by the few officials of the rooms who had been retained as door-keepers and the like in the building from which all life had fled.

Still clad in the torn, somewhat shabby livery of more prosperous days when "Trinkgeld" was abundant, these men would describe to visitors how this Englishman, a man bearing an historic name, had created a sensation at the tables, where he had been notorious for his ill-luck. To all appearance entirely ruined, he had suddenly been left some twenty thousand pounds, which had soon followed the rest of his fortune into the coffers of the bank. Reduced to his last florin, fortune for a moment had seemed to relent, and he had left the rooms with about seven thousand pounds in his pocket. Having deposited this at his banker's, he had then declared his intention of never playing again—in less than a week the sum had been withdrawn and lost.

His friends, now believing him to be incorrigible, settled upon him a small allowance, which was paid quarterly, and with unfailing regularity found its way to the green cloth.

Seemingly stunned by the closing of the rooms, this Englishman lingered on for some years, mournfully marching about the spot which had engulfed his fortune, the loss of which, however, caused him less concern than being deprived of the means wherewith to gratify the passion that had dominated his life.

All the gambling companies had to pay large sums in return for the privileges which they enjoyed, but still they progressed most successfully till they were frightened from their propriety by Monsieur Blanc. This gentleman, after struggling against immense opposition on the part of the Frankfort merchants, who were naturally alarmed at the danger to which their *commis* and cash-boxes would be exposed by the proximity of a gambling-table, obtained a concession from the Elector of Hesse to establish a bank at Homburg-von-der-Höhe. Play was soon in full swing, with the additional attractions of being open all the year round, and of having only a *trente-et-un après* (known as the *refait*) for the players to contend against. Some time after, Wilhelmsbad was opened as a rival to Homburg, with no *après* at all; and the above mentioned, with the addition of Ems, Aix-la-Chapelle, and Cöthen, formed the principal establishments where "strangers were taken in and done for" throughout Germany.

Wilhelmsbad scarcely attracted the outside world at all, being frequented almost exclusively by Germans. Wildungen might have been called a child left out in the cold; the accommodation was indifferent, and the place itself cheerless and devoid of charm, besides which it was not so easy to get at. Modestly conscious of its slender claims to consideration, the authorities presiding over the tables allowed a minimum stake of 10 groschen (1 franc 25 cents), and only enforced a tax of a quarter of the *refait* at trente-et-quarante and a quarter of the zero at roulette, a state of affairs which should have been far from unfavourable to the players.

As a matter of fact, public gaming, whatever may be said against it, left those places where it formerly flourished in a high state of prosperity—the Kursaals and gardens of German health-resorts, such as Homburg and Baden-Baden, owed their inception entirely to gaming, whilst several other insignificant places were converted into agreeable pleasure-resorts by the influence of trente-et-quarante and roulette.

In spite of the doubtful morality of the enterprise carried on by the proprietors of the tables they certainly metamorphosed several miserable German townlets into cities of palaces. They planted the gardens; they imported the orange trees; they laid out the parks; enclosed the hunting-grounds; and, as it were, boarded, lodged, washed, and taxed the inhabitants. Homburg, for instance, was entirely the creation of M. Blanc.

The story of the commencement of the immense fortune accumulated by M. Blanc is curious.

One fine day in 1842 the two brothers Blanc, who were temporarily disgusted with France owing to a daring and unsuccessful speculation connected with the old semaphore telegraph (which electricity rendered obsolete), arrived at Frankfort.

Their stock-in-trade consisted of a few thousand francs, a roulette wheel, and an ancient croupier, a veteran of Frascati's who knew everything worth knowing about gambling and cards.

The purpose of this visit was to convince the authorities of Frankfort that their city would derive great benefit from affording facilities for public play, but with this, however, they were not disposed to agree. In consequence of its cool reception, the little party then wended its way to the obscure village of Homburg, where the elder of the two brothers, after some negotiations, obtained permission to set the roulette wheel going in one of the rooms of the principal inn.

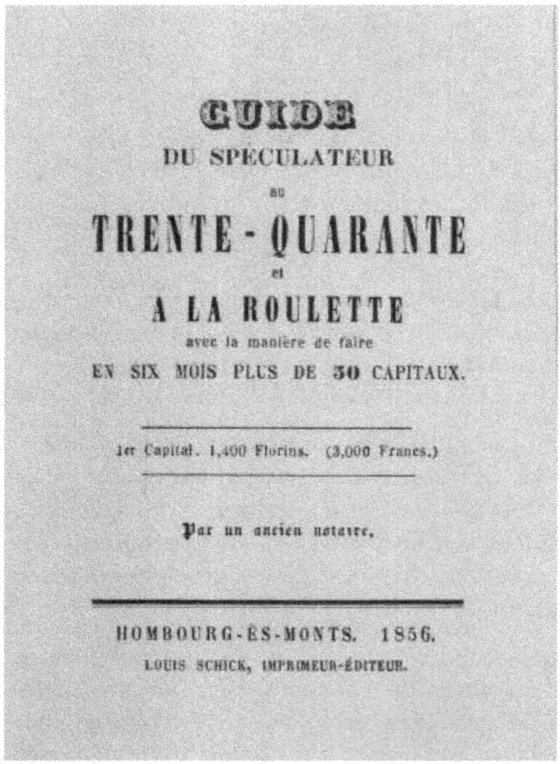

GUIDE

DU SPÉCULATEUR

AU

TRENTE-QUARANTE

et

A LA ROULETTE

avec la manière de faire

EN SIX MOIS PLUS DE 30 CAPITAUX.

1er Capital. 1,400 Florins. (3,000 Francs.)

Par un ancien notaire.

HOMBOURG-ÈS-MONTS. 1856.

LOUIS SCHICK, IMPRIMEUR-ÉDITEUR.

As at Monte Carlo to-day, infallible "guides" to success at the tables were to be obtained in the Homburg book-shops. The above is a facsimile of the title-page of one of the most curious of these booklets.

The next year an exclusive concession was granted to the Blancs to establish games of hazard within the dominions of the Landgraf. They agreed to build a Kursaal, lay out public gardens, and pay about 40,000 florins (something over four thousand a year) to the Landgraf. A company was formed, and soon the fashionable world flocked to Homburg—

ostensibly to drink the waters, but, in reality, to lose their money at trente-et-quarante and roulette.

The general policy pursued by M. Blanc at Homburg was very similar to that afterwards adopted at Monte Carlo, which is still in its essential features followed by the present administration.

The hours allotted to play were from eleven in the morning to eleven at night, which was also the case at Monaco up till quite recent years.

The proceedings at Homburg before play began, that is to say, the counting of money and other preparations for the day's campaign, were also much the same as at Monte Carlo, though the actual opening of the rooms for play was more dramatic. As the clock struck eleven the strains of martial music were heard and the doors of the "salons" were thrown wide open, admitting a stream of people, amongst whom were many officers, a note of colour being struck by their uniforms, which were principally white or green.

In the early days of Homburg, owing to an extraordinary rainfall, a flood of water once made its way into the gaming-rooms and caused the players to beat a precipitate retreat. A fat old German Princess, however, who was devoted to play, was too heavy to get out in time, and had to be hoisted up on to one of the roulette tables, where she placidly remained till matters were put right and the play had resumed its normal course.

In the Kursaal were the Café Olympique, private rooms for parties, and, most important of all, a big saloon and two smaller ones. Here from eleven in the forenoon to eleven at night, Sundays not excepted, all the year round, people from every part of the world came to throw their gold and silver upon the tables.

As a town Homburg was practically created by the Kursaal. The hotel-keepers and tradesmen lived by it as well as the Landgraf, whose main source of revenue was derived from it. This sovereign, of course, was practically sold to the Kursaal, the Board of Directors being the real rulers of Hesse-Homburg. The prosperity which the advent of M. Blanc had brought to his dominions cheered the declining years of this Prince, who was the oldest reigning sovereign in Europe at the time of his death, which occurred on the 24th of March 1866. He had attained the great age of eighty-three when he expired in the arms of two weeping widowed women—one his niece, the Princess Reuss, the other his aged sister, the Dowager Grand Duchess of Mecklenburg-Schwerin. This event caused a temporary cessation of play, which had been continuous since the 17th of August 1843.

The insidious fascination connected with gambling was once strikingly exemplified at Homburg. The story, though a well-known one, will bear repetition.

M. Blanc had been pondering what to give his wife on her birthday, when a peculiarly attractive parasol caught his eye as he was strolling amongst the shops; so he went in and inquired the price, which was twenty marks. The founder of the great gaming establishment was a careful man, and it seemed to him that to pay so much for a parasol was extravagant. Nevertheless, he ordered it to be put aside for him, saying that he would call and pay for it later.

On his way to the Casino the thought suddenly struck him: "To win twenty marks in the rooms is quite easy—numbers of people do it, but they don't stop; which is the reason I make so much money. Why shouldn't I win the price of this parasol—make my twenty marks and walk out?"

Walking up to a trente-et-quarante table and unobtrusively stationing himself behind a group of players, M. Blanc furtively slipped twenty marks on the red—black won. Forty marks on the red—black again won. Eighty marks on the black—red won. He now became excited and, the money he had in his pocket being exhausted, edged towards an astonished *chef de partie*, to whom he was, of course, well-known, and instructed him to place one hundred and sixty marks on red. The croupier dealt the cards, and announced that red had lost. By this time every one had realised that M. Blanc was staking against his own tables, and the whole room flocked to see such an extraordinary sight. The croupiers concluded that their chief had gone mad, for he stood looking fixedly at the cards, entirely absorbed in the effort to recover his losses and win the price of the parasol. To make a long story short, he continued to stake till he had lost about £1000, when of a sudden he realised the situation and rushed out of the rooms. He was, of course, considerably chaffed about this exploit, which was said to have been the only occasion on which he had been known to play. For many a long day afterwards, he used regretfully to say: "That was the dearest parasol I ever bought in my life."

M. Blanc, who was more assailed than any other banker, was once nearly made the victim of a stratagem, which might have entailed serious results. A scoundrel contrived to get into the "Konversationhaus" by night, and blocked up all the low numbers in the roulette machine in such a manner that the ball, on falling in, must inevitably leap out again. On the next day he and his accomplices played and netted a large sum by backing the high numbers. They carried on the game for two or three days, but were fortunately overheard by a detective while quarrelling about the division of their plunder in the gardens behind the establishment. They were arrested and the money recovered. A very dangerous design was also formed against M. Blanc by one of his croupiers, who, being discontented with his lot, determined to make his fortune at one *coup*. The plan he contrived was this. He procured a pack of prearranged cards, which he concealed in his hat, and when it came to his turn to deal he intended to drop the bank cards into his *chapeau* and cleverly substitute the others; but this artfully-concocted scheme was upset by one of his confederates who considered that he might make a better and safer thing of it by telling M. Blanc beforehand.

A great attack was once made by a Belgian syndicate upon the tables at Homburg, and for a time had some appearance of ultimate success. In the end, however, M. Blanc emerged triumphant from the contest, which is mentioned by Thackeray in the *Kickleburys on the Rhine.*

It was at Homburg that the celebrated Garcia once created an enormous sensation by asking the bank to double the limit of 12,000 francs. According to one account a meeting of the Directors was hastily summoned by M. Blanc, who was in favour of letting Garcia have his way; but it was finally decided that no alteration should be made. Another version is that M. Blanc consented to double the limit if Garcia would play sitting down and not standing up, the veteran banker's opinion being that any one standing up was much more likely to depart with winnings than a player seated at the table. Garcia accordingly sat down, and though at first very unlucky, eventually rose a winner.

Garcia is said to have come to Germany with two thousand francs—his whole fortune—in search of employment. Whilst at Frankfort he determined to go and try his luck at the Homburg tables, and being fortunate enough to get on several runs of his favourite colour—red—he won about £20,000 in three weeks. An Englishman, it is said, was so convinced that the runs on red must end, that he watched for what he deemed a propitious moment and began staking maximums on black against Garcia, with the result that in a few days he left Homburg without a penny.

Garcia continued to play on after his rival's defeat, and though at one moment he was reduced to a capital of six thousand francs, he retrieved his fortunes by a run of fourteen reds, and eventually left Homburg with some £50,000—some say more. He now declared that he was determined never to play again; but this resolution was soon broken, for within a couple of years he was trying to break the bank at Baden. Black turned up too often for him, however, and he lost heavily.

He then thought he would try Homburg again, and was there eventually reduced to beggary after a few months' play. This gambler subsequently figured in a most unsavoury card scandal which took place in Paris in February 1863 at the house of Madame Julia Barucci. This lady, who was young and attractive, was always surrounded by a large circle of admirers, and the party which she gave to celebrate her first evening in a new abode was therefore particularly animated, about thirty guests being present, amongst whom was Signor Calzado, the well-known manager of a Paris theatre. Calzado, it should be said, was disliked by the party generally—Garcia alone being on terms of intimacy with him—not only because he was a gamester, but probably because he had the reputation of being a card-sharper, which he was, and a very bold and original one too. (Calzado once went to Havana and bought up every pack of cards in the place, having previously freighted a vessel with marked playing-cards, which arrived just in time to supply the dealers, whose stocks were completely exhausted. With the cards he had prepared and imported, Calzado played incessantly, and for high stakes, being, as an inevitable result, a constant and heavy winner.) The most popular guest was Signor Miranda, Gentleman of the Queen of Spain's household, a constant and honourable gamester, well-known as being capable of losing large sums. He came with about 100,000 francs in his pocket. As soon as possible Garcia arranged a rouge-et-noir table, at which his countrymen, Calzado and Miranda, took their places, the latter soon winning 30,000 francs. After supper baccarat was proposed; whereupon Garcia absented himself from the room for half an hour under the pretext of wishing to smoke a cigar in the air. Retiring into a private chamber, he disposed about his person several packs of cards which he had brought with him, and then returning to the gaming-table began to play for high stakes. His success was extraordinary, and in a short time he won 140,000 francs, chiefly from Signor Miranda. Calzado, who followed Garcia's lead, also won a large sum. The extraordinary good luck of Garcia, and the marvellous character of the cards which he held, aroused the astonishment of the players as well as the suspicions of those looking on, and it was at length perceived that some of the cards in Garcia's hand were of a different design from that of the packs provided by the hostess. He was charged with foul play; whereupon, somewhat confused, he admitted having introduced cards of his own, though stoutly maintaining that he had played fairly, and had brought certain packs from his club merely because they always proved lucky cards to him, which in this instance was certainly true. He offered as a matter of courtesy and as a favour, being, as he said, desirous of avoiding a scandal, to refund his winnings, if the whole affair were hushed up. At the same time he produced the sum of 50,000 francs; but those whom he had cheated were not to be tricked into accepting a third part of their losses in place of the whole, and an extraordinary scene followed. Seeing that his position was desperate, and fearful lest he should be forcibly despoiled of his ill-gotten winnings, Garcia tried to escape. Finding the door bolted, he rushed all over the house, finally hiding himself in a corner of an obscure room, from which he was chased by his amazed pursuers, who seized him and roughly stripped him of all the money in his possession. It was now the turn of Calzado, who was then asked to display the contents of his pockets, or suffer himself to be searched. He refused to do either, but stealthily allowed a roll of bank-notes, to the value of 16,000 francs, to slip down his trousers and fall on the floor. The roll was picked up and handed to him, but he denied all knowledge of it. Eventually the brother cheats were permitted to leave the house, but after their departure it was reckoned that, in spite of everything, they had carried with them at least 40,000 francs.

Garcia and Calzado were both tried for swindling. The former appeared in person; Calzado, however, had fled. Both were convicted of malpractices, Garcia being sentenced to five years' and Calzado to thirteen months' imprisonment, in addition to fines of 3000 francs each. They were also ordered to pay jointly 31,000 francs to Miranda. The hostess, Madame Barucci, escaped punishment, but was placed under strict police supervision, lest she should again allow prohibited games to be played in her house. Garcia died in great misery about 1881.

In 1872 the gambling-establishment at Homburg became a thing of the past. A great number of the townspeople of that resort were shareholders, and all, more or less, derived some profit direct or indirect from the play. During the war between Austria and Prussia they began to be somewhat perturbed, and on their annexation to the latter country, they hoped against hope that Bismarck, whatever he might do with kings, would leave what to them was far more important than dynasties and kingdoms—the bank—alone.

In 1867, however, the blow fell, and the directors of the gambling-rooms, summoned to appear before the Governor, were informed that all play was to cease in 1872.

It should be added that an arrangement of a not unfair kind protected the interests of the shareholders.

GAMBLING AT HOMBURG.
Drawn by the late G.A. Sala. (*Impasse* should of course be *Impair.*)

During these last days of play at Homburg a great crowd had been coming in, but still the tables were not inconveniently crowded, and people were able to stake their money with ease though without comfort. There was, however, a good deal of pilfering and snatching of money, which had always been rather a feature at this resort, shrill-tongued harpies being apt to pounce on the couple of five-franc pieces just won by any simple Englishman ignorant of the German tongue. As the end approached the usual high play still prevailed, but the administration was a good deal disturbed by the advent of workmen, shopmen, and others, a very different class of people from their aristocratic clients of the summer season. These new visitors were sturdy, brutal customers, who became frenzied if they lost a florin, and seemed not unlikely to revenge themselves by some lawless raid. This very unlucrative crowd continued to increase, and it became known that on the last two days the forces would be recruited by yet larger bands. The administration, wisely reckoning that the result might be a general riot organised for purposes of plunder, took measures to avert such a crowning catastrophe. On the Sunday, then, while numbers of speculative individuals at Frankfort and other towns were arranging for one grand final expedition, and were looking forward to being in at the death, it was determined to end play for ever suddenly and without notice. Before five o'clock this had been done, much to the indignant surprise of the new arrivals, and the rage and fury of the less scrupulous. This, perhaps, was no undignified end; and Homburg, from a gambling point of view, may be said to have "died game." The administration maintained its honeyed, courteous phrases to the last, and on the Monday stuck little proclamations all over the walls, to the effect that the "Administration begged to inform *la société* that there would be no play on the 30th and 31st inst. Signed: The Kurhaus Direction." Nevertheless on the back sheet of the Belgian papers was a huge advertisement proclaiming to all whom it concerned that there would be play to the last day of the month. Such an oversight was scarcely fair to the friends and admirers of the tables, some of whom travelled from a great distance to bid a final adieu to the Halls of Chance.

The appearance of the gambling-house on the day after the cessation of play was indescribable, resembling a badly-set scene by daylight. Numbers of charwomen and men-servants hung about in groups; officials, like those of a bankrupt hotel, went about with keys; chairs were piled on the long gaming-tables by irreverent hands; everything looked as though there was going to be a sale by auction. The ball-room, however, still had its chairs all set out in order, as if company were expected, whilst the orchestra played in the gardens, which already presented a neglected air. Even the theatre looked shabby, though behind the frame of wire network was to be read the announcement of the last—the very last in all truth—appearance of the "Diva Patti" in *La Sonnambula.*

Ems was another gambling resort. This was essentially a rendezvous of all the pleasure-loving aristocracy and fashionable financiers of the day—unlike Wiesbaden and Homburg, which were rather the chosen battle-fields of well-known and seasoned gamblers.

A Spaniard at Ems made a very comfortable living by a method of playing he had invented. He placed three louis d'or on the manque, which contains all the numbers to eighteen, and two louis on the last series of twelve; that is, from twenty-four to thirty-six. Thus he had only six numbers and two zeroes against him. If manque gained, he won three louis and lost two; if a number in the last twelve came up, he won four and lost three; but a continuation of zeroes would have ruined his calculation. Russians in particular were very fond of Ems. Many played very high, and a good deal of private gambling was done there on the quiet.

At Geneva in the 'sixties trente-et-quarante was somewhat furtively played in a *Cercle des Étrangers*. Roulette, however, was not allowed. The authorities perhaps feared that the noise of the little ball flying round on its course to a numbered compartment might awaken Calvin from the quiet of his tomb.

There was once what was practically a regular gaming-house on English soil. This was in the 'fifties, when mild roulette was played on the island of Heligoland. A miniature roulette-table there was much frequented by joyous Israelites and English officers from the mainland. In 1856, however, an outraged English tourist wrote a furious letter to *The Times*, complaining of such horrors existing under the British flag. He denounced the scandalous desecration of the English name, and so forth; and in consequence the Governor issued an edict against the roulette. Play, however, on a diminutive scale continued there some time longer.

The closing of the gaming-tables in Germany was the cause of many rumours as to the future of gambling enterprise. The Valley of Andorra in the Pyrenees was said to have been selected by some French speculators as the scene of their operations for the ensuing year, a well-known financier being declared to have obtained a monopoly of theatres, hotels, casinos, railways, and almost everything else that this valley lacked and might be supposed to want. There was also a rumour that efforts were being made to start tables at St. Moritz, in Switzerland, very tempting offers having been made to the authorities.

These anticipations were not, however, realised, and Monte Carlo remains the only regular public gaming-place in Europe, though intermittent public gambling has been tolerated at certain Belgian pleasure-resorts, notably at Ostend. Two or three years ago public gaming was altogether prohibited there, but it now appears to flourish much as before. It is almost superfluous to add that when it was announced that the Belgian authorities had determined to suppress all public play there was much enthusiastic congratulation from this country. The usual time-worn phrases as to the demoralising effects of gambling were unctuously presented to a public whose conscience, it was declared, had too long been outraged by the proximity of such a dangerous temptation; and the Belgians were told that they might anticipate reaping a golden harvest as the result of the high-principled attitude which had been adopted, for the English would now be able to visit their pleasure-resorts without fear of contamination.

A large number of the Ostend shopkeepers really believed that the suppression of play would bring more foreign money into their pockets; but they soon realised their mistake, for when the visitors from across the channel found that there was no chance of enlivening their stay at Ostend (a resort of few natural attractions) with a little flutter, they beat a precipitate retreat, and the prosperity of the town began to suffer severely.

Eventually, as the result of serious protest from the local shopkeepers and others who saw ruin staring them in the face, a species of compromise has been adopted; and baccarat with one tableau (of which more anon) is now allowed in the *Cercle*, election to which is not very difficult.

A short time ago roulette without a zero was here held out as a great attraction to visitors. As a matter of fact this game was only played for a limited number of hours every day, and these were precisely those when visitors would in the ordinary course of events be taking their meals. The game was merely kept going as a lure to the more profitable baccarat, the authorities being well aware that roulette without a zero is unlikely to prove a great source of profit to the bank.

Experience teaches that for some reason not very clearly understood single tableau baccarat would seem to be particularly favourable to the banker. So great, indeed, has been the havoc wrought by this game that the French have given it the name of "La Faucheuse,"—"the mowing-machine"!

Those who cried out so loudly for the suppression of the trente-et-quarante at Ostend have, like so many well-meaning people, done little but harm, for the suppressed trente-et-quarante was a far less dangerous game. Trente-et-quarante, it should be added, is played at St. Sebastian, where up to the present year there was also roulette.

At French watering-places gaming flourishes as merrily as ever during the season. At Trouville, Biarritz, and Aix-les-Bains the game of baccarat forms one of the chief attractions. There is a good deal of high play at Trouville at the time of the races. During the present year one player alone—a very rich gambler fond of high stakes—lost no less than a million francs. No inconsiderable portion of this sum must have gone in the percentage which the French Government now levies upon banks at baccarat. During the last year there was also a great deal of play at Nice, where the game in question was as popular as the classic roulette and trente-et-quarante of Monaco.

It is almost impossible to conceive how the vast majority of French summer pleasure-resorts would contrive to exist were baccarat and petits chevaux to be suppressed, for a certain portion of the large profit derived from play is devoted to the upkeep of the Casinos, which furnish visitors with excellent entertainment. It is, indeed, owing directly and indirectly to the toleration of play that the French *plages* are proving such formidable rivals to the miserably dull English seaside resorts, which offer so little to visitors who are fond of a little exciting amusement.

In 1907 the French Government promulgated a new code of regulations to be enforced at Casinos, all of which were closed for two or three days throughout France—an operation which, of course, evoked a mass of hypocritical and totally inaccurate comment in England.

France was congratulated upon her determination to stop every form of that gambling which had for so many years shocked English visitors, who would, of course, warmly welcome the stern measures about to be enforced, and flock across the Channel in largely increased numbers as a result.

As a matter of fact, the Casinos were closed merely to emphasise the fact that the Government intended to see that the new regulations which they imposed, amongst which was one regulating a tax upon baccarat banks, should be respected.

The very rumour that it was proposed permanently to prohibit gambling terrified the local authorities, a large number of whom at once went up to Paris to ascertain whether there was any foundation of truth in such an idea, which to many a watering-place would mean nothing less than ruin.

They were, however, soon reassured, for in the end only one small and insignificant Casino was permanently closed.

By the decree of June 21, 1907, certain games of chance are permitted at watering-places and health-resorts which have been officially recognised as such by the Minister of the Interior, on the representation of the Municipal Council and the Prefect. These are baccarat, écarté, and the game of petits chevaux and its varieties. A tax of fifteen per cent is levied on the sum produced by the cagnotte at écarté and baccarat.

Counters, which were formerly used at Casinos to represent money, were entirely prohibited, a prohibition which, however, does not apply to Clubs. The reason for this was that players were apt to obtain considerable advances from the *caisse* in baccarat-rooms, a state of affairs not so likely to happen when ready money alone may be staked. Playing in cash is also generally of a more careful kind than play in counters, which for the time being seem nothing at all. A player, of course, has a far greater chance at baccarat than at petits chevaux, where the percentage is very unfavourable to him, one horse out of the nine being the bank's.

According to the new law, fifteen per cent is now levied on the gross winnings of the bank at this game every day; should the bank lose it is allowed to deduct the sum lost from its winnings the next day.

The sum produced by this tax of fifteen per cent is to be devoted to charity, and to various other objects of public utility and affecting the public health.

When this decree was first issued, chemin-de-fer baccarat was not included amongst the list of tolerated games, the French authorities being still horror-struck with the recollection of the single tableau baccarat, called "La Faucheuse" (the game which, thanks to Puritan effort, is played at Ostend), which had provoked such gross scandals in Paris. It was, however, subsequently legalised by a special decree which was promulgated in the *Journal Officiel* of the 18th August 1907, and is taxed at the same rate as other tolerated games.

The main cause of the French Government moving in the matter of gambling at all had been the large increase of so-called gambling clubs in Paris entirely devoted to single tableau baccarat, from which an enormous harvest of gold had been gathered by those holding the banks. It was said that no less than 126 new establishments of this kind had sprung up in Paris, a state of affairs calculated to make the dead proprietors of the long-suppressed and very strictly regulated tables in the old Palais Royal turn in their graves. Many of these Clubs were frequented by women, and it was rumoured that many of the brightest stars of the French *demi-monde* had lost almost everything they had. Paris began to be seriously alarmed. Drastic measures were adopted; the foreign proprietors of the gaming-places expelled from France; "La Faucheuse" forbidden throughout the country; and gambling generally placed upon the strictly regulated footing which has been described. The results of the very sensible action of the French Government appear to be highly satisfactory, for since the promulgation of the decree regulating play no scandals have occurred, whilst it is anticipated that in the course of time a sum well over two million pounds a year will be available for objects of public utility.

Surely the wise regulation of what appears to be an irradicable evil is far more salutary, alike from a financial and a moral point of view, than the unthinking policy of drastic suppression, which, as experience teaches, has ever been powerless to extirpate gambling.

X

The Principality of Monaco—Its vicissitudes—Early days of the Casino—The old Prince and his scruples—Monte Carlo in 1858 and 1864—Its development—Fashionable in the 'eighties—Mr. Sam Lewis and Captain Carlton Blythe—Anecdotes—Increase of visitors and present democratic policy of administration—The *Cercle Privé* and its short life—The gaming-rooms and ways of their frequenters—Anecdotes—Trente-et-quarante and roulette—Why the cards have plain white backs—Jaggers' successful spoliation of the bank—The croupiers and their training—The staff of the Casino—The *viatique*—Systems—The best of all.

Many years before the tables at the German resorts were closed by the Prussian Government, M. Blanc was quietly seeking for a suitable spot where his roulette wheels might whirl free from interference and his croupiers deal in unmolested peace.

Gaming-house proprietors seem in one respect to resemble the monks of old, for almost invariably their establishments have been pitched amidst attractive surroundings commanding lovely views. Thoroughly imbued with this tradition, M. Blanc eventually selected the little Principality of Monaco as being a suitable spot to afford his industry a peaceful and alluring haven. After certain negotiations with the reigning Prince Charles Albert, he obtained the required concession, and a Casino (in its earliest days called the "Elysium Alberti") was erected upon the rocky ground known as the Plateau des Spelugues, which, adversaries of gaming will rejoice to learn, means in Monagasque patois "the plain of the robbers."

The ruling family of Monaco, the Grimaldis, had been exposed to many vicissitudes. During the French Revolution their people rose in rebellion and plundered the Palace, which afterwards served as a military hospital during Napoleon's Italian campaign, and later on became the Dépôt de Mendicité for the Department of the Alpes Maritimes. In 1841, however, Florestan I., the reigning Prince, repaired the home of his ancestors, which was thoroughly restored by Charles Albert after the advent of M. Blanc.

In the turbulent past the Princes of Monaco at times experienced considerable difficulty in holding their own, and often had to defend their rugged old rock against piratical raids, besides occasionally having to cope with internal troubles, the last of which occurred in 1847, when the

Monagasque bitterly resented taxation. The cannon given by Louis XIV. to the Grimaldi of his day may still be seen near the palace. These are fine specimens of the founder's craft, and bear the grim motto "Ultima ratio regum," amidst much ornate decoration.

The armed force which the Princes maintained was much improved in uniform and equipment when M. Blanc brought prosperity to Monaco. Even up to quite recent years there existed a smart little army of something under a hundred men, in all probability the best dressed and least offensive troops in all Europe. Their rifle practice, it was always said, was indifferent, owing to the fact that they could not fire inland, because the boundaries of the Principality were so limited; but whatever may have been their efficiency or non-efficiency as a fighting force, their light-blue uniforms—with old-world aiguillette, neat shako, and picturesque cape—were highly ornamental features, which struck a pleasant note of colour in the streets of the Condamine or about the grounds and terraces of the Casino.

This little army is now but a memory, for within the last decade the reigning Prince, who is a warm advocate of International Arbitration, realising, it is said, that the maintenance of a standing army was inconsistent with his well-known love of peace, abolished the last relic of military strength left to the Grimaldis. Such sentries as are still required are at present furnished by the gendarmerie, whose dainty cocked hat—most military and attractive of head-dresses—was at the same time superseded by an abominable cloth-covered helmet, which for unalloyed ugliness would easily carry off the prize against all competitors. Thus does it constantly happen in the modern world that, whilst there is much prating about art, cultivation, and taste, the very people who should do their best to preserve every distinctive and decorative reminder of a more artistic past are foremost in the work of obliteration.

Old Monaco consisted of a few unattractive streets and a somewhat dilapidated Palace, in which lived the blind old Prince who granted the concession for the tables to M. Blanc, and by so doing converted his poverty-stricken realm into the most prosperous State in the world.

At first, the Prince was somewhat troubled by conscientious scruples as to tolerating gaming, but these were appeased by the large sums which were rendered available for religious purposes and the building of churches—the Church of St. Dévote, which stands in the ravine, for instance, is said to have been erected from funds received in exchange for permission to increase the number of roulette tables, whilst the beautiful little cathedral on the Palace rock would never have been built had not M. Blanc made his descent upon the Principality.

Much abuse has been lavished on the Prince for granting the concession, but it seems a doubtful question whether he did not do more good than harm when he signed it. Certainly his own people of Monaco (who, except on one day in the year—the Prince's birthday,—are not allowed to enter the Casino) gained very largely thereby.

To them the establishment of the Casino has brought lasting prosperity, whilst it has indirectly benefited the whole Riviera, now so popular as a pleasure-resort. On the other hand, a number of people, no doubt, have been ruined at Monte Carlo, but such as these—gamblers at heart—would most probably in any case have lost their fortune in other forms of speculation. It should also be realised that the number of those who have actually been ruined by the Casino is extremely small—as a rule those who lose their last penny at the tables are individuals who, already at their last gasp owing to a long series of gambling reverses, come to Monte Carlo with such funds as they can scrape together in order to indulge in one last desperate plunge.

The old Prince was a kindly man at heart, and did not like to think of visitors losing more money than they had actually brought with them. For this reason he forbade the establishment of any Bank in the Principality, and as a natural consequence, numbers of waiters, who carried on a brisk business in money-lending, made nice little fortunes.

In later years Smith's Bank was established on French territory; this was afterwards absorbed into the Crédit Lyonnais, which (the prohibition having been revoked) is now quite a prominent feature of Monte Carlo.

At the time when M. Blanc made his peaceful conquest of Monaco the place was sparsely populated and miserably poor. The contrast indeed between the Monaco of fifty years ago and the Monte Carlo of to-day is striking in the extreme.

The following description of the Principality at that time was given to the writer by one who has seen every phase of its development.

In 1858 this gentleman and his wife, being on their honeymoon in France, drove from Marseilles to Cannes, then also quite a small place. A report had recently reached the latter place that the celebrated M. Blanc had started gaming-tables at Monaco, and accordingly the Duc de Vallombrosa, who owned the finest château at Cannes, invited several of the English visitors to go over to the Principality on his yacht, and in due course the party climbed up to the rock, on which stands the Palace.

After making inquiries they found the gaming-tables—two roulette and one trente-et-quarante—which were installed in a very unpretentious barnlike edifice somewhere near the spot where the Cathedral is now.

The arrival of manifestly well-to-do visitors created quite a sensation amongst a somewhat limited crowd, mostly composed of Italian tourists who were indulging in a little mild play. M. Blanc, it should be added, had merely started these tables as a preliminary step, being at that time engaged in negotiations with the reigning Prince as to the erection of a more serious gambling establishment in the latter's dominions.

After playing a stake or two the party made their way down to the little town in the Condamine, where, finding that donkeys could be hired, they determined to picnic out of doors. Accordingly, taking the requisite materials with them, they made their way by a bridle path (which more or less followed the present road) to the plateau, on which the present palatial Casino stands to-day.

Monte Carlo (the place was then unnamed) was almost a bare rock covered with rough grass, and here and there a few stunted pine and olive trees, most of the latter of immense age. A few tumble-down hovels were sparsely scattered here and there on the mountain side, in which lived a miserably poor peasantry; the whole spot was as different from the Monte Carlo of to-day as it is possible to conceive.

Just about where is now the ornamental plot in front of the doors of the Casino, the party collected some dry bits of sticks, boiled their kettle, cooked an omelette and drank their tea, whilst they revelled in the lovely view, which remains to-day almost the sole feature which the hand of man has been powerless to change.

Almost the last of the few survivors of this expedition also described to the present writer the marvellous alteration which he found on his next visit to the Principality some six years later. The first Casino had then been built by M. Blanc, and a small Hôtel de Paris stood where the gigantic modern one stands to-day. M. Blanc, in addition to presiding over the rooms, was in supreme command of the hotel, which was managed on the most liberal principles, bills being never sent in unless they were asked for. Since those days the hotel has been much enlarged and altered. It is now being entirely rebuilt on a palatial scale.

When visitors of any standing whatever were about to depart, M. Blanc himself would be present to wish them good-bye, and also to inquire whether they might not like a thousand francs for the expenses of their journey, adding that this could be refunded on their next visit, or sent him at their convenience.

In 1864, except the hotel, there were scarcely any houses in Monte Carlo itself, and most of the visitors had to live on the other side of the Bay in the old town. As the journey from Nice by road took four hours, an abominable and, it was said, unseaworthy, small white steamer, the *Palmaria* (probably the best that could be got), had been chartered by M. Blanc to convey visitors from Nice. This vessel anchored beneath the Castle rock, where its passengers were landed in boats, being met by four-horse omnibuses which plied gratis between the rock and the Casino.

The *Palmaria* made two journeys from Nice a day. If the weather was calm and nothing went wrong, the passage took something like an hour and a quarter. It was a curious sight to see visitors landing in the highest spirits for a flutter, most of them to return in the evening to Nice, weary and sea-sick, without a penny to take a cab to their hotel.

In the early days of Monte Carlo there were two zeroes, and the inevitable result was that the *Palmaria's* evening cargo was usually largely composed of what were facetiously called "empty bottles."

The crowd which thronged to the tables was of a heterogeneous description and not at all smart. There were a number of enterprising damsels in pork-pie hats and a considerable sprinkling of raffish Englishmen, looking as if they had seen better days and were likely to see worse.

Monte Carlo, though a tiny place, already bore evidences of its future expansion. An air of prosperity pervaded it, and the inhabitants had lost the air of hopeless poverty which was formerly such a characteristic of the Principality of Monaco.

In the early days of the Casino not much was heard of its existence, the truth being that M. Blanc, after his experiences at Homburg, feared lest European public opinion might demand the abolition of the tables were their existence to be too prominently thrust before it. In consequence of this as little attention as possible was drawn to the gambling which, if alluded to in the Press at all, was merely mentioned as one of the minor attractions. Knowing the sensitiveness of M. Blanc with regard to publicity, unscrupulous journalists traded upon it, demanding bribes to keep silence, whilst ephemeral newspapers, containing sensational accounts of suicides of ruined gamblers, were published solely in order to extort blackmail.

As time went on, however, Monte Carlo began to be regarded as an established institution, and many visitors took to coming there year after year.

The development of the Riviera as a pleasure-resort steadily proceeded, and at the present time the coast from Genoa to Marseilles is an almost unbroken line of pleasure-resorts filled with villas, not a few veritable palaces, all of which owe their existence to the advent of M. Blanc with his roulette and trente-et-quarante. Abuse gambling as you may, it has in this instance beyond all question brought wealth and prosperity to the inhabitants—not to the rich, for there were no rich—but to the people of the soil, born and bred along this beautiful coast-line lapped by the azure waters of the Mediterranean.

It was after M. Blanc's death in the early 'seventies that the Casino was first enlarged, and the theatre built by M. Garnier. From time to time further additions have been made—an entirely new gambling-room was added only a few years ago, and at the present moment another is being built.

Monte Carlo itself, which even in the 'eighties was quite a little place, has now become a regular town with streets stretching up along the mountain side almost up to the gigantic hotel, which is now such a conspicuous feature of the Principality.

The earthquake of 1887, though it ruined the season of that year, was probably beneficial to the prosperity of Monte Carlo, for it brought the name of the place prominently before the public eye. Shortly after that date the vast crowds which now throng to the place began to make their appearance, and Monaco quite changed its character. New hotels were opened and numbers of houses built, whilst Monte Carlo quite lost its air of reposeful peace and became a sort of cosmopolitan pleasure-town swarming with excursionists. Before this the Casino used to shut at eleven, after which hour every one went to bed, there being no night cafés to go to such as exist to-day.

From about 1882 to 1890 was perhaps the best day of the Principality from a social point of view, for at that time it was the resort of a number of the most distinguished and fashionable people in Europe. All the sporting characters of the day made a point of paying a yearly visit to Monte Carlo—most of them are gone now, including Mr Sam Lewis, who always played in maximums with varying success.

Another well-known figure was Captain Carlton Blythe, who is still alive. He was very successful at trente-et-quarante, where his operations were conducted in a most methodical manner. It was his practice to stake only when sequences were the order of the day. By means of men told off to watch the tables, he was kept informed of this, being sometimes sent for even when not in the Casino. His stakes were high, generally about two thousand francs, which, if won, were increased to six thousand, the next being a maximum (12,000 francs), which was left on till the termination of the run. At times this cheery devotee of coaching was extraordinarily lucky; it is said that he once won as much as £10,000 during a deal.

I believe, however, that in the end this system, like so many others, broke down.

The authorities of the Casino were then rather more particular than at present as to the costume of visitors, and in many cases refused to grant cards of admission to people of the most indisputable respectability on account of their dress not being in conformity with the regulations which they laid down.

On one occasion, indeed, the late Lord and Lady Salisbury, who lived close by at Beaulieu, having been seized with a fancy to look into the rooms, presented themselves at the entrance, where cards of entrée are issued either for the day or longer periods.

They were both dressed in thoroughly country clothes which the official in command viewed with no kindly eye, as his offhand manner showed. When, however, the visitors, in accordance with the regulations, gave their names, he was convulsed with laughter, and at once told the distinguished couple to go about their business and not try their jokes upon him.

The Prime Minister and his wife, who were rather amused at the incident, accordingly retired. Some time afterwards the matter reached the ears of the Administration, who, as a sort of compensation, sent a box at the theatre, but no very profound apology was made. The great gambling monopoly is no respecter of persons, and in the Casino, as on the Turf, complete equality prevails.

In the same year, 1892, a curious incident occurred at a trente-et-quarante table. An individual having staked a maximum on the black, red won. He immediately snatched up his (or rather the bank's) notes from the table and ejaculating, "*C'est la dot de ma fille*," strode out of the rooms before any one quite realised what had happened. For some reason or other he was not followed and got clear away.

Many rich Englishmen annually found at Monte Carlo relaxation and rest from lives of arduous work in the city; some of these regarded play much as sportsmen do shooting, hunting, or yachting.

One of these, now dead, said to the writer: "I have regularly taken a villa here for years, and with hardly an exception have lost the sum which I set apart for gaming every year; but I do not regret it. The amount of amusement which I have obtained has been well worth the money. I might, it is true, have kept a yacht which I should have hated, or taken a shooting which would have been little to my taste. I might, in fact, have spent the money in various ways which would have thoroughly bored me—on the whole I am well content."

Another well-known high player, who from time to time has lost large sums at Monte Carlo, once declared that he considered the money well invested. "Many a large landowner," said he, "is not as lucky as I have been, for he is obliged to spend a large sum every year on the upkeep of his estate for which he obtains nothing in return. I, at least, have had a great deal of amusement."

To this it may be objected that the money which goes into the coffers of the Casino benefits no one—but this is not strictly true, for the shares are held by all sorts of people, who draw their profits in the same way as from any industrial enterprise.

In the 'eighties there were many less hotels than at present and not a great number of villas, whilst the Café de Paris, which has since been rebuilt in an enlarged form, was about the only restaurant apart from the dining-rooms in the hotels. The Gallery, now filled with shops, which is such a favourite morning resort, had not yet come into existence, and except the admirable band in the Casino (which gave two performances a day, free) there was little music in Monte Carlo—a spot which now rings from morning till late at night with the strains of Tzigane bands.

After the tables were closed—at eleven—there were no amusements at all, and, instead of sitting up half the night, every one went to bed—contentedly or discontentedly, as they had won or lost.

The gambling-rooms were much quieter in those days, the flocks of German excursionists having not yet arrived. Many of these visitors, as a rule somewhat undesirable from a decorative point of view, are divided up into little coteries or bands, each of which elects a leader who is entrusted with such funds as the party is desirous of risking at the tables, where the leader alone stakes for all, winnings or losings being divided in proportionate shares.

Of late years the crowds round the gambling-tables have increased to such an extent that except in the early morning or during dinner-time it is impossible to make certain of obtaining a seat. Formerly two or three old men of solemn aspect were always to be found sitting at the trente-et-quarante marking down the run of the game, and on a louis being unostentatiously slipped into their hand they would at once yield up their seat. Of late years, however, they are no longer to be seen, the Administration having banished them from the Casino, much to the discomfort of habitual players desirous of risking substantial sums under comfortable conditions. In old days far more attention was paid in a great many other small ways to visitors who had the appearance of belonging to the upper strata of society. To these the croupiers and other officials made a point of being especially obliging and polite.

The authorities of the Casino, however, seem now to have decided on a more democratic policy, no favour being shown to any one. From a financial point of view this is probably not unsound, a vast number of small players, who drop a certain amount of five-franc pieces and then depart to make way for others, being probably more profitable to the bank than a few heavy gamblers, some of whom may hit it very severely.

It is more than likely that scarcely one in fifty of the individuals who sit with a pile of silver beside the roulette wheel goes away a winner, whereas amongst the high gamblers at trente-et-quarante success is not so rare as is usually supposed. The proof of what has been stated was furnished by the brief existence of the "Cercle Privé"—a new gaming-room which for a short time was highly appreciated by frequenters of Monte Carlo some seven or eight years ago.

The "Cercle Privé" was open only at night in a room upstairs, and men alone enjoyed the privilege of being allowed to play there. There were four tables, three trente-et-quarante and one roulette, a small bar where refreshments could be obtained, smoking was permitted, and the tables, which did not commence operations till the ones downstairs had closed, were kept going very late.

From the point of view of players this innovation was highly successful; for, owing to the comparatively small number of persons who frequented the "Cercle Privé," greater comfort prevailed than downstairs, whilst the conditions in general were far more conducive to calculated and calm speculation.

A large proportion of the frequenters were well known to one another, and the whole thing somewhat resembled a club, the members of which were leagued together against the bank.

Runs, intermittencies, and other tendencies of chance at certain tables could be carefully noted; occasionally there would be no play at all at one table, the whole crowd staking on a run at another; as the room was small, anything of the sort soon reached the ears of every one. Play as a rule was high, and the players, for the most part, were well used to gambling. The results to the bank were most disastrous. On a certain evening it lost more than had ever before been lost in one day by the Casino, and at the end of the year the accounts of the "Cercle Privé" proved anything but an agreeable study for the officials supervising the finances of the great gambling monopoly.

The next year it was closed, and there has since been no inclination on the part of the authorities to repeat what was to them a very unprofitable speculation.

Amongst various causes which in this instance operated to the detriment of the bank was the difficulty, generally amounting to impossibility, of players obtaining a further supply of money when what they had in their pockets had run out. At such a late hour, when the Bank was closed and the *caisse* of most hotels shut up, no matter how rich a man might be, he could not obtain any considerable amount of cash. Consequently, should he lose what he had brought with him, he was reduced to playing with such modest sums as could be borrowed from friends, who naturally could not be expected to make any substantial advance, as any moment they themselves might be in a similar predicament.

The bank, on the other hand, was equipped with ample funds, and its loss—unlike those of the players, which, after a certain point, were limited by necessity—often extended into a very large figure; consequently, when it was in good luck, it only won a comparatively moderate amount, and when in bad lost very heavily.

Another reason for the ill-success of the bank was that the policy pursued in the large rooms downstairs had in the case of the "Cercle Privé" been exactly reversed. In the former there have always been many more roulette tables than tables devoted to trente-et-quarante—upstairs there was only one roulette table as a counter-attraction to the three devoted to the rival game.

Trente-et-quarante is mathematically one of the most favourable of games at which a gambler can play, the percentage against him produced by the *refait* being only 1·28 per cent.

Roulette, on the other hand, is, owing to the zero, highly advantageous to the banker.

The bank's percentage on all-round play at the tables is more than one-seventy-fourth of all the figures staked; the actual winnings of the bank being about one-sixtieth part of all the money actually placed on the board. At the present time the bank's winnings (gross) are, roughly, £1,200,000 per annum.

A large proportion of the gains of the Monte Carlo bank is derived from small players who enter the rooms with the deliberate intention of either making a certain sum or losing what they have in their pockets; these form, as it were, the rank and file of the gambling army which is constantly being decimated by the Casino, and the almost total absence of such an element in the room upstairs reduced the play to a duel between the bank and a number of persons, the majority of whom were, more or less, capitalists and who, as often as not, went home immediately after bringing off one big and successful coup.

The gaming-rooms in the Casino at Monte Carlo have often been described as a hot-bed of vice and debauchery, the tables surrounded by a seething crowd of excited figures whose countenances betray the intense emotions which the vitiating effects of play arouse. "Cries of triumph, imprecations, moans and sobs are heard on every side." In certain highly coloured accounts, suicide is spoken of as being an ordinary occurrence, the crowd making way without comment for the passage of the corpse of some unfortunate gambler who, at the end of his tether, has blown out his brains.

All this is purely fanciful, and conveys no idea whatever of the real state of affairs prevailing in the rooms, where calm and good order invariably reign. There exists, indeed, an almost religious hush in the halls of this great Temple of Chance. After dinner, and towards the time of close of play, the scene, it is true, becomes more animated, but, as a rule, the only sounds heard are those connected with the games played. What conversation there is is almost exclusively devoted to short comments on such matters as the lack or abundance of runs on one particular colour, the persistent recurrence of certain numbers, the amount of winnings or losings of some well-known player, or the like; people rarely speak, when at the table, of their own vicissitudes in the battle with chance.

The real gamblers, that is to say, those to whom speculation is the very breath of life, speak least of all, their whole mind being concentrated upon the system or method of staking which it is generally their practice to adopt. They sit with unmoved faces, which appear neither elated by victory nor depressed by defeat.

A well-known Monte Carlo type—more abundant perhaps in the past than to-day—is the *beau joueur*, the man who plays to the gallery and, let it be added, pays handsomely for his performance. Certain and inevitable ruin is the fate of these individuals, who sacrifice themselves to the spirit of vanity. As a rule, the winnings or losings of such people are a great subject of conversation and discussion amongst the frequenters of the tables—they are said to have either won or lost enormous sums—to be at the end of their tether, or to have an enormous fortune behind them. Their fame, however, is of no enduring kind, being at best a nine days' wonder. They are soon forgotten, and their departure, leaving only too often their money in the vaults of the Casino, and an unpaid bill at their hotel, excites not even passing comment from the crowd of spectators whose approving gaze and fleeting admiration has been so dearly bought.

Some old players remain watching the game for a considerable space of time without risking a stake at all, till the moment arrives when either superstition or calculation prompts them to take the first steps in the campaign. Many of these come provided with memorandum books filled with column after column of figures, records of past runs on colours, and recurring sequences of numbers carefully inscribed as a guide to fathoming the capricious movements of fortune.

Others bring queer little mechanical contrivances, which are manipulated in a manner to show the correspondence between certain chances; whilst yet another section quite frankly display all sorts of fetishes, to some of which they attach a quite serious importance. A piece of the rope which has been used by a hangman is a fetish reputed to be an almost certain passport to good luck. The experience of the present writer with a grim relic of this kind did not, however, give any support to such a belief. As a great favour he was once given a small hempen souvenir by a friend, and armed with the precious talisman he betook himself to a trente-et-quarante table, where a good seat was secured. From the very first, however, it was evident that the gruesome charm was not exercising its occult influence in a direction favourable to its new, and perhaps somewhat sceptical, possessor. When runs were sought for, alternates appeared, and vice versa. *Refaits* were dealt with unnatural frequency; in fact, disaster followed disaster in an unbroken sequence, with the result that the little bit of rope was all that the player had in his pocket as he somewhat disconsolately strode out of the rooms, rather inclined to wish that the hempen relic had been utilised for its original purpose around the neck of its donor.

Gamblers are generally most superstitious folk and swayed by all sorts of whimsical ideas.

Years ago an old lady used to give the authorities a good deal of trouble by repeatedly bringing a small portion of ham into the rooms, and, whilst at play, cutting off slices and eating them. For some reason or other she had the fixed idea that, in her case, ham-eating propitiated fortune.

The rules of the Casino naturally forbid any proceeding of such a kind in the rooms, and whenever the ham was produced the *chef de partie* was obliged to point this out. The old lady in question, who was a well-known character, was, however, very rich, and, being a constant and high player, any drastic action would naturally have been disadvantageous to the best interests of the bank. Some compromise was, therefore, eventually arranged, by which the amount of ham consumed was so infinitesimal as to pass almost unnoticed by the general public.

Certain players attach considerable importance to the numbers inscribed upon the check handed to them by the attendants who look after cloaks and sticks. Now and then, as must of necessity happen in the ordinary course of events, an individual succeeds in winning a good stake by backing a number at roulette corresponding with that on his wooden ticket; more often, however, he fails, and then proceeds to work out all sorts of combinations of numbers, adding, subtracting and dividing, as the fancy seizes him.

The number of the sleeping-berth which has carried the visitor from Paris is also often chosen, as is that of his bedroom in the hotel. The date of a birthday, the sum total of the numbers on a watch, or of the figures on a coin, the number of cigarettes left in a case, or of coins in the pocket, and other similar trifles are all noted with intense interest by a certain class of player, eager for any clue which they believe may assist them in their struggle to achieve success.

It used, at one time, to be said at Monte Carlo that the clergyman of the English Church there never gave out any hymns under number thirty-six, as he had discovered that some of his congregation had made a practice of carefully noting down the numbers with a view to backing them at roulette. Most players, even the least superstitious, have some special lucky number of their own, which they make a point of following. Occasionally it turns up two or three times in succession, which, of course, further confirms them in constantly backing it, and, more often than not, losing far more than they have won.

The present writer's experiences in this direction have not been of an encouraging nature.

Some years ago, being on his way to the Principality, he was much struck by the curiously persistent way in which the number 13 confronted him throughout the journey. His room at Paris was 13; the number of his sleeping-berth in the train to Monaco was 13; and finally he was put into room No. 13 at the Hôtel de Paris on the day of his arrival, the 13th day of the month. All this, to any one with a vestige of superstition, looked as if 13 was a number well worth backing, and accordingly the writer hastened to the rooms, eager to see whether the tip would come off. As a matter of fact the only thing which did come off was the end of his finger, which in his haste to get to the Casino he slammed in his bedroom door. After having been attended to by a surgeon he finally obtained a place at roulette and steadily backed number 13, which, to his intense disgust, appeared rather less frequently than the other numbers. The same unsatisfactory state of affairs prevailed throughout his stay, which on that occasion was a prolonged and unpleasant one.

The curious influence which the advent of certain persons, or the occurrence of trivial incidents, appears to exert in matters of luck is well known to all gamblers. Many of them generally regard a number of trifles with feelings of considerable apprehension at the gaming-table, entertaining the most extraordinary likes and dislikes for various people and things, and cherishing queer fancies at which, in ordinary life, they would be the first to scoff. All this, of course, is akin to the superstition of the savage, a queer atavistic reminder of civilised man's humble descent.

Though the principles of roulette and trente-et-quarante are known to many, it may not be out of place to give brief descriptions of these games as played at Monte Carlo.

Before play begins the money is set out at one end of the table. The gold, after being weighed in scales, is placed in rouleaux, and the bank notes ranged according to their value. Everything is verified by an inspector, who taps each row with a rake and signs his name to a statement on paper.

At trente-et-quarante the minimum stake is a louis, the maximum 12,000 francs (£400), and the capital with which each table begins play £6000. "Breaking the bank" merely means that the money at a particular table is exhausted, and that play has to be suspended while more money is being procured.

Trente-et-quarante is a game of four even chances—*rouge* and *noir*, *couleur gagne* and *couleur perd*. It is played with six packs of cards, which, having been shuffled, are cut by one of the players. There is often a good deal of competition for this ceremony, the cut being by request reserved for some keen player. As a rule, however, others give way when any one who seems in luck—especially a lady of attractive appearance—steps forward to cut the cards.

After every one has staked and "*rien ne va plus*" has been called, the croupier deals the first card face upwards, and continues dealing until the cards turned up exceed thirty pips in number, when he must announce the numbers from "trente-et-un" to "quarante." This top line of cards is black, and when it is less in number than the one which is dealt beneath black wins.

Another line underneath is then dealt for *rouge*. When the two lines are equal in the number of pips—say thirty-six each—the dealer announces an *après*; thirty-one is the *refait* when all stakes are *en prison*. When, however, a *refait* has been dealt, a player may withdraw half his stake if he chooses, or move his money over from the red "prison" to the black "prison." In the case of another *refait*, the money is removed into another space, which is called the second prison. The odds against a *refait* turning up are usually reckoned as 63 to 1. The bank is said, however, to expect it twice in three deals, and there are generally from twenty-nine to thirty-two coups in each deal. By paying one per cent players may insure their stake. A large white counter is placed by the croupier on or near the money insured, which is unaffected by the *refait*. There are high players, however, who consider it bad policy to insure, and prefer to run the risk of 31 being dealt in both lines.

As a matter of fact, from a mathematical point of view, thirty-one is the number which the cards are most likely to make, as any one can easily prove for himself; the combinations formed by the numbers of the pips on the cards being more adapted to produce thirty-one than anything else. It is for this reason, no doubt, that the number in question was chosen for the *refait*, when the game first came into vogue.

At trente-et-quarante, besides the even chances of *rouge* and *noir*, there are also the even chances of *couleur gagne* and *couleur perd*.

The first card dealt determines *couleur*. If, for instance, it is red and *rouge* (the bottom line) wins—*couleur gagne*—the croupier says, "*rouge gagne et la couleur*"; if it is black and *rouge* wins—*couleur perd*—the croupier says, "*rouge gagne, couleur perd*."

The prison, of course, applies to *couleur* just as it does to *rouge* and *noir*.

At certain stated intervals, in the presence of a *sous-directeur* or *chef de partie*, the used packs of cards from trente-et-quarante are carried to a furnace in sealed sacks and scrupulously burnt.

A good many years ago the backs of the cards used at trente-et-quarante were plain white; at the present time, however, a slight design, the pattern of which varies daily, is upon them.

The reason for the change was said to be that the plain backs once facilitated a fraud, which cost the authorities of the Casino many thousands of francs. The story is a curious one.

One morning, as trente-et-quarante was pursuing its usual somewhat monotonous progress, a player with a large pile of money before him, seated next the croupier dealing, entered into an altercation with a neighbour about some stake, in the course of which, owing to violent gesticulations, a whole heap of coins was swept to the ground. Considerable confusion arose, which naturally necessitated the interference of the *chef de partie* (who supervises the game). The attention of everybody, both officials and players, was drawn to the spot where the dispute was taking place; the owner of the fallen treasure loudly declaiming against rough, bullying swindlers being allowed to enter the rooms at all. However, after much chatter, the money having been all found, peace was restored and the game proceeded on its ordinary course.

It was very soon evident that a number of very high players were that morning seated round the table, for quantities of notes and gold began to make their appearance. What was more remarkable was that all the high players seemed to be inspired with the same excellent idea, for every one of them invariably backed the winning chances. So extraordinary was their luck that, after the bank had lost a good deal of money, one of the high officials, who had been watching the game, announced that for the time being further play would be suspended at that particular table, as there was reason to believe that the cards had been tampered with. This naturally provoked a storm of protest, and in the confusion which ensued, the high players slipped unobtrusively away, their pockets well stuffed with the money they had extracted from the bank.

An hour or two later an attempt was made by the authorities to trace them, but, curiously enough, not one was to be found in the Principality. They had all crossed the French frontier and had dispersed in various directions. The cards were afterwards carefully counted and examined, and a thorough investigation of that morning's play is said to have proved beyond all doubt that the whole affair had been a cleverly hatched plot against the bank.

The two men who had quarrelled at the table were professional swindlers, and had carefully rehearsed the disturbance, in order to divert attention from the dealer, who remained apparently quite unmoved whilst the *chef de partie* and other officials were inquiring into the dispute. During this time an accomplice on the other side of this croupier had taken advantage of the general turmoil to slip a portion of a prepared pack into the man's hand. This was furtively exchanged by him for a certain number which he was holding ready to deal. Of these the accomplice relieved him. The high players were all swindlers, well aware how the cards had been arranged. The croupier, heavily bribed, was a rare exception, for, as a rule, Monte Carlo croupiers are above all suspicion. His share in the swindle was detected and he appeared in the Halls of Chance no more.

As was perfectly obvious, a robbery of this kind was greatly facilitated by the plain white backs of the cards in daily use. It was therefore decided that in future every morning a new design should be produced for the backs of these cards, which, known only to a special department, would effectually prevent any chance of prepared packets being interpolated with the packs issued by the authorities.

At roulette as at trente-et-quarante the money is publicly counted out and verified by an inspector before play begins.

The roulette wheels are balanced in the presence of the public, and one of the blue-coated *garçons de salle* goes from table to table with a spirit-level, which is placed upon the rosewood rim of the cylinder, a *chef de table* verifying the accurate adjustment of the wheel by seeing that the air bubble is exactly in the centre.

The maximum stakes allowed on the different chances at roulette are:—

	Francs.
On one number	180
On two numbers (*à cheval*)	360
On three numbers transversal	560
Four numbers (*en carré*)	750
On 0, 1, 2, 3	750
On six numbers transversal	1200
On one dozen	3000
On one column	3000
On all the even chances	6000

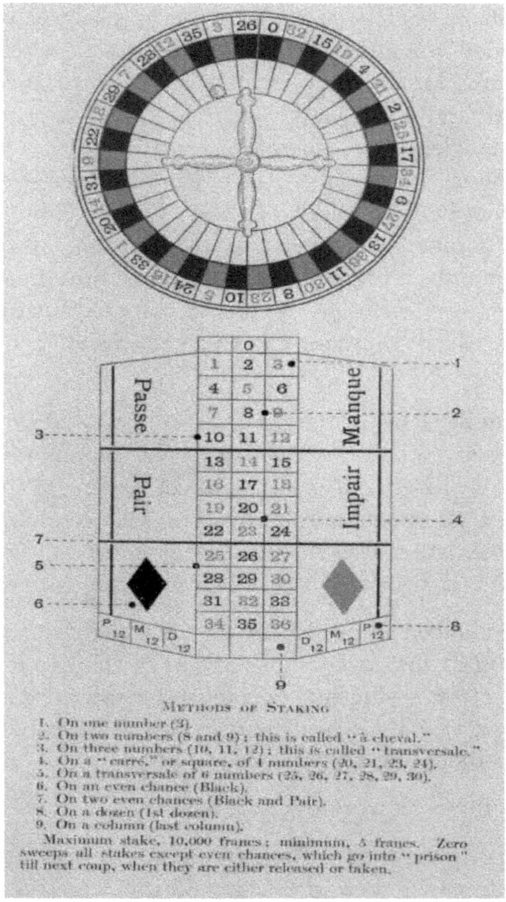

PLAN OF ROULETTE TABLE AS USED AT MONTE CARLO

The amount with which play is begun each day is 80,000 francs, or £3200.

Each roulette table has two boards, on which players may stake, the roulette wheel (a cylinder let into the table) lying between the two. The numbers of the roulette are arranged irregularly, though reds and blacks alternate. Zero, which is not counted as a colour, lies between 32 red and 15 black. There are in all thirty-seven little compartments which receive the ball—eighteen red, eighteen black, and zero. The accurate odds, therefore, are 36 to 1 against any particular division; nevertheless the bank only pays 35 to 1, which causes its profit to amount to 1 in 37, nearly 2·865 per cent.

The lowest stake allowed at roulette is five francs, the highest 10,000 francs, known as a maximum.

The two sides of the roulette table are duplicates of one another, each of them being divided something like a chess-board into three columns of squares, which amount to thirty-six; the numbers advance arithmetically from right to left, and consequently there are twelve lines down, so as to complete a rectangle; as 1, therefore, stands at the head, 4 stands immediately under it, and so on. At the bottom lie three squares marked 12 p, 12 m, 12 d, that is, first, middle, and last dozen. Three large spaces on each side of the numbers are for red and black; even and odd; *manque* and *passe*, that is, the numbers in the first and second half respectively from 1 to 18, and from 19 to 36 inclusive. At the top of each board is zero, which sweeps all stakes, except those on the even chances, into the coffers of the bank.

The stakes having been made a croupier says: "*Le jeu est fait, rien ne va plus.*" The wheel is set in motion. At the same time a croupier sends the ball flying round the cylinder, the roulette wheel bearing the numbers being made to revolve in an opposite direction. The ball eventually falls on to the wheel, and as the latter slackens its speed, enters a compartment, the number of which is announced thus: "*Dix-sept, rouge, impair et manque.*"

When zero is announced all the money on the table is annexed by the bank with the exception of that staked upon the even chances red or black, odd or even, *passe* or *manque*—the sums on these are moved to the edge of the board, being *en prison* till the next coup, when they are taken or released according to the colour and chance which wins.

The odds laid by the bank work out as follows:—

Stakes placed on any number or on zero are paid at the rate of 35 to 1—a player on the numbers is therefore taking 35 to 1 about a 36 to 1 chance, which must be to his prejudice in the long-run—on any four numbers 8 to 1, on any six numbers 5 to 1. Red or black, odd or even, *passe* (the numbers after 18) or *manque* (the numbers before 18) are even-money chances. The dozens and columns are 2 to 1 chances.

Stakes are often placed *à cheval*, that is to say, on two adjoining numbers, which together are paid at the rate of 17 to 1. The red numbers and the blacks are unequally divided in the columns. The centre column contains eight black and only four reds; the first column has six reds and six blacks; while in the last column there are eight reds and four blacks.

Professor Karl Pearson, when making an exhaustive study of the laws of chance, drew up a series of elaborate tables, with the intention of comparing the results of a number of spins of the roulette wheel with those produced by drawing numbers from a hat and tossing with coins.

The conclusion at which he arrived was that, whilst the colours followed the laws of chance as they are generally understood, the other even chances, *passe* and *manque*, *pair* and *impair*, exhibited such capriciousness in their recurrence as could not have been expected had roulette been played continuously through the whole period of geological time.

The roulette wheels of Monte Carlo are perfectly honest machines. The cylinder of each is sheet copper, carefully balanced and strengthened by bands of metal. It revolves in its bed on a vertical pivot of steel, the top of which has a cup-like hollow, into which oil is poured. A mechanic, whose business it is to clean and prepare the wheels every morning, pours oil also into the gun-metal socket which forms the centre of the wheel, and it is then dropped into its place upon the pivot.

The great care which is taken by the authorities to ensure the absolute accuracy of their roulette wheels is based upon very sufficient grounds, for a slight defect in one of those machines once cost them a large sum.

Amongst the frequenters of the rooms at Monte Carlo there is always a large number of astute and none too scrupulous individuals quick to note any little circumstance likely to be of advantage to themselves. For this reason some slight tendency of the roulette wheel to stop in such a way as to cause a certain group of numbers to have an advantage over the rest is very quickly noticed and advantage taken of it.

A mechanic from Yorkshire, Jaggers by name, once cost the Casino some two million francs. Well aware of the difficulty of maintaining a nicely adjusted machine in a perfectly stable condition, Jaggers engaged six assistants, whom he posted at different tables to note the numbers at roulette all day long, whilst he himself undertook to make an elaborate analysis of the results. After a month's play peculiarities were clearly to be discovered in the appearance of the numbers at each of the tables quite out of consonance with the law of average, some numbers turning up more, some less. Having ascertained this fact Jaggers and his men began to play on the numbers which kept ahead of the rest, and won some hundred and forty thousand pounds. The authorities then realised that all was not right, and changed the roulette wheels from one table to another for every day's play, with the result that the bank recovered £40,000. Jaggers, however, was not yet defeated, for by searching observations he discovered minute marks on most of the six wheels, which enabled him to follow them from table to table—a mere scratch was enough.

In a short time he and his assistants knew what numbers would be most likely to recur at certain tables, and the £40,000 which the bank had regained was soon won back.

The authorities controlling the play now began to take a serious view of the situation, and in consequence consulted the manufacturer of the roulette wheels in Paris with a view to constructing cylinders capable of baffling Jaggers and his gang. A new set of wheels were constructed with interchangeable partitions, so that the position of the various receptacles to receive the ball might be changed every evening, when practically a new wheel would be produced, the receptacle which had served for one number on any certain day being utilised for another on the other side the next.

By these means Jaggers was eventually defeated. He was astute enough to perceive that the advantages which he had so cleverly utilised for his own profit no longer existed and, after having lost back some portion of his gains, retired from Monte Carlo some £80,000 to the good.

In order to obviate all chance of anything of this kind happening again, the roulette wheels are carefully examined and tested every day, the most thorough precautions being taken to ensure conditions of the fairest kind.

Whatever objections may be urged against the gambling-rooms as an institution, no accusation of unfairness can be raised against the way in which play is conducted at Monte Carlo. In this respect scrupulous and undeviating honesty is the absolute rule.

A croupier, like a poet, is said to be born, not made. Many of those employed at Monte Carlo, according to current report, are descendants of those who raked in the money of the Allies (and especially of the English officers) in the old gambling-rooms of the Palais Royal in 1814.

A large section belong to great croupier families, members of which dealt the cards and plied the rake in the "conversation houses" and Kursaals of Baden, Homburg, Ems, and other German Spas which have been described. There is something rather stately about these men, most of whom have a peculiar look of detachment not lacking in dignity.

Solemn, courteous, suave, and unmoved, they appear little affected by the monotony which must of necessity attach to their calling. They are, it is said, excellent husbands and fathers, of simple tastes, their chief amusement being playing cards for very modest stakes amongst themselves—for they are a class apart.

A School of Croupiers exists, at which applicants are trained.

The course of instruction in question is located in the Club-room of the Tir aux Pigeons and the Salle d'Escrime. Here during the six summer months are tables exactly like those in the public rooms above, each pupil in turn taking the *rôle* of croupier, whilst others, personating players, stake money all over the table. The novice croupier learns to calculate and pay out winning stakes with sham money, consisting of metal discs and dummy bank-notes.

It takes at least six months to produce a finished croupier.

A roulette croupier receives two hundred and fifty francs a month; whilst dealers at trente-et-quarante are paid three hundred francs. The working-day is six hours, in two spells of three hours each; each man being for three days in succession at one table. Every table is controlled by six croupiers, a seventh being held in reserve as a relief.

At the tables the suavity of manner and impartiality of croupiers in settling disputes is generally above all praise. The difficulties with which a croupier has to contend are sometimes disturbing in the extreme, but his decision is final and, as the players know, admits of no appeal.

Though the tables are surrounded by a mob of persons avid of gain, yet there are times when winning stakes remain unclaimed for several *coups*. When this is observed by the croupiers, the money is set aside for a certain time, after which it goes to swell the funds of the bank. Odd though it may appear, people very often depart leaving winnings behind them on the table—a curious case of this once came under the writer's observation.

A lady, who was leaving Monte Carlo, had been sitting all the morning at the roulette, trying with little success to get on a run, and at last left the rooms to go to lunch with the writer, who afterwards, having escorted her to the hotel to prepare for her journey, strolled again into the Casino.

Just within the door he was accosted by an excited and voluble Englishwoman, who explained that the lady (whom she had observed with the writer) had left two louis on the red when she rose from her chair. Red had won twice, and the attention of the croupiers had been drawn to the unclaimed eight louis, for which the speaker had then assumed the responsibility, saying she was to play them for a lady who had gone out of the rooms. She had then proceeded to play up the eight louis till they had become sixty-four, when, at her request, the whole sum was taken off the table. The *chef de partie* meanwhile declared that the bank would not part with the money till the owner of the original two louis returned.

After waiting for some time, the woman (who frankly said that she hoped to receive a share of the money for having played it up) became much perturbed at not knowing where to find the only owner whom the bank would recognise, and the advent of the writer, to whom she explained the whole thing, was therefore most opportune. The lady when told that sixty-four louis was waiting for her was naturally much pleased, and on drawing the sum on her way to the station, very cheerfully gave the woman a third of what had been won.

Of late years the annual profits of the Casino at Monte Carlo have worked out at about a million, £4000 a day, it is said, flowing into the coffers of the bank during the season. The disbursements, however, are very heavy, amounting literally to hundreds of thousands of pounds. Amongst these must be reckoned £9000 for clergy and schools, £6000 for charity, and £20,000 for police. The arrangement, which was some years ago renewed with the reigning Prince, naturally absorbs a very large sum of money; but, when everything has been paid out, the annual profits do not fall far short of £500,000, the shareholders, even in bad years, receiving something like thirty per cent.

The Casino employs about two thousand officials and *employés*; the general management being carried on by a *directeur-général*, who receives 100,000 francs a year, and three *directeurs*. Three *sous-directeurs*, under whom are the *chefs de table* and the croupiers, have to superintend the gaming-rooms, in which eighteen inspectors walk about the rooms quietly and continually, keeping watchful eyes on *employés* and players. These inspectors are known only to the initiated, and have the appearance of being ordinary onlookers, fond of watching the play. Amongst other duties these men keep an eye upon the people staking, in order to detect any habitual snatchers of other people's money, and also to report on any one who may apply for the *viatique*.

The *viatique*, or sum of money doled out to unsuccessful gamblers by the Casino, consists of the price of a second-class ticket to the applicant's home, together with some small additional funds to enable him to proceed on his journey.

The dole in question was in the earlier days of Monte Carlo generally granted without much demur, but at the present time a successful applicant has to comply with some very unpleasant formalities.

To obtain the *viatique*, the presumably penniless gamester must present himself at a special office, just off a corner of the central gaming-room, and there he must take an oath that he has lost over £300. Inquiries are then made as to whether the applicant has really lost a large sum at play, which is easily discovered by the evidence of the inspectors and officials presiding at the tables. If these inquiries corroborate the story told, he is handed the money, for which he signs a receipt; and until the advance is repaid, the recipient is not allowed to pass the doors which separate the atrium from the gaming-rooms. As a matter of fact, I believe those who have received the *viatique* are now photographed so as to be identified by the door-keepers.

There have been instances of unsuccessful system players, who, after obtaining the *viatique*, have remained at Monte Carlo, constantly vaunting the virtues of their peculiar method of play, indulgence in which has shut them off from the tables.

Whilst the enormous majority of those who frequent Monte Carlo lose, as the princely dividends of the Casino show, certain is it that a number of persons continue to eke out a living by very moderate and careful play. Living in humble lodgings or cheap hotels in the Condamine are many who make it the business of their lives to win one louis, or even ten francs, every day, sitting for hours perhaps in the accomplishment of the task.

Some of these are ruined gamblers, who, being reduced to a modest competency owing to their ruling passion, have more or less learnt wisdom and are content to wait for long periods of time without staking at all, whilst quick to grasp the advantage which can be taken from a well-marked run. Old women, with queer handbags and bundles of what resemble washing-books, abound at the roulette tables, some of them being exceedingly shrewd and in a small way not unsuccessful players.

When a woman really grasps the spirit of play she is undoubtedly far cleverer than a man, who more often than not regards the gambling as a personal combat between himself and the bank, which he thinks of rather as a living thing than the ruthless inanimate machine which, in sober fact, it is.

The majority of women, however, are quite hopeless as gamblers, merely frittering their money away, often quite ignorant of the odds, chances, and general procedure of either trente-et-quarante or roulette, at which their favourite method of staking is to try and back winning numbers.

The methods and systems employed by habitual frequenters of the rooms are of every possible description, some being devised to win but a louis, and others to secure a princely fortune.

The numbers at roulette are very profitable to the bank, for no system or method, no matter how carefully devised (except the one employed by Jaggers), has ever assisted any one to back a winning number or set of numbers. All this is mere chance, and no calculations as to previous numbers and the like are of the least assistance. Every *coup* that is played is an absolutely new *coup*, and quite unaffected by anything that has gone before. There is really no reason why one number should not keep turning up during the whole of one day's play except the fact that such a thing has never been known to happen. It appears certain that the general tendency of chances is to equalise themselves at the end of a certain period, but as the player of necessity cannot possibly tell whether any given chance is on the up or down grade, such knowledge is of no assistance whatever to him.

A certain number is observed not to have turned up for a considerable length of time, and the conclusion is formed that an increasing stake upon it must in the end prove a good investment. More often than not the very contrary is the case, for there have been whole days at Monte Carlo during which a number at one table has scarcely appeared at all. On the other hand, if a record of every *coup* at this table had been kept, the recurrence of every number would, in the course of time, be found to be practically the same. Complicated systems have often been devised, the main principle of which was covering a large proportion of the numbers, only a few, supposed by deduction to be unlikely to turn up, being left untouched. Disaster has invariably followed even a moderate run on such numbers, which, of course, occurs in the end, completely draining the players' pockets.

The even chances, without doubt, afford a player the greatest likelihood of success.

Staking a louis every time on both black and red, or any other even chance, leaving on any winnings in the hope of catching a run, is occasionally not a bad plan. The trouble of staking on both chances can be modified by calculation, though it is somewhat apt to lead to confusion.

A great number of players spend their whole time trying to strike a run at trente-et-quarante—this generally occurs when they are absent from their favourite table. The third *coup* would seem to be the most dangerous: for this reason, when a colour has run twice it is better to withdraw some portion of the sum staked, and then the remainder may be left to double up.

The practice of staking on the dozens at roulette is generally very attractive to those fresh to the tables, who like the idea of landing a two to one chance. The same type of player is, as a rule, at one time or another, fascinated by that system (or rather method of staking) which consists in backing two dozens, that is, laying two to one against the bank. Most of such players, however, soon discover how disastrous this may prove, and it should be realised that it is by no means an unusual occurrence for a dozen not to appear for ten or twelve *coups*—seventeen, I believe, is the record number of non-appearances. The great objection, however, to backing two dozens is zero, which sweeps everything but the even chances.

Another method of play is to stake against the recurrence of any number of even chances in an identical order.

Ten *coups* at trente-et-quarante, for instance, having resulted thus:

- Red
- Red
- Red
- Black
- Red
- Black
- Black
- Red
- Red
- Black,

the player plays black, black, black, red, and so on in an exactly opposite sense, increasing his stake till successful. As a matter of fact it is not very usual for any given number of *coups* to recur in exactly the same succession, and played with discretion this system occasionally yields fair results.

Another simple method is to stake red, black, alternately, doubling up till the winning colour is caught. This has the advantage of ensuring profit from a run, but a directly opposite series of alternate reds and blacks must, of course, prove ruinous in the extreme.

The martingale, which is merely going "double or quits," is the simplest of all systems. There are two martingales, the small and the great. In the small martingale the aim is to get back all previous losses in one *coup*, and to leave you a winner of one unit at the finish.

The progression is as follows: 1, 2, 4, 8, 16, 32, 64, 128, 256, 512, 1024. If you played this system at a roulette table with a unit of five francs, it takes eleven consecutive losses to defeat you, and one loss less at the trente-et-quarante table, where the minimum stake is 20 francs.

You may go on playing this martingale for weeks at a time without encountering an adverse run of sufficient magnitude to enable the bank to capture your stake. The only thing you have to fear is a run of 12 against you; you can only double up eleven times, and your last stake will be 5120 francs. Runs of 12, however, are rare.

The great martingale aims at getting back all the previous losses and winning one unit for every *coup* played. The progression is 1, 3, 7, 15, 31, 63, 127, 255, 511, 1023, and the player is defeated by ten consecutive losses at roulette, and nine at trente-et-quarante.

When playing the little martingale the player has to double his stake every time he loses, in order to recover his losses and be one unit to the good. Whereas, in the great martingale he not only doubles his stake but adds one unit to each *coup*, and only stands one chance in 1024 of losing at each *coup*, that is, of encountering an adverse run of ten.

A popular system is that known as the Labouchere system. Its main principle is to keep scratching out the top and bottom figures whenever you win, till no figures are left, and always to put down your loss when you lose, which, added to the topmost number, forms the next stake.

Before beginning to play write down on a card 1, 2, 3, in this order:—

- 1
- 2
- 3

Your object is to win six units, and you always stake the sum total of the top and bottom figures—1 + 3 = 4. If you win, you strike out the 3 and the 1:—

- ~~1~~
- 2
- ~~3~~

Your next stake will now be 2. If you win again, your task is over, for you have won your six units. Suppose, however, as alas! most frequently happens, that you lose your first stake 1 + 3, you must add the figure 4 at the bottom of your score thus:—

- 1
- 2
- 3

- 4

Your next stake will now be 1 + 4 = 5. We will then say that you win, in which case cross out the 1 and the 4, making your score:—

- ~~1~~
- 2
- 3
- ~~4~~

The next stake would be 2 + 3. You lose, and your score stands:—

- ~~1~~
- 2
- 3
- ~~4~~
- 5

The next stake would be 2 + 5. You win, and you cross out 2 and 5:—

- ~~1~~
- ~~2~~
- 3
- ~~4~~
- ~~5~~

The next stake would be 3, and if you win you cross out 3, and have won the six units that you started out to win.

Not infrequently this system, after very nearly proving successful (one number only being left), goes entirely wrong and runs into very big figures, and in such a case the player is very lucky if he succeeds in regaining his losses and winning the six units originally sought for. More often than not he finds himself obliged to desist through lack of capital.

The writer's own experience of this system, which he has thoroughly tested on several occasions at Monte Carlo, was that very frequently the six units would be won several times in succession with comparatively slight difficulty—at times, indeed, it appeared almost ridiculously easy to win. In the end, however, there invariably came a day when a very contrary state of affairs prevailed, and the money won returned, with interest, to the bank.

It should be added that before the writer embarked upon his efforts to defeat the bank at Monte Carlo by means of this system, he gave it a thorough trial by dealing out the required number of packs of cards at trente-et-quarante, and noting the results of the various *coups*. In almost every case the system proved completely successful, as systems generally do when they are not being played for money.

An exception to this was Lord Rosslyn's defeat by Sir Hiram Maxim, when the former's system, played for sham money, was beaten at the 3080th *coup*. Nevertheless the system in question is not a particularly bad one, were it not that it requires a considerable capital. Ten thousand units or more are essential, with £16,000 on the basis of a one-louis unit.

If fortune should favour the player, the profit would be from five to six hundred louis a day.

The principle of this system is to increase the stakes by one unit every time, without ever decreasing, until all previous losses are wiped out and one louis as well is gained for every *coup* played.

Two exceptions to this rule, however, exist. The first stake is always "one," but if you lose this, instead of your next stake being two, it is three; after that it should be four, five, six, seven, eight, etc., until your task is accomplished. The game is finished when you can wipe out all minus quantities from your score sheet and bring the result to +1. Suppose, therefore, your score sheet shows you to be -3, and your stake in the ordinary way ought to be 7; instead of staking 7 you would only stake 4, in order to arrive at the result of +1 if you win. In the event of your losing the stake of 4, your next stake will be 8, just as if you had staked 7 in the ordinary course of the game the previous *coup*. If you lose the 8, you would continue with 9, 10, 11, and so on.

If you win two or three stakes of 1 at the commencement, they are considered as definite gains, and put away quite apart from your capital.

In the event of your losing the first two stakes of 1 and 3, your position is:—

First loss	-1
Second loss	-3
	—
Total loss	-4

The object of the system being to win a unit per *coup* as well as to recover any loss, in order to keep a clear record of the amount you require to win, it is best to add one unit to your losses after every *coup*.

Supposing that the game is begun with four losing and three winning *coups*, it will be scored as follows:—

First loss	1	to which add 1 more.
	1	
	—	
Total	-2	
Second stake	-3	and lose.
	—	
Lost	-5	to which add 1 more.
	1	
	—	
Total	-6	
Third stake	-4	and lose.
	—	
Lost	-10	to which add 1 more.
	1	
	—	
Total	-11	
Fourth stake	-5	and lose.

—

Lost	-16	to which add 1 more.
	1	
	—	
Total	-17	
Fifth stake	+6	and win.
Lost	-11	to which add 1 more.
	1	
	—	
Total	-12	
Sixth stake	+7	and win.
	—	
Lost	-5	to which add 1 more.
	1	
	—	
Total	-6	
Seventh stake	7	and win.
	—	
Result	+1	

Result.—*Coups* played, 7; *coups* lost, 4; units won, 20. *Coups* won, 3; units lost, 13. Total won, 7.

The last stake, it will be observed, is only 7 instead of 8. This is because you only require to arrive at a result of +1. Had 8 been staked in the ordinary course and won, you would have won a unit more than you needed, but would have taken some unnecessary risk.

Those desirous of giving various systems a trial should not omit to study the method of staking set forth in Mr. Victor Bethell's lively little book, *Ten Days at Monte Carlo*. A merit of this system is that it only seeks to win a certain moderate amount every day, and does not allure the player with hopes of immense and impossible gain.

Most systems as a rule prove successful for a short time, and while this happy state of affairs prevails, the player, not unnaturally, congratulates himself upon having discovered an infallible method of overcoming the wiles of chance. Sooner or later, alas, comes the day when his laborious calculations prove quite powerless to defeat the bank, and clearly demonstrate that the success, which at one time seemed so certain and easy, was merely the result of having hit upon a vein of good luck.

In all probability the best method of staking is the following, which was once carried out for some two months with complete success. The method in question was successfully worked by a gentleman (known to the present writer), who owing to the illness of a relative, was obliged to remain at Monte Carlo for a rather lengthy period of time. He was, it must be understood, very well off, and by no means a gambler. His plan was this: every day he put a hundred-franc note in his pocket, which he changed into five-franc bits in the Casino. With these twenty coins he commenced to play. His stake was usually but one or two of these coins at first, though sometimes he would lose his whole capital in a few moments trying to back winning numbers.

If successful, any notes he might receive were put in his pocket-book not to be used for play. It was no uncommon thing for him to leave the Casino with a profit of a thousand francs.

On the other hand, it would often occur that for a number of days in succession he would lose his hundred francs without hardly having won a stake at all. In the long run, however, he was a very considerable sum to the good, a comparatively small number of winning days having far more than compensated him for the large number of those on which the hundred francs had been speedily lost. Under no circumstances did he ever risk more than a hundred francs in one day. It was, of course, the system of putting all paper money in the pocket which caused this method to succeed. It should be added that when the hundred francs had rolled up into twenty or thirty louis at roulette the player often tried his luck with them at trente-et-quarante. The essential advantage of this method of staking is the limit imposed upon loss; under no circumstances can more than one hundred francs a day be lost, whilst when in luck a very large sum may be won.

The method described above is not a bad one for any one who is making a prolonged stay at Monte Carlo, and is not desperately anxious to indulge in serious gambling; a better course to be adopted by those who are, is to decide exactly how much they are prepared to lose, take the whole of sum in question into the rooms one morning, divide it into a certain number of stakes, and with these play a limited number of *coups* on the even chances. If successful, repeat this operation the next day with the winnings alone, and so on until a fairly substantial sum has been amassed, when the wisest course is to cease all further gambling for that visit.

It must never be forgotten that the fewer *coups* which are played the more chance there is of winning.

Long sittings at the trente-et-quarante or roulette table are absolutely certain to end in loss, besides being inexpressibly tedious, trying to the eyes, and destructive to health.

A man who plays a great part of the day and all the evening after dinner must certainly end by being a loser; whereas he who merely plays for a few minutes at a time has a very fair chance of ending up a winner, always provided, of course, that the fates are propitious.

In the long run nothing is to be gained by making a toil of gaming, the only justifiable defence of which is that in moderation it affords a good deal of pleasurable though generally costly excitement.

There are good methods of staking and bad methods; but there is not, and, so far as can be foreseen, never will be, a thoroughly reliable system. The best is that which minimises loss, acting as a check in the case of an unfavourable run. All complicated mathematical calculations undertaken with a view to defeating the bank are vain, for none of them take into consideration that most important and mysterious factor—*luck*—which so often seems to shun serious gamblers.

"If I were resolved to win," said a lover of systems, "I should go very soberly with a hundred napoleons, and be content with winning one." "That would never do," was the reply of a player well versed in the fallacies of gamesters' calculations. "Better go, after a good dinner, with one napoleon, resolved to win a hundred."

XI

Difficulty of making money on the Turf—Big wins—Sporting tipsters and their methods—Jack Dickinson—"Black Ascots"—Billy Pierse—Anecdotes—Lord Glasgow—Lord George Bentinck—Lord Hastings—Heavy betting of the past—Charles II. founder of the English Turf—History of the latter—Anecdotes—Eclipse—Highflyer—The founder of Tattersall's—Old time racing—Fox—Lord Foley—Major Leeson—Councillor Lade—"Louse Pigott"—Hambletonian and Diamond—Mrs. Thornton match—Beginnings of the French Turf—Lord Henry Seymour—Longchamps—Mr. Mackenzie Grieves—Plaisanterie—Establishment of the Pari Mutuel in 1891—How the large profits are allocated—Conclusion.

In the course of some remarks on racing made by Lord Rosebery at the 131st dinner of the Gimcrack Club he said:—

"I don't think any one need pursue the Turf with the idea of gain."

This statement, though a discouraging one for sportsmen, is nothing more than the plain, unvarnished truth, as any one who cares to look into the matter can find out for himself. A quicker and more convincing method, open to those with plenty of funds, is to own race-horses.

The Turf, as a means of making money, is indeed not to be considered seriously. Certain bookmakers, of course, have made, and do still make fortunes, but bookmaking cannot properly be called going on the Turf.

Owners have also existed who, for a time, have reaped a rich harvest by the success of their horses. Over Hermit's Derby Mr. Chaplin is said to have landed an enormous stake, something between a hundred and a hundred and twenty thousand—he never received the whole of the amount which he won. Mr. John Hammond was also at times very successful in winning large sums. He is said to have cleared over £70,000 by the victory of Herminius in the Ascot stakes of 1888. This horse he had bought for two hundred and forty guineas! A singularly lucky owner was Mr. James Merry, who is supposed to have cleared over £80,000 when Thormanby won the Derby. Another big win was that of Mr. Naylor, who is supposed to have won £100,000 over Macaroni for the Derby of 1863.

Nevertheless, from a financial point of view betting on horse-races is almost without exception disastrous, and, whether they know too much or know too little, men who systematically indulge in it to any great extent stand an excellent chance of being left with empty pockets.

As for the general public, a number of whom are more or less given to risking an occasional bet, their chance of winning is absolutely infinitesimal. An individual who bets throughout the year is indeed very lucky if he loses only two-thirds of the money he has risked—as a rule he does far worse than this. The sporting papers, on which many rely, are of course genuinely anxious to assist their readers to find winners, but do not pretend to be infallible guides. Sporting journalists themselves, who should be in an excellent position to obtain reliable information, are not infrequently peculiarly unsuccessful in their own bets; probably few end the year on the winning side. The most expensive guides of all are, of course, the advertising tipsters, some of whom make quite large sums by issuing thoroughly unreliable vaticinations to a touchingly confiding clientele. Some time ago one of these men very cleverly took advantage of a newspaper competition, when a prize had been offered by a sporting paper for naming the most popular tipster of the day. Purchasing some thousands of coupons he put his own name on them, of course varying the writing to prevent suspicion. As a result of these tactics he was eventually adjudged to be the prize tipster, and, though the scheme cost him a good deal of money, it eventually brought considerable grist to his mill.

The circulars and letters issued by these prophets are generally admirably calculated to increase the number of their followers.

Not infrequently they adopt a high-flown style. One for instance, moved by purely philanthropic motives, declares that "when he casts his practised eye on the broad surface of struggling humanity and witnesses the slow and enduring perseverance or impetuous rush of the many to grapple with a cloud, he is seized with an intense desire to hold up the lamp of light to all." Another adopts a bluffer style and writes:—

> DEAR SIR—DON'T WASTE YOUR MONEY. Let me entreat you not to miss to-morrow's GOLDEN PADDOCK WIRE; it will be honestly worth a £10 note.
>
> My RELATION connected with a certain WELL-KNOWN STABLE says, "Frank, my boy, get your money on at once; this is another 20 to 1 chance." A GOLD MINE is before us—miss this and you will miss a pile of GOLD and silver.

> OWNER and TRAINER HAVE planked their money down; both will travel with the GRAND ANIMAL (the name of which I will forward for 5s.) to-morrow by special train.
>
> Send a postal order and secure the name of the smartest three-year-old that ever came under the starters' orders or romped past the judge's box lengths ahead of all the favourites, winning clients and myself many HUNDREDS OF POUNDS.

Yet another offers infallible information if clients will merely put a small portion of their stake on for him. As some of the horses he gives must win he probably does fairly well. Whilst most of such tipsters are but sorry guides, some are undoubtedly honest men and try to do their best for their clients.

Such a one was Old Jack Dickinson, a thoroughly honest sporting tipster, who will be remembered by all race-goers of some years ago. This well-known character, who was a fine sprint runner in his day, bore a quite unblemished reputation, though a backer of horses and a professional vendor of tips. Old Jack was a regular church-goer in his own parish, where his death caused genuine sorrow. Though in his capacity as a Turf tipster he was at times compelled to issue his circulars on Sunday, this he did not like, and by way of salving his conscience in the matter he is said to have made a practice of devoting all the money he received from the Sunday information to church purposes, it being put into the collection box.

On the Turf, exclusive of betting men, jockeys, and trainers, there are three classes—men of large fortune, with well and old-established studs, fixtures as it were; sporting men of moderate fortune, who confine themselves to four or five horses at a time, and run merely in their own part of the world; and lastly, men of small or no fortune, who run for profit more than amusement. It is the conduct of many of this last class which has at times been injurious to the Turf.

The sporting owner, who has to pay large trainers' bills and meet the other inevitable charges incident to the sport of which he aspires to be a pillar, cannot reasonably hope to make a profit on his racing; even the sharp betting man is in many cases out of pocket at the end of a year. Expenses, such as travelling, hotel bills, and the like, amount to a considerable sum, and for this reason every supporter of the Turf is greatly handicapped before he even makes a bet.

Layers as well as backers have large disbursements which they cannot avoid—as a matter of fact the vast majority of bookmakers who have died rich men have made their fortunes through commercial enterprises, though, of course, the moderate capital originally invested was made in the Ring. To acquire any considerable sum in this manner is by no means an easy thing. Much is heard about successful bookmakers; little of those who fail and disappear.

If betting can ever be made profitable, it must be carried on in a most systematic and restrained manner. A few points in the odds make the difference often of some thousands; and it will require a man's whole time and attention to take advantage of any turn in the market.

A young man who goes racing with the idea of making money is of necessity quickly disillusioned in the most unpleasant of ways. If he knows no racing men he is, of course, hopelessly at sea; but should he have means of obtaining really good information, his fate is generally even more deplorable, for some untoward incident almost invariably happens when a big *coup* is on and the good thing goes down.

Not a few, in despair at continual losses, make up their minds to wait for "absolute certainties," and lay heavy odds on some horse which it would seem cannot possibly be beaten, a method which usually proves very expensive in the end.

Of all meetings Ascot seems most fatal to gamblers of this description. A particularly disastrous meeting was that of 1879. In the Vase, Silvio, 9 to 4 on, fell before Isonomy; Peter, 5 to 2 on for the Fern Hill Stakes, was beaten by Douranee; Victor Chief, 7 to 4 on, was fourth to Philippine for the Seventeenth New Biennial; Valentino second for the Maiden Plate at 5 to 4 on; Silvio, 6 to 4 on, was beaten in the Hardwicke; and Aventurier, 2 to 1, was defeated by Royal for the Plate of one hundred sovereigns, which concluded this woeful meeting.

Another "Black Ascot" was that of 1882. 8 to 1 was laid on Geheimniss, which could only obtain second place in the Fernhill Stakes; 9 to 2 on St. Marguerite, third in the Coronation Stakes; 11 to 8 on Rookery, second in the New Stakes; and 9 to 4 on Foxhall, second in the Alexandra Plate. An appalling series of disasters for the unfortunate backer!

Layers of odds on again suffered at Ascot in 1894, when 5 to 1 was laid on Delphos for the All Aged Stakes, and 5 to 1 on La Flèche for the Hardwicke on the Friday. The odds in each case were upset, both being second.

At Ascot this year backers as usual did not fare particularly well, for notable upsets occurred in the Coventry Stakes, won by the Admiration colt at 20 to 1, and in the All Aged Stakes, in which 100 to 15 was laid on Hallaton which succumbed to his only rival Hillside.

When everything is said and done, there can be no doubt that the individual who starts out, either as bookmaker or backer, with the idea that he is going to make a fortune must, as an old racing character (Billy Pierse, whose father fought at Culloden) used to say, "want it here."

This expression was very popular with "T' au'd un" or the "Governor," as Billy was commonly designated on the Yorkshire courses. Once at Doncaster, when Sir John Byng had to decide a dispute as to jostling to the prejudice of a horse trained by "T' au'd un," the latter insisted that Sir John could not distinguish between a race and a charge of cavalry, and that he could by no earthly explanation be made to comprehend in what a "jostle" in racing consisted. So cantankerous was Billy on the subject that he accosted an old gentleman, whose erudition he held in high esteem, in the following manner: "Tell me, sir, wasn't this Sir J. Byng's father or grandfather hanged?" "No, Mr. Pierse," was the reply, "not hanged; probably you allude to the Admiral, who was shot." "I thowt," rejoined Billy, "it was sommat o' t' sowort, an' it's much of a muchness between hanging and shooting; but I'll uphoud ye that this Sir John Byng will never do for the Turf—he may be well enough for a General, but he'll never do for the Turf! He wants it here, sir," added Billy, putting his finger in a most expressive manner on his forehead, "he wants it here!"

The maxims of "T' au'd un" were held in great respect, and the Duke of Cleveland, for whom he won several races on Haphazard, used frequently to ask the old man (who had had his last mount in the St. Leger of 1819) to Raby. Concerning these visits Billy used to say, "I never forgot that I was Billy Pierse—I was useful or I wouldn't have been theer." This was to some extent true, for the Duke had a high opinion of his judgment in Turf matters. A favourite saying of Old Billy, and one which afforded him much comfort, was, "I've done as many as have done me." Nevertheless he was straight enough, according to the Turf ethics of his day.

Within the last twenty-five years there have been many changes in connection with Turf speculation. Ante-post betting, for instance, is now practically obsolete, whilst starting price betting, unknown in old days, has come into vogue; and, finally, the huge wagers formerly quite common have become things of the past, a state of affairs which would be little to the taste of men of the type of the fifth Lord Glasgow did they still exist. This nobleman's love of wagering enormous sums excited attention even in an age when high gambling was not generally viewed with anything like the severity which prevails to-day, when Stock Exchange speculation is the favourite mode of attaining complete and speedy impecuniosity.

The evening before the Derby of 1843 Lord Glasgow, then Lord Kelburne, was at Crockford's, when Lord George Bentinck inquired if any one would lay him three to one against his horse, Gaper. Lord Kelburne said he should be delighted.

(THE PRINCE REGENT.) (COLONEL O'KELLY.)
BETTING.
By Rowlandson.

"Remember," said Lord George, "I'm not after a small bet."

"Well," rejoined Lord Kelburne, "I suppose £90,000 to £30,000 will suit you."

This staggered the owner of Gaper, who was obliged to admit that he had never dreamt of taking such a large bet.

Lord Kelburne was rather annoyed. "I thought you wanted to do it 'to money,'" said he sharply; "however, I see I was wrong."

As early as 1823 this sporting peer had created a sensation at the Star Inn at Doncaster, by offering to lay 25 to 1 in hundreds against Brutandorf for the St. Leger, afterwards repeating the offer in thousands.

On the St. Leger of 1824 Jerry won him some £17,000, but three years later he lost £27,000, Mr. Gully's much-fancied Derby winner, Mameluke, being beaten by Matilda. The victory of this filly, which was very popular with the Yorkshire crowd, is commemorated at Stapleton Park, near Pontefract—where her owner, the Hon. E. Petre, lived—by a chiming clock placed over the stables, known as the "Matilda clock," which is appropriately surmounted by a "race-horse weathercock."

Lord George Bentinck is said to have won no less than £100,000 by betting in one year (1845), but his racing expenses amounted to an enormous sum.

He won £12,000 by the victory of Cotherstone in the Derby, and it is said would have profited to the extent of some £135,000 had Gaper proved the winner of that classic race. His successes as an owner, though considerable, hardly compensated him for the immense amount of time, thought, and money which he expended upon racing matters. Crucifix, it is true, won the Two Thousand, the One Thousand, and the Oaks in 1840, but Lord George never won the Derby, though if he had not parted with his stud in 1846 he would in all probability have done so, for Mr. Mostyn in his purchase acquired Surplice, who became the winner in 1848. The victory much agitated his former owner when he heard of it.

Sir Joseph Hawley was a very heavy better in his time, though at the end of his Turf career he began a crusade against the evils of plunging—nevertheless, not very long before, he had taken £40,000 to £600 about each of the fillies he had entered for the Derby.

The enormous bets made by the ill-timed Marquis of Hastings are notorious. Now and then he hit the Ring very hard—when Lecturer won the Cesarewitch, for instance, he was a gainer of no less than £75,000—and his Turf winnings in stakes were also considerable for two or three years. In 1864 they amounted to £10,000, in 1866 to £12,000, and in 1867 to over £30,000. Hermit's Derby, however, in the same year is said to have cost him £140,000; and even had Marksman, who was second, won, he would have lost £120,000.

This spendthrift nobleman was anything but shrewd as a plunger. He had made his book so badly that, though he stood to lose heavily, he would only have profited to the extent of a few thousands had Vauban, which was his best horse, been first past the post. In 1868 the Marquis, a broken-down, ruined man, passed to his grave at the early age of twenty-six.

There was very heavy betting in the old days. Davies, the celebrated bookmaker, for instance, more than once made a Derby book amounting to £100,000. As a matter of fact he is said to have generally lost money over the Derby and Oaks, and won it over the St. Leger. When Daniel O'Rourke won the Derby he lost about £50,000 (some say almost double this sum), having laid a great deal of money at 100 to 1. Catherine Hayes also hit him hard, and over West Australian he lost £48,000, of which £30,000 went to the owner, Mr. Bowes. In his latter years Davies rather avoided ante-post betting, especially on the Derby. The victory of Teddington in 1851 took something not far short of £90,000 out of his pockets, one cheque alone sent out by him to Mr. Greville being for £15,000. The Derby in question was very costly to the Ring in general, which lost something like £150,000. The most considerable sum, however, ever won by the great racing public of small means was when Voltigeur won the St. Leger in 1850. The excitement during the deciding heat with Russborough was probably the greatest ever seen on any race-course; and on the evening of the following day, when he won the Doncaster Cup, beating the Flying Dutchman, many of the Yorkshiremen caroused all night. As one of them said, "Who'd go to bed when Voltigeur's won the St. Leger and the Cup?"

Whilst racing possesses some claim to be considered a serious sport owing to the undoubted improvement which it has effected in the breed of horses, its most ardent supporters have been men of pleasure. The founder of the English Turf, indeed, was the "Merry Monarch," though there had been horse-racing for bells long before his time.

Charles the Second did everything he could to improve horsemanship in England. He it was who induced a celebrated French riding master, Foubert by name, to come over and settle in England. This Frenchman set up a riding academy near what is now Regent Street. His name is still perpetuated by "Foubert's Passage."

Charles, who knew a good deal about most things, possessed, it is said, much knowledge of horses, and was himself an experienced and able rider. He became a great supporter of the Turf, gave many prizes to be run for, and delighted in witnessing races. When he resided at Windsor the horses ran on Datchet-mead; but the most distinguished spot for these spectacles was Newmarket, a place which was first chosen on account of the firmness of the ground.

Remains of the house in which Charles lived at what became the head-quarters of the Turf still exist. It was originally purchased by the "Merry Monarch" from an Irish Peer, Lord Thomond.

Here it was that Nell Gwynne is supposed to have held her infant out of the window as Charles passed down the Palace Gardens to his stables, and apostrophised him to the effect that if the child was not made a Duke upon the spot she would drop it.

When the King went to see this palace, as it was called, which he had caused to be built at Newmarket, he thought the rooms too low; but the architect, Sir Christopher Wren, who was of small stature, did not agree. Walking through the rooms he looked up at the King and said, "Please your Majesty, I think they are high enough." The King squatted down to Sir Christopher's height, and creeping about in that posture, cried, "Aye, Sir Christopher, I think they are high enough."

During his visits to the little town Charles usually spent the morning in coursing or playing tennis, repairing to the Heath about three to witness racing, it being the custom for the King and his retinue of courtiers and ladies to ride alongside or after the contending steeds, which on their arrival at the winning post were saluted with the blare of trumpets and the beating of drums. Most of the races in Charles' day would appear to have consisted of matches to decide wagers previously laid.

The Whip which is annually run for at Newmarket has sometimes been said to be the identical one which Charles II. (not George II.) was in the habit of riding with, and which he presented to some nobleman, whose arms it bears, as being the owner of the best horse in England.

The whip itself is of very antique appearance, and by no means "a splendid trophy." The handle, which is very heavy, is of silver, with a ring at the end of it for a wristband, which is made of the mane of Eclipse.

During this reign the Turf became a popular and aristocratic institution. The Merry Monarch even condescended to ride himself, and rode a match at Newmarket in 1671, on which occasion his horse Woodcock was beaten.

Charles kept and entered horses in his own name, and by his attention and generosity added importance and lustre to the institution over which he presided. Bells, the ancient reward of swiftness, were now no longer given; a silver bowl or cup of the value of one hundred guineas succeeded the tinkling prize. On this royal gift the exploits of the successful horse, together with his pedigree, were usually engraven to publish and perpetuate his fame.

James the Second is reputed to have been a good horseman, but his reign was too short and troublesome to permit him to indulge his inclinations as regards horses. He was a lover of hunting, and ever preferred English mounts, several of which he had always in his stables after he became an exile in France.

When William the Third ascended the throne, he not only added to the plates given at different places in the kingdom, but made every attempt at improving horsemanship. Though he was a monarch of considerable austerity, this king once matched a horse of his own for a stake of two thousand guineas.

Queen Anne continued the bounty of her predecessors, with the addition of several plates. Her Consort, George, Prince of Denmark, is said to have taken infinite delight in horse-racing, and to have obtained from the Queen the grant of several plates allotted to different places.

Towards the beginning of the eighteenth century a statute of Queen Anne was enacted with a view to the restriction of betting. Very great sums of money changed hands owing to a match run at Newmarket between the gentlemen of the South and those of the North. It is almost superfluous to add that the proverbial shrewdness of the Northerner was fully demonstrated on this occasion.

Queen Anne herself was, however, a supporter of the Turf, running horses in her own name in matches at Newmarket and York.

Towards the close of the reign of George the First he discontinued the plates, and in lieu of each gave the sum of one hundred guineas.

In the middle of the eighteenth century the Turf had fallen into some disrepute, but the Duke of Cumberland did much to revive the glories which had somewhat languished since the days of Charles II. He it was who first instituted the race meeting at Ascot.

The Duke was a born gambler, and used when out hunting to play at hazard with Lord Sandwich, throwing a main on every green hill and under every green tree whenever the hounds checked.

Though cheery enough in the hunting field, he was anything but tender-hearted when pursuing his avocation as a soldier; indeed his severity at times became cruelty, which gained for him the nickname of "the Butcher."

The day after the decisive battle of Culloden, in the year 1745, the General, or as he was popularly styled, Duke William, was riding over the scene of battle in company with his officers, among whom was Colonel Wolfe, afterwards the hero of Quebec, then a young man. Among the dead and dying stretched on the stricken field, one was so far recovered as to be able to sit upright. Looking at the poor wretch, the Duke said to the young Colonel by his side; "Wolfe, shoot me that rebel." Wolfe glared back at his prince and commander, and, with a flushed countenance which showed his indignation, replied: "Your Royal Highness, I am a soldier, not an executioner." The Duke turned his back upon Wolfe and did not utter another word.

If, however, the Duke, as the saying went, was a "very devil in his boots," he was all right out of them and good-natured enough when racing. Being at a Newmarket meeting just before the horses started, he missed his pocket-book, containing some bank-notes. When the knowing ones came about him and offered several bets, he said he had lost his money already and could not afford to venture any more that day. The horse which the Duke had intended to back was beaten, so he consoled himself, as he said, with the thought that the loss of his pocket-book only anticipated the evil, as if he had betted, he would have paid away as much to the worthies of the Turf. The race, however, was no sooner finished than a veteran half-pay officer presented His Royal Highness with his pocket-book, saying he had found it near the stand, but had not an opportunity of approaching him before. To this the Duke most generously replied; "I am glad it has fallen into such good hands—keep it. Had it not been for this accident, it would have been by this time among the blacklegs and thieves of Newmarket."

In 1764 the Duke of Cumberland matched his famous horse, King Herod, against the Duke of Grafton's Antinous for £1000 over the Beacon Course at Newmarket. This contest excited intense interest, and more than £100,000 is said to have changed hands over the victory of Herod, who won by what was then called half a neck. In the annals of the Turf, however, Duke William is best remembered on account of the fact that he bred the greatest horse of all time, "Eclipse."

This animal, whose wonderful powers as a racer have won him unparalleled fame, was got by Marske (a son of Squirt) out of Spiletta, a bay mare foaled in 1749 by Regulus, a son of the Godolphin Arabian. Eclipse was foaled in 1764, during the great eclipse of that year. When, at the death of the Duke, His Royal Highness's stud was brought to the hammer, Eclipse was purchased as a colt by Mr. Wildman (who appears to have had some insight into his value), under very curious circumstances. Mr. Wildman, who had, it was reported, been put into possession of the extraordinary promise evinced by a particular chestnut colt when a yearling, adopted the following questionable measures in order to make sure of him. When he arrived at the place of sale, he produced his watch and insisted that the auction had commenced before the hour which had been announced in the advertisements, and that the lots should be put up again. In order, however, to prevent a dispute, it was agreed by the auctioneer and company that Mr. Wildman should have his choice of any particular lot. By these means, it is generally believed, he became possessed of Eclipse at the moderate price of seventy or seventy-five guineas. Eclipse did not appear upon the Turf till he was five years old, and so invincibly bad was his temper that it was for some time uncertain whether he would not be raced as a gelding. It is by mere accident, indeed, that the most celebrated of English stallions was preserved to adorn the Calendar with the glories of his descendants. In the neighbourhood of Epsom Downs there lived a man of the name of Ellerton, who, however, was better known by the sobriquet of Hilton, and who united the occupations of poacher and rough-rider. To him, after all else had signally failed, Eclipse was handed over as an incorrigible, and he had recourse to the kill-or-cure system. He was at him day and night, frequently bringing him home at daybreak, after a poaching excursion, with a load of hares strung across his back. Twelve months of this regimen brought him sufficiently to his senses to fit him to be brought to the post, and once there, he ran because it was his pleasure to do so. Still he never could be raced like any other horse. Fitzpatrick, who rode him in almost all his races, never dared to hold him, or do more than sit quiet in his saddle. All through his Turf career his temper was wretched, and very seriously interfered with his value as a racer. His extraordinary superiority was also so palpable that latterly no odds could be got about him save by stratagems. One of these was very clever. For a race in which there were several horses engaged, when O'Kelly failed in getting any money on no-matter-what odds, he took them to a large amount that he placed every horse in it! This he did by naming Eclipse first and all the others nowhere, winning by his horse distancing the field. In 1769, Wildman and O'Kelly were joint-owners of Eclipse, the latter, however, soon after becoming the sole owner at the price of 1750 guineas. At a late period of his life, when an offer to purchase him was made to O'Kelly, these were the terms demanded—£20,000 down, an annuity of £500 for his (O'Kelly's) life, and the right of having three mares every year stinted to him as long as he lived.

This "horse of horses" was short in the forehand, and high in the hips, which gave elasticity to his speed. Upon dissection the muscles were found to be of unparalleled size—a proof of the intimate relation between muscular power and extraordinary swiftness. No horse of his day would appear to have had the shadow of a chance against him.

Eclipse died February 26th, 1789, aged twenty-five, at Cannons, in Middlesex, to which place he had been removed from Epsom about six months previously, in a machine, constructed for the purpose, drawn by two horses, and attended by a confidential groom. When his owner, old O'Kelly, died at his house in Piccadilly on December 28th, 1787, he bequeathed Eclipse and Dungannon to his brother Philip.

Another famous horse was Highflyer, which received his name from having been foaled in a paddock, in which were a number of highflyer walnut trees. He was named by Lord Bolingbroke at a large dinner-party at Sir Charles Bunbury's. The horse in question was the cause of considerable jealousy between Colonel O'Kelly, the owner of Eclipse, and Mr. Tattersall, the founder of the celebrated institution at Hyde Park Corner, whose prosperity was greatly increased by the purchase of Highflyer. "The Hammer and Highflyer" indeed became a favourite toast of the day. Both owners felt the necessity of crossing by the blood of their respective stallions, but each was afraid of increasing the celebrity of the other's horse thereby. The two men were widely different in character. Colonel O'Kelly (of whom an account has already been given) piqued himself upon being descended from the first race of Milesian kings, although he had served for the greatest part of his life some of the humblest offices. It was his boast that he bred and ran his horses for fame. He certainly sacrificed many thousands of pounds in aspiring to the glory of being the Jehu of the day. Mr. Tattersall bred for profit. The former never sold anything before he had trained and ran it at Newmarket; the latter never trained anything, with the exception of one mare early in life, which was of no note. The Irishman matched everything—the Lancashire man sold everything. The one was hasty and impetuous in betting upon the descendants of Eclipse. The other was cautious, and left it to those who had bought them to risk their money upon the progeny of Highflyer. In a word, they resembled each other in nothing, except, it was wickedly said, their total ignorance of horses and extreme good fortune. Mr. Tattersall in the decline of life was more than usually anxious that his son should persevere in keeping stallions and breeding race-horses. O'Kelly directed by his will that all his stud should be sold as soon as possible after his death. Mr. Tattersall's son and heir sold the whole stud after his death. O'Kelly's nephew and executor was obliged to sell under the direction of the will, but he bought most of the horses for his own use. He was a cultivated man, and had been well brought up by his uncle.

Mr. Tattersall used to say that there was no part of Colonel O'Kelly's conduct which he wished he had imitated except that in giving an excellent education to his heir.

Mr. Tattersall was a very economical man. When Highflyer died, many suggestions were made that the horse should be skinned and stuffed, as had been done by Colonel O'Kelly in the case of Eclipse. Mr. Tattersall, however, replied that he did not see the use of stuffing him with hay after he was dead, as he could no longer cover; he had stuffed him full enough with hay and corn when he was alive and producing money. Mr. Tattersall had very practical ideas about such things, and when inspecting his cattle whilst they were fattening, was often overheard to say, "Eat away, my good creature! eat away, and get fat soon. The butcher is waiting for you, and I want money."

Mr. Tattersall's prosperous career arose in a great measure from a successful speculation in Scotland. Having heard that a Scotch nobleman's stud was to be sold there, he applied to a friend to go his halves in the purchase. "If you will find money, for I have none," said he, "I will find skill, and you shall have a good thing." The sum was deposited, and he went to the sale, partly by coach and partly on foot, buying nearly all the horses for a trifle. Upon his return, he sold a few at York for more money than the whole of them had cost, making several hundred pounds out of the rest from purchasers at Newmarket and in London. Mr. Tattersall used often to say this was the first money he ever possessed above a few pounds. Having thus acquired a little capital, he soon increased it by similar means, and also, of course, by his business at Hyde Park Corner.

At that time, though sales of horses by auction were occasionally held, there was no regular repository or fixed sales at stated periods, the lack of which was much felt in the sporting world. Perceiving that a golden opportunity lay ready to hand, Mr. Tattersall, who was well-known to the gentlemen of the Turf and to the horse-dealers, offered his services as an auctioneer, and solicited their patronage. Lord Grosvenor warmly espoused his cause, and built for him the extensive premises at Hyde Park Corner, where Mr. Tattersall died. His success was astonishingly rapid. He soon enlarged the premises and built stands for carriages, which were sold by private contract; as well as kennels for hounds and other dogs, which were sold by auction. He converted a part of his house into a tavern and coffee-house, and fitted up two of the most elegant rooms in London for the use of the Jockey Club, who held their meetings there for some years. He allotted another apartment to the use of betting men. This was supported by an annual subscription of a guinea from each member, and was called the betting-room. Here prominent Turfites assembled every sale-day to lay wagers on the events of future races, and here they met to pay and receive the money won and lost at what were called country races, in contradistinction to the races at Newmarket. His sales were not confined to Hyde Park Corner; he constantly attended the Newmarket meetings and the races at York, where he had considerable employment, and thereby kept up his connection with the jockeys in different parts of the kingdom, who sent their horses to him from all the various districts.

Racing as carried on in the eighteenth century was on a very different scale from that of the present day. Our ancestors were contented with very small stakes and but few races in a day.

In 1755 there were but three meetings at Newmarket, which gave fifteen racing days. Thirteen stakes were run for, the gross amount of which was £1255. There were twenty heats.

Besides the stakes there were twenty-nine matches, which made the daily average of races something over three.

E.O. ON A COUNTRY RACE-COURSE.
By Rowlandson.

In those days noblemen and gentlemen met to enjoy each other's society and test the merits of their horses rather than for purposes of gain, the stakes being, from a pecuniary view, a matter of comparative indifference.

At the small country meetings the racing was spread over a greater space of time than at present; all of them lasted three days and many a week. Dinners and balls were the order of the day, the race meeting being an event which was looked forward to throughout the year.

A number of the more aristocratic spectators were mounted, and followed the horses as they ran. So great, indeed, became the disorder caused at race meetings by this riding with and after the horses during racing, that the Chief Magistrate of one provincial town (who, it should be added, had Irish blood in his veins) caused a placard to be posted up just before the races, intimating "that no *gentleman* would be allowed to ride on the course, *except the horses* that were to run."

Racing was formerly a very rough-and-ready affair, and much was tolerated on a race-course which would be sternly dealt with to-day. Gambling-booths and E.O. tables were easily to be found, whilst little order was maintained on the course. At Tavistock Races in 1815, a sailor with one arm, who had just been paid off, exhibited his skill in horsemanship, to the no small annoyance of everybody, till at length, checking his Bucephalus at full gallop, he was thrown with great violence, by which his right leg was dreadfully fractured.

Cocked-hat races and other eccentric contests were not infrequent features at race meetings. At Hereford races in 1822 a race between three velocipedes, commonly called hobby-horses, created much mirth. They were ridden by three men, dressed in scarlet, yellow, and white jackets. Much skill was displayed, and every exertion used, with the result that white won, scarlet and yellow being both upset, and the riders each receiving a hearty bump, to the great diversion of all the spectators.

The Turf of former days eased the aristocracy of a good deal of money, and many a fine estate changed hands owing to the vicissitudes of racing. Fox of course lost very large sums. He used to declare after the defeat of his horses that they had as much bottom as other people's, but that they were such slow, good animals that they never went fast enough to tire themselves! Occasionally, however, he was lucky. In April 1772 he won nearly £16,000—the greater part of which was the result of bets against the celebrated Pincher, who lost the match by only half-a-neck, two to one having been laid on him. At the Spring meeting in 1789 Fox is also said to have won about £50,000; and at the October meeting next year he realised £4000 by the sale of two of his horses—Seagull and Chanticleer. In 1788 Fox and the Duke of Bedford won eight thousand guineas between them at the Newmarket Spring meeting. Fox and Lord Barrymore had a match for a large sum; this was given as a dead heat, and the bets were off.

On taking office in 1783, Fox sold his horses, and erased his name from several of the Clubs of which he was a member. In a short time, however, he again purchased a stud, and in October attended the Newmarket meeting, when a King's messenger appeared amongst the sportsmen on the Heath in quest of the Minister, for whom he bore despatches. The messenger, as was usual on these occasions, wore his badge of office, the greyhound, and his arrival created quite a stir on the course.

In 1790, Fox's horse, Seagull, won the Oatlands Stakes at Ascot of one hundred guineas (nineteen subscribers), beating the Prince of Wales's Escape, Serpent, and several of the very best horses of that year. The Prince was much mortified at this, and immediately matched Magpie against the winner, two miles, for five hundred guineas. This match, on which immense sums were depending, was, four days later, won with ease by Seagull. At this time Lord Foley and Mr. Fox raced together.

Lord Foley died in 1793; he entered upon the Turf with a clear £18,000 a year, and some £100,000 in ready money—he left it without ready money, with an encumbered estate, and with a constitution injured by cares and anxieties which embittered the end of his life.

Many other patricians were practically ruined on the Turf at about the same time, some by continuous ill-luck, but more owing to the machinations of the many doubtful characters who were experts at what was then known as "throwing the bull over the bridge"—a cant phrase formerly used by frequenters of the race-course to indicate a sporting swindle.

The phrase in question, it may be added, had its origin in the cruel pastime of bull-baiting. When such an orgy of cruelty was over, and the militia of hell which had witnessed it surfeited with blood, the carcass of the bull was dragged to a bridge, over which his quivering remains were thrown into the water beneath!

Many were the queer freaks and fancies of the great pillars of the Turf of the past. Sir Charles Bunbury, for instance, who trained his horses privately under his own eye, made the lads who groomed them wear his colours whilst at their task, in order to accustom the animals to the racing jackets and prevent all chance of nervousness in public. His horses were never allowed to be sweated or tried on a Good Friday, on account of an accident which had on one of these anniversaries happened to a couple of his racers, who had both fallen and broken their backs, each jockey having got a fractured thigh.

All this, however, has been written of time after time; indeed, the fascinating story of the Turf has found many admirable chroniclers. Nevertheless, these have hardly touched upon some of the more obscure figures, who seem to have escaped notice.

Such a one was Major Leeson, a well-known sporting character at the close of the eighteenth century, who may be taken as typical of the sharp racing man of humble origin, and who, having by astuteness attained a certain prosperity, was eventually reduced to beggary by the allurements of gambling. An Irishman of obscure birth, Mr. Leeson originally obtained his commission through the patronage of a Scottish nobleman, by whose munificence he was sent to school at Hampstead, and afterwards to the French military academy of Angers. Whilst at this seminary he fought a duel with a well-known baronet, and both combatants displayed great courage. Leeson was soon after appointed a lieutenant in a regiment of foot, in which he conducted himself as a soldier and a gentleman.

During his military career, Leeson was especially popular with his men, whose liking for their young officer almost amounted to adoration, owing to his ardent championship of their interests. While they were quartered in a country town, one of the sergeants, a sober, steady man, was wantonly attacked by a blacksmith, who was the terror of the place. The sergeant defended himself with great spirit as long as he was able, but was obliged, after a hard contest, to yield to his athletic antagonist. This intelligence reached Mr. Leeson's ears the next morning, and without delay he set out in pursuit of the victor, whom he found boasting of the triumph he had gained over the "lobster," as he called the sergeant. The very expression kindled Leeson's indignation into such a flame, that he aimed a blow at the fellow's temple, which was warded off and returned with such force that Leeson lay for some minutes extended on the ground. Leeson, however, renewed the attack; and his onslaughts were made with such rapidity and success, that the son of Vulcan was eventually stretched senseless on the ground. In order to complete the triumph, Leeson placed him in a wheel-barrow; and in this situation he was wheeled through all the town amidst the acclamations of the populace. Soon after this, Mr. Leeson exchanged his lieutenancy for a cornetcy of dragoons.

He now began to be attracted by the seductions of gaming and the Turf, both of which exercised a fascination over his mind which he was unable to resist. Fortune was kind, and an almost uninterrupted series of success led him to Newmarket, where his evil genius, in the name of good luck, converted him in a short time into a professional gambler. At one time he had a complete stud at Newmarket; and his famous horse Buffer carried off all the capital plates for three years and upwards, though once beaten at Egham, when 15 to 1 was laid on it. Major Leeson's discernment in racing matters soon became generally remarked, and he was consulted by all the sharpest frequenters of the Turf on critical occasions.

In later years, however, Major Leeson experienced the ill-fortune which is too often the lot of gamblers. A long run of ill-luck preyed upon his spirits, soured his temper, and drove him to that last resource of an enfeebled mind—the brandy bottle. As he could not shine in his wonted splendour, he sought the most obscure public-houses in the purlieus of St. Giles, where he used to pass whole nights in the company of his countrymen of the lowest class. Overwhelmed by debt and worn-out body and soul, he was constantly pursued by the terrors of the law, and alternately imprisoned by his own fears or confined in the King's Bench, till, a broken and miserable man, he welcomed death as a friend come to relieve him of an almost insupportable load.

An eccentric supporter of the Turf, who died in 1799, was Councillor Lade. It was his highest ambition to be thought a distinguished member of the sporting world; but in this, as in the more contracted circle of private life, he was not destined to cut a conspicuous figure, being by nature much better calculated for an obscure place in the background. During the last twenty years of his life he kept a miserable lot of spindle-shanked brood mares, colts, and fillies at Cannon Park, between Kingsclere and Overton in Hampshire—a place which, owing to its barrenness, was quite unsuited for breeding horses.

His successes on the Turf were insignificant. During the last twelve years of his life he hardly ever brought less than six, seven, or eight horses annually to the post for country plates (never till the last two or three years presuming to sport his name at Newmarket); nevertheless, few of them, if any, ever realised his expectations, or paid one-third of the expenses in the way of breeding, breaking, training, running, or sale. Councillor Lade's almost constant sequence of disappointments originated in one single cause strikingly palpable to every eye but his own, which was their breeder's parsimony. His mares were in a wretched and deplorable state of emaciation during the whole time of bearing their foals, whilst a systematic starvation of both dams and offspring when foals, and a miserable sustenance barely enough to support life when weaned, totally nullified his chances of success upon the Turf.

It was no uncommon thing to see the Councillor's favourite brood mare, Laetitia, and many others with their foals, in the fertile months of May and June, upon the side of a barren, burnt-up hill, with barely pasture sufficient to keep even the dam in existence, without even a possibility of affording half the nutriment necessary for the unfortunate foal. Owing to these highly injudicious and cruel methods, his stud, even when of superior blood, was always inferior in bone and strength to its rivals, there being in it never more than one horse in every eight or ten with constitutional stamina sufficient to bear the training necessary before going to the post.

When after his death the Councillor's wretched stud were on their way to be sold by auction they excited universal pity from the humane in the towns and villages through which they passed. Many of the horses sold for the trifling sum of two or three guineas each, owing to the wretched condition of the poor animals. Councillor Lade, in his Turf transactions as elsewhere, was so consistently parsimonious even to those whom it would have been good policy to conciliate that every man's hand was against him, even that of his own servants.

One of his manias was to run his horses as much as possible at race meetings near his home, in order to avoid the expenses of travelling.

The years 1797 and 1798 were the most prosperous of his Turf career. Seven of his horses went to the post for twenty-four plates and purses, of which Truss, Will, and Grey Pilot won seven fifties—two at Ascot, two at Abingdon, and one each at Reading, Winchester, and Stockbridge.

Councillor Lade was in himself a singular and unsociable man, seldom seen in company, upon the race-course or elsewhere. Cynically cold and innately parsimonious, few cared to sojourn beneath what might be justly termed, in more senses than one, a habitation without a roof. Hospitality was alien to the spirit of Cannon Park, and the building itself was one entire mass of chilling frigidity which betokened a total lack of good cheer. The owner was constantly involved in pecuniary disputes and lawsuits with his dependents, in which he was usually worsted.

It was not infrequently his practice to drive his curricle and greys without a servant the fifty-seven miles to Cannon Park, not even taking them once out of the harness; a handful of hay, and two or three quarts of water at Salt Hill, and Spratley's, the Bear, at Reading, in addition to the turnpikes, constituted the entire expense of the journey, it being an irrevocable opinion of his that servants on the road were more troublesome and expensive than their masters.

The Councillor was married to a lady of excellent family, who, owing to mental trouble, lived in seclusion. This, however, did not trouble him much, for he took care to make up for the lack of a wife's society by a profusion of female friends, who enlivened his elegant house in Pall Mall, his rural cottage near Turnham Green, and even his unadorned inhospitable mansion at Cannon Park.

Another unpleasant Turf character about this date was "Louse Pigott," a man of good Shropshire family. The slovenly manner of dressing and general unkempt appearance of this gentleman had obtained for him his unsavoury nickname. He had originally been possessed of some wealth, but going racing soon lost practically his whole fortune. Devoid of means, and prompted apparently by the same spirit which induces unsuccessful modern gamblers at Monte Carlo to apply to the authorities for a sum sufficient to enable them to leave the Principality of Monaco, Mr. Pigott conceived the original idea of making representations to the Jockey Club, with a view to receiving pecuniary aid. Needless to say his petition was treated with a complete lack of consideration which, it was said, so enraged him that in revenge he wrote the libellous work called *The Jockey Club*, a volume of short but scandalous biographies of persons well known in the sporting world. Though Pigott appears to have escaped punishment for this, the publishers, Messrs. Ridgway & Symonds, were incarcerated in Newgate.

"Louse Pigott" appears to have been an eccentric character in many ways, for one September evening in 1793 he got into great trouble at the London Coffee-House, Ludgate Hill, where, sitting with a friend, Dr. William Hodgson, he became very vociferous in giving toasts of a disloyal kind, finally loudly proposing success to the "French Republic." This was immediately resented by a gentleman present, who, rising to his feet, proposed "The King," a toast which was drunk with cheers by all present except Pigott and his companion, who made use of such improper expressions that peace officers were sent for, who removed the apostles of revolution to the lock-up.

The next morning they were charged with drinking "the French Republic and the overthrow of the present system of Government and all Governments of Europe except the French; likewise of speaking disrespectfully of the King, the Duke of York, Lord Mayor, and other persons in high authority. They had," it was deposed, "called the Prince of Hesse a swine-dealer, and Ministers in general robbers and highwaymen." Finally, when being conveyed to the cells, they had shouted from the coach windows, "The French Republic, and Liberty while you live."

Being unable to find bail, the two prisoners were sent back to prison, to remain there till tried at the ensuing Old Bailey Sessions. The bill preferred against Pigott, however, was eventually thrown out and he was discharged. The general comment upon his release was that "he who is born to be hanged will never be drowned," and vice versa. His companion, Dr. Hodgson, was less fortunate, and received some punishment for the advanced sentiments which he had uttered.

Probably the shrewdest nobleman who ever went racing was the eccentric but highly astute "Old Q." At the time when he owned race-horses he was generally hand-in-hand with his jockey, Dick Goodison, with whom he had a perfect understanding. During a lengthy connection with the Turf, "Old Q." never displayed the least want of philosophy upon the unexpected result of a race. As a matter of fact he never entered into an engagement but where there was a great probability of his becoming the winner. In all emergencies his Grace preserved an invariable equanimity, and his cool serenity never forsook him, even in moments of the greatest surprise or disappointment. A singular proof of this occurred at Newmarket just as the horses were about to start for a sweepstakes. His Grace was engaged in a betting conversation with various members of the Jockey Club, when one of his lads, who was going to ride (in consequence of his light weight), tactlessly called him aside, asked him, too soon and too loud, How he was to ride that day? Perfectly convinced this had been overheard, his Grace, with well-affected surprise, exclaimed, "Why, take the lead and keep it to be sure! How the devil would you ride?"

Matches were a great feature of the period, and very large sums were staked. An historic match was that between Sir Harry Vane's Hambletonian and Mr. Cookson's Diamond for three thousand guineas, run over the Beacon Course during the Newmarket Craven meeting of 1799. Hambletonian, who was ridden by Buckle, carried eight stone three pounds, and Diamond, ridden by Dennis Fitzpatrick (Deny), eight stone; the betting was five to four on Hambletonian.

Though both gallant steeds have now long since mouldered into dust, together with the gay company of sportsmen who assembled to see them run, the memory of their desperate neck-and-neck struggle over that terrible last half-mile is not forgotten, and will ever shine amongst the chronicles of equine fame as the most sporting and gamely contested match of all time.

Hambletonian, a bright bay and a grandson of Eclipse, was a wonderful horse. He was only once beaten, at the York August meeting 1797, when he ran against Deserter and Spread Eagle, and took it into his head to bolt out of the course and leap a ditch.

Diamond, a beautiful brown bay, smaller than Hambletonian, was got by Highflyer. He was the more compact horse of the two.

Hambletonian being a Yorkshire bred horse, the Yorkshiremen backed him for prodigious sums, whilst Diamond was strongly supported by the Newmarket people, the horse being well-known in the neighbourhood.

Every bed in Newmarket (which could not hold a tenth of the visitors) was occupied, whilst Cambridge and all the towns and villages within twelve or fifteen miles were also thronged with people. Stabling was not to be had, and no chaise or horse could be procured on any of the roads, all having been engaged three weeks before.

The weather was most auspicious, and the general scene on the Heath highly interesting and attractive. All the gentlemen of the Turf, as the phrase ran, from the neighbouring counties were collected on the course, and many of the nobility of England, which was then a real and powerful nobility, including the Duchess of Gordon, were assembled to see the race.

At the start the horses kept tolerably close, Hambletonian retaining the lead till the last half-mile, when Diamond got abreast of him. The two horses then raced home in a most desperate manner, the nose of one or the other being alternately in front till Hambletonian won in the last stride. Both horses were terribly whipped and spurred, particularly Hambletonian. The four miles one furlong and one hundred and thirty-eight yards were covered in about eight minutes and a half.

Every one declared that this match was the most exciting ever known, and it was acknowledged even by the losers (who were described as being as much pleased as losers could be) to have been thoroughly fairly contested, each jockey having made the best of his horse.

As soon as the race was over, Sir Harry Vane Tempest, who, besides the stakes, had won about three thousand guineas, declared on the course that Hambletonian should be taken out of training the next morning, and in future he would ride him only as a hack. Sir Harry afterwards travelled to town in a post-chaise and four, and arrived at the Cocoa Tree at half-past eleven at night. The news of his victory, however, was already known, Mr. Hall, of Moorfields, who had three horses on the road, having got to town between nine and ten.

A bronze penny token of fine medallic design—now very scarce—commemorates this famous match. An inscription is on one side and a picture of the race on the other.

Mr. Cookson, the owner of Diamond, did not lose any enormous sum over the race. He was well-known for his shrewdness, and in one year, 1798, is said to have realised nearly £60,000 by the victories of Ambrosia and Diamond.

Hambletonian became the sire of over a hundred and forty winners.

Another match between Diamond and Mr. R. Heathcote's Warter strongly excited the sporting world, which was much puzzled how to bet. Warter having beat Diamond in the Oatland stakes of 1800, the latter was to receive seven pounds in the projected race. This, according to the knowing ones, was an advantage of the utmost importance, and Diamond became a strong favourite, his backers flattering themselves with the opinion that one of Warter's legs would fail him in running, and that consequently they were on the right side. Till about a fortnight before the meeting betting was equal; six to four was then betted in favour of Diamond, and was at first very cautiously accepted.

So highly was the gambling mania roused that, till a late hour on the Saturday night previous to the meeting, all the sporting houses near St. James's, and even more to the eastward, were crowded with betting-men of every description. The bolder sort dashed at the odds, whilst others more cautiously hedged, and all waited the event with the most anxious expectation.

The whole of Sunday the Newmarket road was crowded with carriages and cattle of every description, from the dashing curricle to the humble buggy, and from the pampered hunter to the spavined hack.

When every mouth was opening to bet, and expectation was on tiptoe, it was declared in the Coffee-room, that Warter, by reason of a kick, had declared forfeit, and the famous match was off.

Another match, which excited enormous interest at the beginning of the nineteenth century, was that between Mrs. Thornton, wife of the celebrated Colonel Thornton of Thornville Royal (now Studley Royal, the seat of Lord Ripon), and a gentleman well known in sporting circles, Mr. Flint by name. This was run at York in 1804, and is memorable as being the only race chronicled in the *Racing Calendar* in which a woman's name is mentioned. The entry, dated August 25, 1804, runs thus:—

> Mr. Flint's Brown Thornville by Volunteer out of Abigail, aged, rode by the owner, beat Colonel Thornton's ch. h. Vinagrillio, aged, rode by Mrs. Thornton, four miles, five hundred guineas.

The weights were catch weights, and before the race five and six to four were laid upon the lady, which increased during the early portion of the race to seven to four and two to one, it seeming likely during the first three miles that Mrs. Thornton would secure an easy triumph. During the final mile, however, things entirely changed, and the victory of Mr. Flint appearing certain, odds were laid upon him. Over two hundred thousand pounds, it is said, were lost and won over this race, which excited a vast amount of interest. The lady's horse, it may be added, was a very old one.

Mrs. Thornton's dress was a leopard-coloured body with blue sleeves, the rest buff, and blue cap. Mr. Flint rode in white. The race was run in nine minutes and fifty-nine seconds. In the published account of the race it is stated that "No words can express the disappointment felt at the defeat of Mrs. Thornton, the spirit she displayed and the good humour with which she has borne her loss having greatly diminished the joy of many of the winners."

The fortunate individuals in question seem, however, to have been under some misapprehension as to the lady's equanimity under defeat, as she subsequently sent an angry letter to the *York Herald* complaining that she had been treated with scant courtesy.

Though the lady signed herself Alicia Thornton she seems to have had no legitimate claim to the name—she was a Miss Meynell, and her sister was by way of being the wife of Mr. Flint. The race engendered much ill-feeling between the two couples.

The year after the race on the Knavesmire a fracas occurred between Colonel Thornton and Mr. Flint, the latter being very indignant at not having received £1000 of the £1500 wagered by the gallant Colonel on his wife's success. Mr. Flint vigorously applied a new horsewhip to the soldier's shoulders. The aggressor was taken into custody, Colonel Thornton afterwards making an application in the Court of King's Bench for leave to file a criminal information against Flint, who (he deposed) had challenged him to fight a duel, and horse-whipped him on the race-ground at York. The Colonel maintained that the bet of £1000 was a mere nominal thing, intended to attract people to the race-course, and that it was understood that only £500 of the £1500 should be paid. The case was eventually dismissed, the Colonel apparently sticking to his £1000.

Mrs Thornton.
Pub. Feb 1, 1805, by J. Wheble, Warwicksquare.

In after-life Flint became miserably poor, and eked out a living as a manager of a horse bazaar at York. He eventually committed suicide by taking a dose of prussic acid.

At the York August meeting in the following year Mrs. Thornton rode another match against Buckle, the celebrated jockey. Mrs. Thornton, in the highest spirits, appeared dressed for the contest in a purple cap and waistcoat, long nankeen-coloured skirts, purple shoes, and embroidered stockings. Buckle was dressed in a blue cap, with blue bodied jacket, and white sleeves. Mrs. Thornton carried 9 st. 6 lb., Mr Buckle 13 st. 6 lb. At half-past three they started. Mrs. Thornton took the lead, which she kept for some time; Buckle then exercised his jockeyship, and took the lead, which he retained for only a few lengths, when Mrs. Thornton won her race by half a neck. On this occasion Mrs. Thornton rode Louisa, by Pegasus, out of Nelly; and Buckle rode Allegro, by Pegasus, out of Allegranti's dam.

As the English Turf began to rise in importance some attempt was made to introduce racing into France. As early as the reign of Louis XV. a number of the French nobility had frequented Newmarket. The well-known sportsman, Hugo Meynell, much resented this, and grimly declared that he wished the peace was all over and England comfortably at war again. A particularly unpopular visitor was the Comte de Lauraguais, who purchased the celebrated race-horse, Gimcrack, took him over to France, and for a big bet ran him twenty-two and a half miles, it is said, within an hour.

At the end of the eighteenth century Philippe Égalité raced at Newmarket, where he seems to have created an unfavourable impression. Though he entered a good many horses, he was not particularly successful as an owner. In France the sporting exploits of this Prince and of the Comte d'Artois excited a good deal of indignation. They were declared to be the associates of grooms, and to enter into scandalous combinations in the races which they organised, whilst treating the onlookers with the most ineffable contempt and savage ferocity. It would certainly appear that at times they used their whips on the spectators as well as on their horses; and not only encouraged the officers to maltreat the crowd, but employed such grossness of speech, and offensive oaths, as showed that these Princes were not unskilled in the language of the vilest part of the nation. High betting was general, and noblemen turned jockeys and rode their own racers. When the Comte de Lauraguais appeared at Court, after a long absence, the King coldly inquired where he had been for so long. "In England," the Count replied. "What did you do there?" "I learnt there, please your Majesty, to think." "Of horses," retorted the King.

The early days of the French Turf were unedifying. In a match between the Duc de Lauzun and M. de Fénelon the latter fell from his horse, broke his arm, and lost his wager. The same gentleman betted with another nobleman as to which of them could reach Versailles and return to Paris the quicker in a single-horse chaise. The horse of the first died at Sèvres, and the other expired in the stable at Paris, a few hours after his return.

Frivolous courtiers, not satisfied with exercising their inhumanity on their horses, exposed themselves to the derision of Paris by other kinds of races. The Duc de Chartres, the Duc de Lauzun, and the Marquis FitzJames once betted five hundred louis who could first reach Versailles on foot. Lauzun gave up the foot-race about half way; Chartres about two-thirds; FitzJames arrived in an exhausted state, and was saluted as conqueror by the Comte d'Artois. The hero in question was near expiring in the arms of victory and had to be put to bed. Blood-letting was resorted to, and though he won his wager he contracted asthma.

Marie Antoinette, not satisfied with foot and horse racing, instituted contests of speed in which donkeys were bestridden, the successful jockey being rewarded with three hundred livres and a golden thistle.

During the first Empire, Napoleon, probably with an eye to the horsing of his cavalry, decreed that there should be races, and races of a sort there were, chiefly in the Department of the Orne and at a hippodrome at Le Pin, the seat of a Government stud established by Colbert in the days of the Roi Soleil.

After the restoration of the Bourbons, racing was intermittently carried on at Vincennes, at Fontainebleau, in the Champs de Mars, and at Satory-Versailles, which were the chief places of racing near Paris. The ground at both was detestable. At Satory-Versailles, in wet weather, the course was so deep in mud that the horses could hardly move. At the Champs de Mars the ground was often "so hard as to endanger the strongest legs," and "when the horses galloped the jockeys were liable to be blinded by a cloud of dust and small pebbles." As a matter of fact the races were more often than not won by the mounted gendarmes, who rode with the horses from start to finish.

In the early days of the French Turf the fields were, of course, small, and so was the value of the prizes. For this reason, in order to eke out a fair number of races with very few horses, the practice of running races in "heats" was grossly abused. In 1840, Madame de Giraudin wrote: "The races on Sunday were favoured with superb weather, and the extraordinary sight was seen of nine horses running together—nine live horses, nine rivals—a rare spectacle in the Champs de Mars. Generally one horse runs all alone, contending against no opponent, and always coming in first. But this does not signify; it excites the admiration of those who love sport, and especially of the philosophers among them; it is so noble to strive against and overcome oneself!"

The foundation of the French Turf as we see it to-day dates back to 1833, when the French Jockey Club was founded.

Before this there had existed in the Rue Blanche an English Jockey and Pigeon Shooting Club founded by a Mr. Thomas Bryon, who acted as secretary. In 1830, of the eighteen members, four were English, including that very original character. Lord Henry Seymour, and in course of time he took a leading part in originating a Members' Club, which should resemble the English Jockey Club, and should be lodged in a luxurious Club-house.

The twelve founders of the French Jockey Club were soon joined by a large number of sportsmen, among whom were the novelist, Eugène Sue, Lord Yarmouth, and Mr. John Bowes, who passed most of his life in Paris. The latter gentleman won the Derby four times. On the first occasion, in 1835, when Mundig beat Ascot (which belonged to the writer's grandfather, Lord Orford) by a head, Mr. Bowes was still an undergraduate at Cambridge—in subsequent years he won it again with Cotherstone, Daniell O'Rourke, and West Australian.

The French Jockey Club, at its institution, consisted of Royal Princes, noblemen, ordinary men of property, all persons of considerable influence interested in horse-breeding and in the improvement of the breed of horses by means of horse-racing and the "selection of the fittest." Most of them were good horsemen, who rode their own horses on occasion. M. de Normandie, for instance, was the winner of an improvised race which took place at Chantilly in 1833 between himself, Prince Lobanoff, Viscount de Hédouville, and others. This is said to have suggested the idea of forming the present beautiful race-course there. This gentleman, who must be ranked as one of the fathers of the French Turf, frequently acted in the earliest days of the French Jockey Club as steward, judge, and starter; and though he does not appear to have introduced any famous strain of blood into the studs of his country, greatly contributed to establish French racing on its present prosperous footing.

M. de Normandie is said to have won the first regular steeplechase ever run in France on English principles. This took place in 1830, near St. Germain, and in December 1908 a gentleman was still living who was supposed to have taken part in it.

This was Mr. Albert Ricardo, J.P., who spent his early days in Paris. A great supporter of sport, Mr. Ricardo, who died on the last day but one of the year, had won the Cambridgeshire with The Widow as far back as 1847. He had also been a keen cricketer in his youth, and was one of the two first members of the I Zingari.

There was steeplechasing at the Croix de Bernay as early as 1832, and at La Marche some little time later.

The Auteuil steeplechase course, which is now the head-quarters of the sport in France, was not inaugurated till after the war of 1870.

Through the influence of the Duc d'Orléans, the son of Louis Philippe, who was killed in a carriage accident in 1842, the French Jockey Club obtained leave to hold regular meetings in the Champs de Mars; and he it also was who, in 1834, arranged the creation of the race-course at Chantilly, which, till Longchamps was started in 1856-57, was without doubt the best course in France. At Chantilly was run the first French Derby (Prix du Jockey Club) in 1836, and the first French Oaks (Prix de Diane) in 1843.

The stables of the Duc at Chantilly were presided over by an English trainer, George Edwards, and his principal jockey was Edgar Pavis. In 1840 his English-bred horse, Beggarman, won the Goodwood Cup. Besides this the Duc d'Orléans won a number of French races. As a matter of fact, racing in France, from 1834 to 1842, was more or less of a duel between the Prince in question and Lord Henry Seymour.

The latter extraordinary personage was born in Paris in 1805, and is believed never to have set foot in England. Lord Henry Seymour was said to be related on his mother's side to "Old Q." or George Selwyn, or both, and from either or both of them he probably inherited some of his numberless eccentricities as well as his taste for the Turf. He was a well-known figure in Paris and its neighbourhood, for it was his constant practice to drive about in a carriage with four horses, postilions, and out-riders. After *Mardi Gras*, he would sit with other congenial spirits at the window of the noted "Vendanges de Bourgogne," watching the *descente de la Courtille* (the return from the ball) in the early morning, when he would scatter heated pieces of gold among the crowd of returning "maskers." Lord Henry is said to have been the original of the eccentric character described by Balzac, who delighted in furtively administering drastic medicines to his dearest friends, the very unpleasant effects of which afforded him intense amusement. He delighted also in giving away cigars with something explosive inserted at the end, afterwards watching the effect of a light applied by the unsuspecting smoker. He died in Paris in 1859.

In 1856 the French Turf entered upon a new and important era, a promise being obtained from the Government and the municipality of Paris that a race-course should be included in the projected plan for the transformation of the Bois de Boulogne. In the Longchamps meadows, on the borders of the Seine, an expanse of level and unencumbered ground was allotted to the Société d'Encouragement, and by an arrangement with the municipality of Paris, the Société became lessees of the race-course for fifty years, undertaking to pay an annual rent, as well as to build stands, which, at the expiration of the lease in 1906, should become the property of the city. The old stands, which during the last three years have been replaced by magnificent new ones, were erected by the architects of the city of Paris, at an expense of 420,000 francs (£16,800), and subsequent expenses brought the amount up to 1,284,981 francs (about £51,395). The race-course was opened on the last Sunday in April 1857, and the first Grand Prix was run in 1862, when the Ranger won.

The moving spirit in the institution of this race, now the richest in the world, is said to have been the Emperor Napoleon the Third, represented by the Duc de Morny, the creator of Deauville. The first Grand Prix was worth £4000 and an *objet d'art*; the amount of the stakes for the same race in 1909 was some £16,000.

When the Grand Prix was first inaugurated, many vigorous protests were made in England against the race being run on a Sunday, but by these the French declined to be swayed. As a matter of fact, notwithstanding Anglo-Saxon plaints at the iniquity of Sunday racing, the beautiful courses at Longchamps and Auteuil are very popular with visitors from across the Channel on many a fine Sabbath day, when Englishmen, known for their stern and unflinching moral rectitude, are not infrequent spectators on such occasions. One of these, a public man, notorious for his advocacy of every form of puritanical restriction, whilst exhibiting some confusion at being recognised by a friend, could only make the defence: "Well, after all, it doesn't matter, as I am not betting." In all probability, however, he, like other visitors, had backed his fancy!

An important share in the laying-out of Longchamps race-course was taken by the late Mr. Mackenzie Grieves, who, originally an officer in the Blues, took up his residence in Paris, became a member of the French Jockey Club and played a prominent part in the organisation of French racing. Mr. Mackenzie Grieves, whose memory is preserved by an important race to which his name has been given, was personally known to the writer, who retains pleasant recollections of his great charm and dignified appearance, both of which were highly characteristic of one of the last of the fine old school. He was a most graceful rider and a master of the *haute école*.

Though racing in France was naturally suspended during the war, it was once more in full swing in 1872, when the Grand Prix was won by Cremorne. In consequence of the downfall of the second Empire a number of the important races were renamed. The Prix de l'Impératrice, for instance, became the Prix Rainbow; the Prix du Prince Impérial the Prix Royal Oak. The Prix Gladiateur, one of the oldest French prizes, has under its various names strikingly reflected the vicissitudes of French politics. Originally it was the Prix Royal, then Prix National, then Grand Prix de l'Empereur, till, with the rise of the third Republic, it was called after the famous race-horse.

In 1885 there was great jubilation amongst French sportsmen at the victories of Plaisanterie, which won both the Cesarewitch and Cambridgeshire, as well as twelve out of thirteen events in France.

The appearance of the daughter of Wellingtonia and Poetess in the Cesarewitch was said at the time to be owing to two bookmakers, T. Wilde and Jack Moore, who made it worth the while of the filly's owners (M.H. Bony and Mr. T. Carter) to start her, guaranteeing them 33 to 1, though they themselves had only got 20 to 1 in England. Wilde, it was declared, brought back to France after the race nearly five million francs (£200,000), won by backing Plaisanterie, of which Jack Moore paid out some 600,000 (£24,000) in five-franc, ten-franc, and twenty-franc pieces to French backers who had been on the good thing.

In common with the rest of the fraternity, these two very sporting layers have now long disappeared from the French race-course. Bookmaking in France practically ceased to exist with the introduction of the Pari Mutuel in 1891.

Previous to that time bookmakers had pitches provided for them some way behind the stands, where they were allowed to exhibit lists of the horses running in the various races, against which were chalked the odds, the variations in which were thus easily shown. The whole thing was most decorously conducted, and the system worked fairly well. Nevertheless, from time to time, rumours were rife as to an intended suppression of the bookmakers by the French authorities, and at last in 1891 they were definitely bidden to cease plying their business. The new decree was rigorously enforced, crowds of police in uniform and plain clothes being present on the Parisian race-courses, and any one found openly making a bet was ruthlessly arrested—a perfect reign of terror, indeed, prevailed amongst betting-men, and very great dissatisfaction ensued amongst habitual frequenters of the French Turf. On several occasions, notably one Sunday at Auteuil (when the writer was present), a large force of military were on the ground, regiments of cavalry being in reserve outside the race-course. Feeling ran very high, and the races were run amidst hoots, yells, and other demonstrations of indignation, some of which most unjustly took the form of missiles hurled at the jockeys. The cabmen and proprietors of the char-à-bancs who drive the public to the various race-courses around Paris, the keepers of the small restaurants along the various lines of route, loudly complained that the new era of restriction which had dawned would completely ruin them. The saddest people of all, however, were very naturally the bookmakers, most of them English, who for many years had made a living on the French race-courses, for, whilst the public generally were more or less certain that some new method of betting would be devised, they fully realised that the suppression of their business was no mere outburst of outraged morality on the part of the Government, but a well thought-out scheme for appropriating their spoils and diverting them to public purposes. The golden days were gone, and ruin stared them in the face.

In a very short time public indignation was allayed by the announcement that French racing was not, as it had been averred, about to be stamped out by the high-handed brutality of those at the head of the State. Betting would be allowed, but only through the medium of the Pari Mutuel or Totalisator, which would be established on a legal basis on every race-course in France; and after the passing of the law, which definitely laid down the manner in which speculation on the French Turf was in future to be conducted, the beautiful courses round Paris were once more thronged by crowds of relieved race-goers.

The law in question, passed on 2nd June 1891, expressly prohibited any form of betting on race-courses except through the medium of the Pari Mutuel, and strictly defined the conditions on which the latter was to be worked. For a few years after this law came into operation a certain toleration was extended to a few of the principal bookmakers, who still continued to make bets in an unobtrusive way, but of late years the authorities, considering that such a state of affairs tends to decrease the receipts drawn from the Totalisator, have become exceedingly stern in repressing any attempts at such a form of speculation.

The percentage levied on the sums staked at the Pari Mutuel is now eight per cent for the race-courses round Paris and that at Deauville, and ten per cent for race-courses in the provinces. Of this sum the five great Parisian racing associations and that of Deauville are allotted four per cent, the rest being applied to charitable and other public purposes. A different scale applies to the provincial race-courses, where the receipts are naturally not so remunerative.

The official figures issued on 7th June 1909, show that £160,000,000 has been staked by the public by means of the Pari Mutuel since its institution in 1891. During the last eighteen years no less than £4,000,000, produced by the percentage levied on this sum, has been applied to public purposes; besides this, various charities and the Racing Societies have profited to an enormous extent.

To-day, owing to the large sums which are available from this source, there is to all intents and purposes no poor-rate in France—the Pari Mutuel takes its place.

As regards the racing itself, it is shown by the official statistics to be in a more flourishing condition than ever before.

In 1891 there existed in France 253 Racing Societies, which held 526 meetings; on the 31st of December 1904 an official statement showed that 396 societies held 906 meetings. During this period more than twenty-nine millions of francs, considerably more than a million pounds sterling, produced by the percentage levied on the Pari Mutuel, had been devoted to racing prizes and the general encouragement of horse-breeding in France. Since the institution of the Totalisator the race-courses and stands have been much improved, funds being abundant.

As a means of speculation for the casual visitor to a race-course the Pari Mutuel is a most convenient form of betting. An excellent organisation exists on every French race-course for enabling those desirous of backing any horse to do so by taking their ticket at one of the many bureaux, above which are inscribed the amount which any ticket represents.

Separate betting bureaux exist for ladies in the special stands which are on some courses set aside for them, and everything is done to render the public thoroughly comfortable.

A list of the horses running is clearly displayed, and there is when possible place betting. On some race-courses the field can be backed, which, in the event of an outsider winning, is not unprofitable. The lowest sum for which a ticket is issued is five francs, the highest five hundred francs. There is, of course, no limit to the number of tickets which any one who wishes to do so may take. Should a backer not be desirous of changing a winning ticket into cash upon the race-course he can keep it till his return to Paris, where, on presenting it at a Central Office at certain fixed hours (defined on the ticket), he receives his money without any inconvenience. In justice, however, to the French race-course authorities it should be added that, considering the huge amount of money carried by those going racing in France, robberies are extremely rare.

Admission to the "pesage," the best and most expensive enclosure, is only 20 francs for a man, 10 francs for a woman. There is also a cheaper stand, and admission to the course costs a franc.

Though a certain number of heavy betters complain of the lack of bookmakers, the general public appears satisfied.

On the Grand Prix day of the present year, when the race was for the first time won by a French jockey, £185,326 passed through the Pari Mutuel at Longchamps, out of the percentage levied on which the poor received no less than £3700. Whatever may be urged against the Totalisator in France, it is bound to benefit a certain number of people, which is a good deal more than can be said for any other form of betting, gambling, or speculation.

Those who in the pages of this book have wandered through the gaming-houses of Europe, and have briefly surveyed the careers of most of the chief gamblers of the past, will, it is hoped, do the writer the justice to admit that he has in no wise sought to minimise the grave evils which are the almost inevitable result of worshipping the goddess of Chance.

Nothing, indeed, is more striking than the almost universal ruin which has ever overtaken the vast majority of gamblers, except the complete failure which has invariably attended all attempts to stamp out this vice by means of coercive measures.

The futile and ineffectual results which, during the last two hundred years, have invariably followed all drastic repression, are clearly demonstrated by hard facts; at the present time speculation, gambling, and betting all flourish as they never flourished before.

In open combat, the strong arm of the law is resistless; but there is no possibility of its ultimate triumph or power of eradicating the desire of gaming from the human mind; and more especially in a country where speculation on the Stock Exchange is regarded with the greatest tolerance by those who denounce the race-course and the card-table.

The anathemas of well-meaning and unworldly ecclesiastics, the plaints of zealous philanthropists, the strident declamations of social reformers, who call for legislative measures of drastic restriction, can only cause the philosophic student of human nature to deplore that so much well-meaning effort should be devoted to such a futile end.

In sober fact the gambling mania is one for which no specific remedy exists—it is possessed by those who are well aware of its dangers, and realise that in the ordinary course of events it must prove ultimately destructive. Repress it in one direction and it reappears—more often than not worse than ever—in another.

It is impossible to dragoon human nature into virtue. The leopard cannot change its spots, or the Ethiopian his skin. Man with his craving for strong emotions will assuredly find means of gratifying them, and it is mere hypocritical rubbish to assume that in the future milk and water is to be the elixir of life.

The well-meaning altruist, who looks with contempt on the frivolous occupations which appear to amuse a great part of mankind, should remember that they, on the other hand, are equally at a loss to account for the pleasure which he derives from the more elevated pursuits in which their lower mental capacities forbid them to indulge.

As a matter of fact the strongest motive with all mankind, after the more sordid necessities are provided for, is excitement. For this reason gambling will continue—even should all card-playing be declared illegal and all race-courses ploughed up.

Repugnant as the idea may be to the Anglo-Saxon mind, regulation, not repression, is without doubt the best possible method of mitigating the evils of speculation; and, moreover, such a system possesses the undeniable advantage of diverting no inconsiderable portion of the money so often recklessly risked into channels of undoubted public benefit.

The time is not yet when English public opinion is prepared to face facts as they are; but though it may be at some far distant day, that time must come, when a wiser and more enlightened legislature, profiting by the experience of the past, will at last realise that the vice of gambling cannot be extirpated by violent means. Reluctantly, but certainly, it will endeavour to palliate the worst features of gambling by taking care that those who indulge in it shall do so under the fairest conditions, whilst at the same time paying a toll to be applied for the good of the community at large.

Such is the inevitable and only solution of a social problem which from any other direction it is absolutely hopeless to approach.

CPSIA information can be obtained
at www.ICGtesting.com
Printed in the USA
LVHW040956020323
740706LV00007B/714

9 789356 892361